EU-Japan Joint Project ／日本・EU共同企画

主催：「日本・ヨーロッパ建築の新潮流」委員会

New Trends of Architecture in Europe and Japan
日本・ヨーロッパ建築の新潮流 2002
2002

Organized by "New Trends of Architecture in Europe and Japan" Committee
主催：「日本・ヨーロッパ建築の新潮流」委員会

Preface

Juan Leña
Ambassador of Spain

It is with no small pride that I have the pleasure, as Ambassador of Spain and present holder of the European Union Presidency in Japan, to introduce the second edition of the Exhibition / Symposium "New Trends of Architecture in Europe and Japan."

The fulfillment of last year´s commitment to follow up this event in a yearly basis, which has never been an easy task, must be acknowledged as a major success, and as a solid step towards the continuity of this event.

We must then acknowledge the opportunity of this important encounter between Japan and Europe. Truly, this joint cultural event is one of the first, if not the first, to take place after the signature of the ten years Action Plan for EU-Japan Cooperation, during the 10th EU-Japan Summit in Brussels on December 8th, 2001. Thus, we can be proud of having achieved an early start in what seems to be fundamental in the promotion of a wider and deeper understanding between our societies, that is, the need to develop civil society links and exchanges by bringing together people and cultures. The exposure in Japan and Europe during a period of months of the works and ideas from young outstanding European and Japanese architects clearly follows this direction.

We must now plan for the future in the true spirit that informed this initiative since the beginning, and I want thus to underline my wish that it evolves definitely into a people-to-people event, autonomous and independent, fully grown, in which the support from our official entities will no longer be indispensable.

Lastly, I wish to thank all those persons and institutions that have once more cooperated in the project, with a special mention to Art Front Gallery and arc en rêve centre d'architecture, and to convey to all of you present here today my appreciation for your time and enthusiasm.

Hakuo Yanagisawa
Chairperson, Japanese Committee for
New Trends of Architecture in Europe and Japan

It is a great pleasure that the second edition of "New Trends of Architecture in Europe and Japan" can be realized. This EU-Japan joint project, which was launched by a group of European cultural and press counsellors to Japan, is an epoch-making enterprise in which all the 15 EU member states, united to one body while retaining their own characteristics, endeavored to open up a cultural project in cooperation with Japan. The first edition created great response in Japan and over 4,000 people visited the exhibition. The participating young architects from Europe, invited by 17 universities and cultural institutions to give lectures, enjoyed exchanges with students. Among these architects, some have started working on projects in Japan. Furthermore, the event has brought about a new network of students and universities. We are now entering the phase to consider what kind of support we should request from official organizations in correspondence to Europe, in order to continue and develop this meaningful project, which has been led and shouldered by a private organization and individuals in this country.

The spirit of "United Europe," to respect cultural diversity of each region while unifying the continent in political and economical terms, is represented by the system of "cultural capital," which this exhibition chooses as European venues.

Europe is going through a period of "state to state" and, through culture, started networking "city to city" and "city to the world." From "EU-Japan" to "EU-Asia." To extend this initiative from Japan to Asia as a project of interregional exchange, we can learn much from this inspiring idea: "cultural capital."

Last but not least, I would like to express my heartfelt gratitude to EU embassies and cultural institutions, Japanese foundations, the commissioners, the participating architects and all those involved in realizing this project.

はじめに

ホァン・レニャ
スペイン大使

柳澤伯夫
「日本・ヨーロッパ建築の新潮流」日本委員長

少なからぬ誇りをもって、私は、駐日スペイン大使および現在の欧州連合議長として、第2回「日本・ヨーロッパ建築の新潮流」をご紹介させていただきます。

この事業を毎年継続するという昨年の約束を実行することは、決して生易しいことではありませんでしたが、かなりの成功をおさめ、事業の継続に向けた確固とした一歩を築くことができたと認めざるをえません。

私たちは、この日本とヨーロッパの重要な出会いの場を感謝しなければなりません。実に、この共同文化事業は、2001年12月8日、ブリュッセルのEU・日本サミットで「EU・日本共同の十年」のアクションプランが調印されてから最初の事業となるのです。かくして、日欧間のより広く深い理解を促進するための基本と思われること、つまり、人と文化をつなげることにより市民社会の連携と交流を発展させる必要性において、早いスタートを切ることができたことを、私たちは誇りに思うのです。日欧の傑出した若い建築家たちの作品と思想が数ヶ月にわたって日本とヨーロッパで展示されることは、まさにこうした方向性に沿ったものであるのです。

私たちは今、このイニシアティブを初発のときから特徴づけてきた真の精神において、未来にむけた計画をたてていかなければなりません。私は、このプロジェクトが民と民の自立的なイベントとして成長し、もはや私たちのような官の機関の支援が不可欠ではなくなる日がくることを強く願っております。

最後に、このプロジェクトに今一度ご協力くださったすべての個人、諸団体の皆様、特に、アートフロントギャラリーとアルカンレーヴに対し感謝申し上げたいと思います。

この度、第2回「日本・ヨーロッパ建築の新潮流」開催を迎えることができますことは、大きな喜びです。EU加盟国の駐日文化・報道参事官が中心となって組織されたこの日欧共同事業は、それぞれの個性を堅持しながら今や一体となったEU15カ国に日本が加わる形でひとつの文化事業を展開しようとする点で画期的な試みでありました。第1回展は日本でも大きな反響を呼び、4000人を超える人が展覧会を訪れました。ヨーロッパの若い建築家たちは17の大学や文化機関でレクチャーを行い、学生たちと交流しました。また日本との仕事に関わり始めた建築家もいます。さらに、このプロジェクトを契機に学生や大学のネットワークも生まれつつあります。日本では民によって担われてきたこの意味ある事業を継続・発展させるために、EU側に対応してこれから官にどのようなサポートを求めていくべきかが今後の課題となってきたと考えます。

政治・経済の統合を進めながらも、各地域の文化的多様性は維持していこうという「欧州統合」の精神は、この展覧会が巡回先とする「欧州文化首都」という制度にも象徴されております。もはやヨーロッパでは国と国ではなく、都市と都市、都市と世界がダイレクトにつながり、「文化」によるネットワークをつくりあげていこうとしています。「EU―ジャパン」から「EU―アジア」へ。この展覧会を「地域と地域」の交流プロジェクトとして日本からアジアへと展開させていくうえで、「文化首都」という概念は大変刺激的で、大いに学ぶべきものであると思います。

最後に、この事業を実現するためにご協力くださったEU各国大使館、文化機関、日本の各財団、コミッショナー、出展建築家他、すべての皆様に心より感謝を申し上げたいと思います。

credits
クレジット

EU-Japan Joint Project
New Trends of Architecture in Europe and Japan 2002

<Tokyo>　June 1-30, 2002
　　　　　Hillside Terrace
<Salamanca>　October 10 – November 10
　　　　　Palacio de Abrantes
　　　　　and Centro Hispano Japones de
　　　　　Salamanca
<Belgium>　Undecided
<Bordeaux>　Spring 2003
　　　　　arc en rêve centre d'architecture

Commissioners:
Toyo Ito (Japan)
Alejandro Zaera-Polo (Spain)
Bob Van Reeth (Belgium)
Participating Architects:
15 groups of architects from 15 EU member states
and 5 groups of architects from Japan
Organized by:
"New Trends of Architecture in Europe and Japan"
Committee
Co-organized by:
University of Salamanca (Spain)
Ordem dos Arquitectos (Portugal)
Secretariat:
Art Front Gallery (Japan)
arc en rêve centre d'architecture (Europe)

<Exhibition in Tokyo>
Co-organized by:
Hillside Terrace
Patronage:
Ministry of Foreign Affairs
Ministry of Land, Infrastructure and Transport
Support:
Asahi Beer Arts Foundation
Association Française d'Action Artistique (AFAA)
The British Council
Building Contractors Society, Japan
Delegation of the European Commission
Embassy of Austria/Cultural Forum
Embassy of Denmark
Embassy of France
Royal Netherlands Embassy
Embassy of Portugal
Embassy of Spain
Embassy of Sweden
EU-Japan Fest Japan Committee
European Commission
Government of Flanders (Culture Administration)
Instituto Camões – Tóquio
Istituto Italiano di Cultura
Japan Federation of Architects & Building Engineers
Associations
The Japan Foundation
The Tokyo International Foundation
In Cooperation with:
ANA, Yamato Transport

日本・EU共同企画
「日本・ヨーロッパ建築の新潮流2002」

<東京展>　2002年6月1日〜30日
　　　　　ヒルサイドテラス
<サラマンカ展>　2002年10月10日〜11月10日
　　　　　Palacio de Abrantes/
　　　　　サラマンカ日西センター
<ベルギー展>　検討中
<ボルドー展>　2003年春
　　　　　アルカンレーヴ建築センター

コミッショナー：
伊東豊雄（日本），アレハンドロ・ザエラ＝ポロ
（スペイン），ボブ・ヴァン・レート（ベルギー）
出展建築家：
EU15カ国15組　日本5組
主催：
「日本・ヨーロッパ建築の新潮流」委員会
共催：
サラマンカ大学，ポルトガル建築家協会
事務局：
アートフロントギャラリー（日本）
アルカンレーヴ建築センター（ヨーロッパ）

<東京展>
共催：ヒルサイドテラス
後援：外務省、国土交通省
助成・協賛：
（財）アサヒビール芸術文化財団
フランス芸術文化活動協会
ブリティッシュ・カウンシル
（社）建築業協会
駐日欧州委員会代表部
オーストリア大使館／文化フォーラム
デンマーク大使館
フランス大使館
オランダ王国大使館
ポルトガル大使館
スペイン大使館
スウェーデン大使館
EU・ジャパンフェスト日本委員会
欧州委員会
フランダース政府文化部
インスティテュート・カモンイス（ポルトガル文化院）
イタリア文化会館
（社）日本建築士会連合会
国際交流基金
（財）東京国際交流財団
協力：全日本空輸㈱、ヤマト運輸㈱

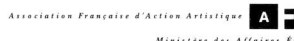

contents
目次

Preface p. 2
はじめに

Juan Leña
ホァン・レニャ

Hakuo Yanagisawa
柳澤伯夫

Introduction p. 6
序文

Alejandro Zaera-Polo
アレハンドロ・ザエラ＝ポロ

Bob Van Reeth
ボブ・ヴァン・レート

Toyo Ito
伊東豊雄

Profiles p. 94
プロフィル

Data & Credits p. 98
作品データ・クレジット

Ireland　アイルランド
O'Donnell + Tuomey Architects p. 70
オードネル＋トゥミ・アーキテクツ

United Kingdom　イギリス
Allford Hall Monaghan Morris p. 30
アルフォード・ホール・モナハン・モリス

Belgium　ベルギー
evr. Architecten p. 42
evr.アーシテクテン

Luxembourg　ルクセンブルグ
Ney & Partners sarl p. 66
ネイ・アンド・パートナーズ

The Netherlands　オランダ
Architect Agency Cepezed B.V. p. 38
アーキテクト・エージェンシーCEPEZED

Denmark　デンマーク
Dorte Mandrup Arkitekter p. 58
ドーテ・マンドルップ・アーキテクテー

Sweden　スウェーデン
Studio Grön arkitekter ab p. 46
スタジオ・グレーン建築事務所

Finland　フィンランド
Sanaksenaho Arkkitehdit Oy p. 82
サナクセンアホ・アーキテクツ

Greece　ギリシャ
Yannis Aesopos p. 22
ヤニス・アエソポス

Austria　オーストリア
Riegler Riewe Architects Pty. Ltd. p. 74
リーグラー・リーヴェ・アーキテクツ

Italy　イタリア
UdA – Ufficio di Architettura p. 86
UdA

Germany　ドイツ
b&k+ p. 34
b&k+

France　フランス
Anne Lacaton & Jean Philippe Vassal p. 54
アンヌ・ラカトン＆ジャン・フィリップ・ヴァッサル

Spain　スペイン
Abalos y Herreros p. 14
アバロス＆エレロス

Portugal　ポルトガル
Aires Mateus & Associados LDA. p. 26
アイレス・マテウス＆アソシアードス

Japan　日本
Atelier Hitoshi Abe p. 18
阿部仁史アトリエ

Japan　日本
Kazuhiro Kojima／C+A p. 50
小嶋一浩／C+A

Japan　日本
Mikan p. 62
みかんぐみ

Japan　日本
Kazuyo Sejima + Ryue Nishizawa／SANAA p. 78
妹島和世+西沢立衛／SANAA

Japan　日本
Motomu Uno + Phase Associates p. 90
宇野求＋フェイズアソシエイツ

Introduction

Reconstructing Europe
Alejandro Zaera-Polo

Europe provides now very interesting opportunities for architectural experimentation. As a continent undergoing an intense process of transformation, culturally, socially and economically, Europe is being physically reinvented. And in this reinvention, the spatial practices are becoming a critical device, suddenly required to develop also new formats, new techniques, new procedures... to cope with this continental reorganization.

Primarily, Europe is a continent traditionally characterized by a rich diversity of well developed local cultures and traditions, now undergoing a process of homogeneization as a result of the new European Union rules, regulations and standards. Far from erasing the former local specificity, this new layer of genericness is also proliferating the local cultures into previously inexistent realms. This European diversity can no longer be interpreted as the "collage" of cultures, patchwork of "locals" that was the European trademark not long ago, but as an increasingly consistent field of differences. The oscillation between variation and homogeneity has been traditionally a feature of European space, and the very essence of its remarkable cultural development since the middle ages, when the globalizing Roman Empire collapsed and the mighty Asian bureaucracies begin to stall precisely as the outcome of their streamlined sophistication.

We could list a number of very important current processes that will require increasingly sophisticated capacities to shape the environment:
1. The articulation between entrepreneurial economies and interventionist policies that characterizes the European "third way."
2. The articulation between national and supranational states and policies of territorial and urban planning.
3. The incorporation of the former communist countries, and the impact in the re-location of entire sectors of production.
4. The massive immigration from Northern African and Asian workers, creating large demand for housing and services.
5. The emergence of unprecedented relationships between work and leisure due to the economic growth of the zone, advanced work regulations and shift of the economy towards the tertiary sector.
6. The need to articulate heritage and tourism, as complementary aspects of a new important sector of the economy.
7. The specialization of North and South into production and leisure centers, and the progressive interdependence between them that is producing an overhaul of the transportation and communication infrastructure.
8. The processes of negotiation and hybridization between traditionally strong cultures and their articulation in the new European identity.

What is most important, Europe's political and social background has become a guarantor of the possibility of planning the built environment. As neither a free-market nor an autocratic regime, the planning of the built environment in Europe is still possible but requires complex and sophisticated techniques. This ecosystem is the origin of truly complex and sophisticated new architectural and urban species.

The complexity of these current European processes put forward a rich field of possibilities that are being considered and exploited by a new generation of European architects. Their work no longer needs to become visionary nor overtly theoretical, as the pragmatics of these processes are already sufficiently intricate and problematic to produce innovation. But they are neither blindly compliant with the volatile mandates of capital nor enslaved to the mere replication of bureaucratic regimes and regulations or to the mere replication of models of profitability.

It is important to see the work of the emerging European architects in the light of these developments to understand the kind of work that is being produced. Their compromise with the pragmatics of construction, but also the recognition of the social and political value of architecture is probably the most interesting characteristic of their work. This is a kind of work that is fundamentally precise and rigorous in the modest resolution of problems, offering an alternative to the schizophrenia between spectacular extravagance and corporate replication, more common in the American and Asian domains (with the remarkable exception of Japanese architecture and some interesting but isolated examples in other Asian countries). It is also sometimes less evident than those more obvious models that concentrate on exploiting the profits of an extravagant image or of the straight market compliance, and requires the well educated public that European architects still enjoy.

One can perceive a certain withdrawal, a certain distance from the work; almost the search for anonymity in many of these projects. The work is modest and to the point, driven still by need rather than excess, and in that sense quite consistent with some of the Japanese contemporary currents after the burst of the bubble. One can also perceive the homogeneizing orders of the new Europe at work, and yet, the differences are quite clear, for example between a more market-oriented profession in the UK and a more state-run profession in Spain, or between a more industrialized construction in the Netherlands to a more artisanal construction in Portugal. It is on those differences embedded in the new generic European conditions that the potentials of the emerging European architects rely. One only wonders whether this rigorous and experimental new European – and perhaps Japanese – architecture will have the capacity to engage the public in the after-Guggenheim era.

Alejandro Zaera-Polo
Born in Madrid in 1963
Studied at E.T.S. of architecture in Madrid
Graduate School of Design, Harvard University, U.S.A.
Established Foreign Office Architects in London with Farshid Moussavi in 1992
Design Professor at the Hoger Architectuur Instituut Sint-Lucas, Gent (1993 -1995)
Japan Grand Prize for Yokohama International Ferry Terminal

Selected works:
Yokohama International Ferry Terminal, Yokohama (1995 - 2002)
Blue Moon, dwelling unit and temporary railway station canopy, Groningen, Netherlands (2000 -2001)
Central Police Station Complex and surrounding landscape, Villa Joyosa, Spain (2000 -)
Mahler 4, office complex, Amsterdam (2000 -)
Publishing Headquarters, Paju City, Korea, (2000 -)
New Belgo restaurants, London, NewYork, and Bristol, (1998 -1999)

序文

ヨーロッパの再構築
アレハンドロ・ザエラ＝ポロ

ヨーロッパは現在、建築的実験に対し非常に興味深い機会を提供している。ヨーロッパは、大陸として文化的、社会的、経済的に激しい変容の途上にあり、物理的に改革されようとしている。そしてこの改革の中で、空間的な実践は重要な装置となりつつあり、大陸の再編成に対処するための新たな形式、新たな技術、新たな手続き..を作りあげることをも突如として要求されている。

本来、ヨーロッパはローカルな文化や伝統が、豊かな多様性をもって発展してきたという特徴をもった大陸であったが、現在は新たなEUの規則、規制と規格の結果として均質化のプロセスを経験している。この新たな一般化のレイヤーは、かつてのローカルな特性を消失させることなく、これまでなかった領域にまでローカルな文化を増殖させつつある。ヨーロッパの多様性は、つい最近までヨーロッパのトレードマークであったような、文化の"コラージュ"や"地方"のパッチワークとはもはや呼べず、ますます普遍化する差異のフィールドとなりつつある。多様性と均質性の間の振幅は、ヨーロッパの空間の特徴であり、グローバル化するローマ帝国が崩壊し、強力なアジアの官僚主義が合理化と洗練によって行き詰まった中世以降の、目覚しいヨーロッパの文化的発展の核心そのものであった

環境を整えるためにますます洗練された能力を必要とする、現在ともても重要なプロセスを列記しようと思えば可能である。
1. ヨーロッパの"第3の道"を特徴づける、干渉主義政策と企業家的経済との接合
2. 民族国家と超民族国家との接合、および地域・都市計画に関わる政策
3. 旧共産主義国家の編入、および生産セクター全体の再配置における影響
4. 北アフリカとアジアの労働者の膨大な流入が生み出す住宅とサービスの大幅な需要
5. この地帯の経済成長、進んだ労働規定と第3セクターへの経済の移行による、かつてない労働と余暇の関係の出現
6. 経済的に重要な新しいセクターの補完的要素としての、文化的遺産と観光事業の接合の必要性
7. 北と南の生産と余暇の中心地としての特化、および両者の増大する相互依存がもたらす、輸送と通信のインフラストラクチャーの点検整備
8. 伝統的に強い文化間の折衝と混成のプロセス、および新しいヨーロッパのアイデンティティにおける複数の文化の接合

何よりも重要なのは、ヨーロッパの政治的・社会的背景が、建築的環境を計画する可能性の保証人となったことである。自由市場でも独裁体制でもなく、ヨーロッパでは建築的環境を計画するのは依然として可能であるが、複雑で精巧な技法を必要とする。このエコシステムは、本当に複雑で精巧な、新たな建築的・都市的種族の起源である。

こういった現在のヨーロッパの複合的なプロセスは、ヨーロッパの新しい世代の建築家たちが、考察し開拓しつつある豊かな可能性のフィールドを提示している。彼らの作品は、もはや空想的であったり、露骨に理論的である必要はない。何故ならこれらのプロセスのプラグマティックス はすでに十分に錯綜し問題提起的であるため、革新性を生み出さざるを得ないからである。しかし彼らは、資本の気まぐれな指図に盲目的に従順であるわけでも、官僚的な体制と規制を単に反復したり、収益性のモデルを単に複製することに隷属っしているわけでもない。

重要なのは、新たに登場してきたヨーロッパの建築家たちの作品を理解するためにはこういった展開に照らして見るべきだということだ。建設のプラグマティックスとの妥協があったとしても、建築の社会的・政治的価値の認識が、多分彼らの作品の最も興味深い特徴である。それは問題の穏やかな解決に際して基本的に緻密で厳格であり、アメリカやアジアの地域でより顕著な（日本建築のすばらしい例外と、他のアジアの国々の興味深いが孤立した事例を除いて）甚だしい浪費と企業の複製との間の精神分裂症に代わるべきものを提示している。それはまた、行き過ぎたイメージや、徹底した市場の追従による利潤を搾取することに焦点を絞ったもっと露骨なモデルに比較すれば、明白さに欠けることもままあるし、ヨーロッパの建築家が依然として享受している教養ある大衆を必要とする。

彼らの作品の多くからは、ある種の撤退、作品との距離、ほとんど無名性の探求ともいえるものを感じるかも知れない。作品は控えめで、いまだ過剰より必要に駆られており、その意味ではバブル崩壊以降の日本のある種の傾向と一致していると言える。新たなヨーロッパの均質化の秩序が作用しているとも感じられる。しかしながら差異は極めて明快である。例えば、より市場志向の強いイギリスにおける職能と、より国営的な状況にあるスペインにおける職能。より工業化されたオランダの建設と、より職人的なポルトガルの建設。新たな包括的なヨーロッパの状態に埋め込まれたこういった差異こそが、新しいヨーロッパの建築家たちの潜在力が拠って立つところなのである。果たして、この厳密で実験的な新しいヨーロッパの――そしておそらく日本の――建築に、グッゲンハイム後の時代にある人々を引きつけるだけの能力があるのかどうか...。

アレハンドロ・ザエラ＝ポロ
1963年　マドリードに生まれる
マドリード建築大学、ハーバード大学大学院で学位を取得
1991年から1992年　OMAに勤務
1992年ファシッド・ムサビと共にフォーリン・オフィス・アーキテクツをロンドンに設立
1993年から1995年　ゲントのシント・ルーカス・インスティテュート建築学科教授
横浜国際フェリーターミナルで最優秀賞受賞

Introduction

Cultural Sustainability
Bob van Reeth

What is architecture? In my view, architecture is the search for architecture. There are many different ways of searching, which result in rather varied and interesting types of architecture. Not everything that is built qualifies as architecture.

The most important idea of the last century (in terms of city planning, urban development and architecture) was focused on the future. This was the insight that the construction and use of infrastructures, buildings and cities themselves, has extremely far-reaching effects which come at an enormously high environmental cost, and that this is untenable so that we must all investigate means of bringing about change.

Just as all problems are so-called limitations, so this awareness too offers a new source of creative energy to urban and architectural designers. Sustainability – that is, sustainable urban development, sustainable architecture, cultural sustainability will, in my opinion, be the design challenge in the years to come.

The architectural discourse based on pure formulae and aesthetic issues (still far too often carried out in architecture courses and by building inspectors, heritage councils – even in architectural criticism) should perhaps evolve towards a more intrinsic discussion about how and on the basis of what sustainable architecture, sustainable buildings and objects may be conceived and evaluated. Perhaps institutions should forget for a time that architecture is art. With energy, being as conservative as possible means not using it. Reducing pollution as far as possible means not producing waste. The most ecological house is the house that is never built. This should be our starting point.

Our most valuable resource is space and in particular, the open spaces, the countryside. It is quite simple not to consume this resource anymore: it suffices no longer to build there. This is a necessity, which may be easily accomplished. Increasing population, urban growth, changes in the standard of living must be dealt with through the consolidation of municipalities and cities. This I call sustainable construction, conservative re-use of existing space.

A sustainable architectural concept is not possible without quality-related terms such as: permanence, inflexibility, durability and (multifaceted and apparently contradictory) changeability. Sustainability must be seen as a basic characteristic of architecture. The fundamental structure of a building, its carcass, its skeleton, its frame, consists of the load-bearing structure and the skin. This primary construction should be built to last for many hundreds of years.

Urban development, architecture, consists of several layers:
- the location, the place, the footprint, which is permanent
- the load-bearing structure + the exteriors, which should last at least 400 years
- the building's interior floor plan, its installations and its finishing treatments, which are designed to last a much shorter time.

Builders and architects should make long-lasting structures, "intelligent ruins," as I call them. This is the key to sustainable buildings. History has shown us how to do this. Sustainability is about added, collective value, achieved by the factor of time. This is what I call cultural sustainability.

In order to last, for the sake of continuity, change must be a built-in architectural quality. Change upholds the unchanging. Evolution reveals a curious permanence, and this is sustainability. This is cultural sustainability: something, which does not change, but nevertheless summarizes the passage of time. Because given time, buildings designed for varied functions become, as it were, "occupied." We are all of us, as a generation, a squatter's movement which has taken over the city. We conceive buildings, which are ready to be lived in, not living itself. In my view, one should emphasize the contrast between the transient and the long term in architecture, between the impermanent and the permanent. We should attempt to overcome functional program when designing buildings. The stated requirements are mainly short term, often they don't even last until the building itself is completed. The program itself must be seen as an alibi for designing buildings with an option for change, with many different scenarios for their continued use. Sustainable buildings are buildings designed for unpredictable events.

New concepts sometimes give rise to resistance, dislike and even rejection. Perhaps my sustainability concept will result in buildings which do not, in the first instance, have a place in the mental landscape of many people who may find the buildings ugly. I believe that "finding something" is part of looking for something. Looking for something is the relative autonomy of an architect's profession.

Sustainable architecture is also concerned with the intellectual and emotional needs of inhabitants and users. Great precision, intelligence and intuition is expected from designers for these, more than for practical needs. We must produce generous designs. We must give to architecture the perspective of improvement. We must transcend our profession to do so.

Bob van Reeth
Born in Temse, Belgium in 1943
Studied at the Hoger Architectuur Instituut Sint-Lucas at Schaerbeek, Brussels
Established AWG (ArchitectenWerkGroep) in 1972
Professor in architectural design studio at the Henry van de Velde Institute, Antwerp
Regular visiting critic at various schools of architecture in Belgian and abroad
Member of the Fine Arts Division of the Royal Academy for Science, Literature and Fine Arts of Belgium
Eugene Baie Award for Architecture, Antwerp, 1987
Architect of the Flemish Government

Selected works:
Woning Botte, Mechelen (1969-1971)
Begijnhofwoning Van Reeth, Mechelen (1969-1971)
New wing for the Onze-Lieve-Vrouwecollege, Antwerp (1973-1978)
New black-and-white Van Roosmalen house, Scheldekade, Antwerp (1985-1988)
New Zuiderterras café restaurant, Scheldekade, Antwerp (1987-1991)
Uitgeverij-en drukkerijgebouwen, 1° ontwerp in Averbode, (1992-1993)
De Ark, conversion of barge into floating theatre café, Antwerp (1992-1993)
240 apartments for the Ceramique project, Maastricht (1993-1998)
54 new dwellings and public space "Mariaplaats-Walsteeg," Utrecht (1994-1998)
New exhibition and guest rooms Seppenhuis, Zoersel (1994-1997)

序文

文化的サステイナビリティ
ボブ・ヴァン・レート

建築とは何か。私の見解は、建築の探求こそが建築である。探求の仕方には多くの異なる方法があるから、多様な興味深い建築のタイプが結実する。建設された物が、すべて建築と呼ぶに値するわけではない。

前世紀の最も重要な概念（都市計画／都市の発展、建築において）は、未来に焦点を合わせていた。そこから洞察されるのは、インフラストラクチュア、建物、都市自体の建設と利用が、極めて長期的な影響をもち、とてつもなく高い環境コストを払っていること、そしてそれが危機的な状況にあり、私たちは皆、変化をもたらすような方法を模索しなくてはならないということであった。

あらゆる問題は、いわゆる制限であるから、この認識も都市や建築のデザイナーに、新たな創作のエネルギーを与える。文化的なサステイナビリティーそれは、サステイナブルな都市の発展、サステイナブルな建築であり、文化的サステイナビリティは私の見解では、今後のデザインのまさに課題となるだろう。

純粋な公式や美学的な問題に根ざした建築のディスクール（現在でも目に余るほど、建築の講義や建築の検査官、文化遺産協議会、あるいは建築批評でさえ行われている）は、おそらくどのようにして、何に基づいてサステイナブルな建築や建物や物品を考え、評価すべきなのかという本質的なディスカッションに進化することだろう。多分、建築に関係する機関は一旦、建築が芸術だという認識を捨てるべきなのである。

エネルギーについては、できるだけ保存するためには使わないべきである。汚染をできるだけ減らすとは廃棄物をつくらないことである。最もエコロジカルな住宅とは、決して建てられることのない住宅である。これが私たちの出発点だ。

私たちの最も価値ある資源は空間であり、特に広々した田舎の空間である。この資源をこれ以上消費してはならないことは、全く明らかである。そこにはこれ以上建設してはならない。これは必要事項であり、意外に簡単に達成できるかもしれない。

人口増加、都市の成長、生活水準の変化等は、自治体や都市の統合によって克服されなくてはならない。これを私はサステイナブルな建設、保守的な既存空間の再利用と呼んでいる。

サステイナブルな建築の概念は、永久性、不変性、耐久性、（多角的で実際、矛盾するが）可変性といった質的な項目なしでは、可能ではない。サステイナビリティは建築の基本的特徴だと見なされなくてはならない。建築の基礎的な仕組み、その胴体、躯体、骨組みは、荷重を受ける構造体と表皮からなっている。この一義的な建設物は何百年も耐えられるようにつくられなくてはならない。

都市の発展や建築は、いくつかのレイヤーからできている。
- 永久的である、場所性、配置と建物の専有部分
- 400年は持ちこたえられる、荷重を受ける構造体と建物の外壁
- 仮設的であり短期間存続する、室内のプラン、建物設備、仕上げの取扱い

建設者と建築家は長持ちする構造をつくらなくてはいけない。私はそれを"知的な廃墟"と呼んでいる。ここがサステイナブルな建物の鍵である。歴史がそれをどうやって実現するか示している。サステイナビリティとは時間によって積み重ねられた、集合的な価値に関わるものである。これが私が、文化的サステイナビリティと呼ぶものである。

長続きするため、継続するために、変化は建築の特性に組み込まれていなくてはならない。変化が不変なものを支える。進化は興味深い永久性をあらわにする。そしてそれがサステイナビリティである。それが文化的サステイナビリティである。変わらないが、にもかかわらず時間の経過を要約するもの。

与えられた時間により、多様な機能のため設計された建物は"占有"される。私たちは皆、世代として、都市を占拠した無断居住者である。私たちは建物を、住むためのものと捉え、建物自体が生きているわけではない。

私の考えでは、建築の中の変化する部分と長期的な部分、永続しないものとするものとの対比を重要視する必要がある。建物を設計するとき、私たちは機能的なプログラムを解こうとする。定められた条件は主に短期的なものであり、しばしば建物が完成するまで持たないことさえある。プログラム自体を建物を設計するためのアリバイとして捉え、継続して利用するためには、変化の余地、多くの異なるシナリオを準備しなくてはならない。サステイナブルな建物とは、予期せぬ出来事のためにデザインされた建物のことである。

新しい概念は、よく抵抗や反感、拒絶の対象となる。多分私の唱えるサステイナビリティの概念による建物も、当初は、醜いと考える多くの人々の認識の地形には登場し得ないものとなるだろう。私は"何かを見つけること"は何かを探すことの一部だと考えている。何かを探すことは、建築家の職能に関わる自律性である。

サステイナブルな建築は同時に、居住者や利用者の知的・感情的な必要にも関わるものだ。デザイナーには、実用的な要求に接する時以上に、卓越した精密さ、知性と洞察力が求められる。私たちは、豊かなデザインをしなくてはならない。建築に改良の展望を与えなくてはならない。そのためには職能の枠を越えて行かなくてはならない。

ボブ・ヴァン・レート
1943年　ベルギー、テムゼに生まれる
1972年　ARCHITECTENWERKGROEPを設立
ブリュッセルのシント・ルーカス・インスティテュートで建築を学ぶ
アンリ・ヴァン・デ・ベルデ建築学科教授
ベルギー王立科学・文学・芸術アカデミー会員
1987年　ユーゲン・ボーア建築賞受賞
フランダース政府建築家

Introduction

Five Architectural Teams on the Abstract and the Concrete
Toyo Ito

People have been saying the Japanese economy is in trouble for quite some time now and local governments actively involved in construction administration are burdened with heavy debts. But even under these circumstances architecture is still being built in Japan. Compared to Western Europe it is still easier and faster to build in Japan.

In most cases in Japan architects are told the budget and the completion date as soon as they begin the design process. In the case of public architecture these must be strictly upheld; failure to do so creates problems in the local city council or prefectural legislature. This means that the suitability of the space for each function and the avoidance of problems of the functional level are prioritized over program innovation and creativity in the production of space.

As a result clients feel most comfortable with respectable and reliable design and construction firms with good track records.

The current state of Japanese architecture deriving from this situation might be thought of as a kind of "modernist sophistication." One building after another goes up with flawless insulation, lighting and sound proofing thanks to highly precise construction technology. And for most people this is equated with high quality. But there is very little enjoyment for those who experience these spaces and they never really come to life. Instead they are devoted entirely to controlling the people who use them, allowing them to carry out only certain designated functions in the space allotted.

This kind of controlled, in some sense sophisticated, meekness and apathy is characteristic of most young architects today. At the risk of over-generalizing, I think it is fair to say that most young Japanese architects are smitten with an ideal of architecture best described as "minimalist, highly abstract, beautiful cubes." Enveloped in such spaces one senses a pure aesthetic without sweat or odor, an abstraction so great as to make people feel they should keep their voices down. It is not so much that there is something in these spaces which actively sucks the life out of them, but that they are simply filled with a silence like the furthest extreme of entropy. One wonders how much further this can go.

The five architect teams I will be discussing here are not necessarily part of the younger generation, but all of them have established and conducted their careers out of both a taste for and abhorrence of this brand of sophistication.

To take the question of "abstraction" as an example, the work of Sejima Kazuyo and her partner Nishizawa Ryue, and Kojima Kazuhiro (Coelacanth) stands in clear opposition to that of Abe Hitoshi/Onoda Yasuaki and the members of "Mikan."

Sejima and Nishizawa employ an exceedingly abstract style. By "exceedingly" I mean to say that they have gone far beyond the level of sophistication. Their architecture would be aptly described as "hyper-abstractism." Their buildings are not composed of the conventional elements of roof, walls, and windows. Instead they strive towards a composition consisting exclusively of abstract surfaces. Of course they do have to perform the same functions as ordinary buildings and stand up to actual use. So where necessary they have standard sashes and doors. But the details and choices of materials are all made in order to facilitate the composition of abstract surfaces. This intention is clearly expressed in the way they draw plans with a single line.

The result is that Sejima and Nishizawa's plans have nothing conventional about them, but are more like abstract diagrams. And this is why their architecture is so radical. Spaces rendered with a single line do not express relationships among separate rooms but appear only as a series of differing volumes (SPACE A, SPACE B, etc.) appropriate to various functions.

Plans are usually full of hierarchies relating rooms to rooms, and conventions as shorthand for architectural elements. But Sejima and Nishizawa seem to have reached this level of abstraction by doing away with these systemic restrictions in order to create a kind of nonhierarchical zero-degree space. Their architecture sometimes comprises extremely homogenous spaces and sometimes extremely dehumanized spaces. But the essence of their work is in this unrelenting insistence on extremes.

Kojima Kazuhiro and his colleagues in Coelacanth also employ abstraction in their composition of space. Their built architecture expresses "objects" much more concretely than Sejima and Nishizawa. Whether concrete, wood, or steel, their work is scattered with tangible expressions of the materials themselves. In this sense the space does not seem abstract in the least.

And yet their architecture is astonishingly logical and precise. They believe that the secret to creating innovative architecture lies in the arrangement of spaces. Their work departs from a keen understanding of just how tedious it can be to make architecture from a modernist planning perspective that seeks simply to arrive at the "optimal solution" in the commonplace relations of commonplace functions. In other words, they try to think of architecture as a site for a whole variety of human activities without the restrictions imposed by the concept of function. This allows for an unprecedented variety of activity units to be set up within the space. The arrangement of these innumerable units is then simulated and tested. As their numbers grow their permutations expand into infinity. It is through the repetition of these dizzying simulations that Kojima and his colleagues create their own unique spatial compositions.

Their recent Miyagi Prefecture Hakuou High School (2001) is a superb example. Its 200 activity units are completely nonhierarchical but arrayed neatly across the two-level 120-square-meter space. The spaces linking them are also sites of flexible activity, in mutually supplementary relation to each unit. "Miyagi" represents a singular achievement arrived at through experimentation with how a school can be programmed.

Abe Hitoshi and Onoda Yasuaki are more real and concrete. Not only do they concentrate their activities in the northeastern city of Sendai, but they are unique as a partnership between an architect and a planner. Like Kojima and his colleagues they have developed their methodology out of a painful awareness of the limits of modernism. Their work uses a method based on "dialogue" to make manifest the suppressed internal energy characteristic of northeastern Japan. Dialogue may suggest a kind of democratic egalitarianism, but this

序文

＜抽象＞と＜具体＞をめぐる5組の建築家
―― 日本・ヨーロッパ建築の新潮流2002 ――
伊東豊雄

日本の経済が深刻な状況にあると言われてから久しい。建設行政を積極的に推進してきた地方自治体も多くの負債に苦悩している。しかしそんな状況下でも、日本では未だに建築が建つ。西欧に比較して、建築はお手軽に建つし、実に短期間のうちに完成する。

日本では、建築家は設計を開始する時点でほとんどの場合に予算と完成時期を宣告される。とりわけ公共施設の場合には、これら2つの事項はきわめて厳正に守られねばならず、守られないと議会で問題となる。逆に言えば、プログラムの新鮮さや、空間の創造性よりも、各機能に対応した空間の性能が問われ、性能的に問題の起こらないことが最優先される。そしてその性能を確保すべく、優れた施工技術に大きな価値が求められる。その結果、穏当で実績の豊富な、安心して依頼できる設計組織や施工組織が信頼を得ることになる。

このような状況に由来する日本の建築の現況は、「モダニズムのソフィスティケーション」という言葉で括ることができよう。断熱、採光、遮音等々の性能に問題がなく、きわめて精度の良い施工技術に支えられた建築が次々に建つ。それらは一般的には高度な質を備えているように受けとられる。だがその空間を体験しても、決して楽しくはないし、生命力を喚起されることもない。人々は与えられた空間で指示された行為のみをひたすら行うようにコントロールされている。

このようなコントロールされ、或る意味ではソフィスティケートされた従順さ、無気力さが若い世代の建築観をもカバーしていると言ってよいだろう。あくまで一般論でしかないが、日本の若手建築家の建築嗜好を端的に表現すれば、＜ミニマルで抽象性の高い美しいキューブ＞に憧れている。その内に浸っているとピュアな美しさに満たされて、汗も臭気も感じられず、人間の生まな会話すら憚られるような抽象的な空間である。何か生命を奪いたたせるエネルギーを喚起される、というより、エントロピーの極限状態のような静謐さに満たされた空間である。その先には一体何があるというのか。

ここに名を連ねる5組の建築家達は、最早や若手とは必ずしも言えない世代であるが、そうしたソフィスティケーションへの嗜好と反発からその建築活動を展開している。

例えば＜抽象＞という言葉をめぐって、妹島和世＋西沢立衛、小嶋一浩（シーラカンス）という2チームと阿部仁史＋小野田泰明、＜みかんぐみ＞という2チームの意図は鮮明に対立の構図を描く。

妹島和世＋西沢立衛の表現は優れて抽象的である。優れて、と述べたのはソフィスティケーションのレベルをはるかに超えるほどに、という意味である。彼らの建築を＜ハイパー・アブストラクティズム＞と呼ぶこともできる。屋根、壁、窓といった慣習的なエレメントで構成されない。ひたすら抽象的な面による構成のみが求められる。無論それは通常の建築と同じように或る性能を備え、使用に耐えなくてはならないから、既成のサッシュやドアも用いられる。しかしディテールも素材の選択も、すべては抽象的な面の構成の意志に統合されている。シングルラインで描かれた図面がその意図を明快に表現している。

その結果彼らの平面図は、もはや従来の意味でのプランを超え、より抽象的なダイヤグラムを示すに到っている。そしてここに彼らの建築の尖鋭さがある。即ちシングルラインで描かれた空間は部屋の関係を示すのではなく、機能に対応した異なるヴォリューム（SPACE A, SPACE B, etc.）を単に並列しているに過ぎないように見えるのである。

プランには通常、部屋の関係としてのヒエラルキーや、建築エレメントの省略としての約束事が満載されている。彼らはそうした制度的な規制を排除して、もっとヒエラルキーのない零度の空間を生み出したいと考え、あのような抽象性に到達したに違いない。彼らの建築は時には超均質空間かもしれないし、時には超非人間的空間かもしれない。だが、この超…へのこだわりにこそ、彼らの真骨頂がある。

小嶋一浩に代表される＜シーラカンス＞の建築も、空間の構成において抽象的である。実現された建築空間を見ると、妹島達に比較して、＜もの＞ははるかに具体的に表現されている。コンクリートも木も鉄も、各素材そのままのリアルな表現が随所に見られる。決して抽象的な空間には見えない。

しかし小嶋達の空間構成は驚く程論理的かつ緻密である。彼らは新鮮な建築を生み出す源泉が空間の配列にあると考えている。ありふれた機能のありふれた関係によって＜最適解＞を設定してしまう近代主義的計画論から出発することが、いかに退屈な建築しか生まないかを痛感することから彼らは出発した。即ち機能という概念によって人間の行為を省略せず、もっと多様な振る舞いの場として把えようと試みる。その結果従来よりもはるかに多くのアクティヴィティの単位が設定される。そしてそうした無数の単位の配列をシミュレート、検証する。単位が増加すれば、配列の可能性は無限に近く拡大する。この気の遠くなるようなシミュレーションを繰り返した結果として、彼らの空間構成は成立しているのである。

近作である「宮城県迫桜高等学校（2001）」はそうした方法に基づいて実現した優れた例である。200近い単位がほとんどヒエラルキーを持たずに、しかし整然と120m四方の2層の空間に並列している。これらの単位を結ぶ連結空間もフレキシブルな行為の場として、各単位と補完し合う関係を生み出している。「宮城」は、学校というプログラムの下でいくつかの試行を重ねた末に、彼らが到達したひとつのゴールとすらいうことができよう。

阿部仁史＋小野田泰明の建築はもっとリアルで具体的である。彼らは「仙台」という東北の地方都市に活動の拠点を置くという特異性を持つが、それ以上に建築家＋計画学者によるパートナーシップに特徴がある。彼らも小嶋達と同様に近代主義的方法の限界を痛感したところから自らの方法を発展させた。東北地方独特の沈潜する内的エネルギーの発露を「対話」による方法に彼らは求める。「対話」というと何かデモクラティックな平等主義を思い浮かべるが、彼らの対象は人だけではない、＜もの＞との直接的な対話も包含する。即ち、現代建築は人間の行為やものを抽象し、記号のみに置き換えた空間として表現する、その結果人やものの持つ直接的な情感や力を喪失してしまった、その力を取り戻す行為にこそ建築の課題がある、と彼らは考える。

阿部＋小野田は、地域の住民、自治体の人々を交えたワークショップを繰り返すことによって、生きた対話の内から、人間の生の鼓動を伝える建築を立ち上げたいと試みる。この点において彼らの方法は、小嶋一浩等の方法よりも直截であり、かつ具体的、内在的である。社会内の存在としてその内側に止まったまま変化し続ける対話

Introduction

does not involve humans alone. There is also direct dialogue with "things." Contemporary architecture has abstracted human actions and things to be expressed as space converted into mere signs. As a result it has lost the sensuousness and power of a direct relation with people and things. But for Abe and Onoda it is the task of architecture to recapture that power.

Abe and Onoda work to create architecture with a human pulse through lively workshops and discussions with local residents and officials. In this sense their method is more direct, more concrete, and more immanent than that of Kojima et al. They strive to make architecture that directly expresses a continually changing dialogue which nonetheless remains inside and internal to society. No matter how complex and alive the activities are that Kojima tries to grasp he first steps into an abstract space and puts together a method based on rational operations. He tries, in other words, to supersede modernism with a further elaboration of modernism. Abe and Onoda's method, on the other hand, begins with the renunciation of the modernist notion of the "optimal solution." Their recent work, provisionally named Reihoku Community Hall (2002), came together out of a series of workshop discussions. In fact these workshops themselves, that is to say the process leading from design to construction, were already making explicit "use" of the architecture. I look forward to what this radical method will bring.

Mikan is a team with multiple partners and none of their work is released under individual names. This is most likely a statement denying the idea of architecture as the artistic expression of any one individual. They want to create architecture that is anonymous and light rather than trying to overawe people or move them with emotion. For Mikan the greatest contemporary critical potential of architecture is to be found in its levity.

Like Abe and Onoda, Mikan realize their architecture through workshops. But for them this means something very different. While Abe and Onoda look to workshop dialogues as a way to discover the joys of connecting with the passions of people and things, Mikan intentionally limit the scope of their workshops to the level of the quotidian and the practical. It is a method one might call urbane.

They are concerned that methods seeking the profundities of creation inevitably tend to exclude people. They believe that there is more than enough pleasure and interest even in relatively standard levels of society. Their recent publication *Plans for the Rebirth of the Housing Complex Renovation Project: Mikan Renovation Catalogue* (INAX) is a collection of just these kinds of ideas out of daily life.

Their recently completed Hachiyo Nursery School (2001) completely avoids obtrusive expression. Lumber is left exposed both in structural elements of beams and pillars and finishing elements of the floors and ceilings, and no particular operations of abstraction are apparent in the details. Things retain their material aspect as things. And unlike Sejima/Nishizawa and Kojima, there is no abstraction in the planning either. They look for concrete solutions on a concrete level. In other words they consistently reject turning their buildings into "works."

Uno Motomu's work resembles that of Mikan in its concreteness. But as an academic architect with a position in the university few of his projects have been built.

His most recent building is the Villa Fuji (2000), a guest house in a natural setting. Unlike the architects I have discussed thus far, Uno does not try to erase roofs, beams, and openings as architectural elements, but expresses them as such. He is close to Mikan in that he does not perform any operation of abstraction. But whereas Mikan's buildings are unapologetically materialist, Uno's work seems to want to maintain a qualitative depth. And yet this is different from the kind of "thing-like" quality that someone like Abe Hitoshi is after. It is a more natural, relaxed, and leisurely expression. The fact that he talks about this building in reference to a European villa gives a sense of his faith in "architecture."

But I get a better sense of Uno's fundamental orientation from the book *Tokyo 2001*, which he published in collaboration with his friend Okagawa Mitsugu. The book introduces fourteen projects that encompass the characteristic aspects of Tokyo as a city.

The book describes the near future of Tokyo through hyper-architecture like the "highway residences" planned to go above the freeway along Tokyo Bay, "one room skyscrapers" consisting solely of one-room apartments for individuals or couples, and the seamless integration of convenience stores and houses known as "convenience housing." The vision articulated here might be said to have been partially realized already in the ultra-abstract architecture of Sejima and Nishizawa.

The five architectural teams I have discussed here oppose and approach each other, each with their own topology. And yet somehow they are linked together. I can only hope that this cross section of the diffuse scene of contemporary Japanese architecture will help elucidate the nature of that connection.

Toyo Ito
Born in Seoul in 1941
Graduated in 1965 from Tokyo University
Worked with Kiyonori Kikutake (1965 -1969)
Established Urban Robot (Urbot) in Tokyo in 1971
Name changed to Toyo Ito & Associates in 1979
Honorary Fellowship of AIA
"Academician" from The International Academy of Architecture - IAA (2000)
Good Design Awards 2001 Grand Prize for Sendai Mediateque
From Japan Industrial Design Promotion Organization.
Honorary Professor of University of North London

Selected works:
Hôpital Cognac-Jay, Paris (planning stage)
Mediatheque Project in Sendaï, Miyagi (2000)
Community activities + Senior Citizen Day Care Centre, Yokohama (1997)
Yatsushiro Municipal Museum, Kumamoto (1991)
Tower of Winds in Yokohama, Kanagawa (1986)
Silver Hut, house of the architect, Tokyo (1984)

序文

がそのまま表現になっていくような建築をつくろうとするのである。小嶋がいかに複雑な生きたアクティヴィティを把えようとしても、一旦客観的な抽象空間に出て、そこでの理性的操作として方法を組み立てる、つまり近代主義の延長上で近代を超えようと試みるのに対し、阿部＋小野田の方法は、近代主義的＜最適解＞の否定から始まると言える。近作「（仮称）苓北コミュニティーホール（2002）」は正しくそうしたワークショップの繰り返しから実現した建築である。言い換えれば、そのワークショップ自体が、つまり設計から施工に到るプロセス事態が、即に建築を使用しているのである。この尖鋭な方法がいかなる表現を生むのか期待される。

＜みかんぐみ＞は複数のパートナーによるチームであり、すべての作品も個人名で発表されることはない。恐らくそれは、建築が個人の芸術的表現となることへの否定の表明であると思われる。彼らは重く人を圧倒させたり、感動させるような作品を否定し、もっとアノニマスで軽い建築をつくりたいように見える。建築の存在の軽さにこそ、現代の最大の批評性があると考えるように見える。

阿部＋小野田チームのように、＜みかんぐみ＞もワークショップから建築の現実化を試みる。しかしその意味合いはかなり異なっている。阿部達がワークショップによる対話のなかから、人間やものの情に触れ合う喜びを発見しようとしているのに対し、＜みかん＞の、人々との対話はもっと日常的でプラグマティックなレベルに意図的に止まっている。都会的とも言えよう。

創造と呼ぶ深遠さを求める方法こそが、人間の排除に向かうと彼らは危倶する。社会のもっとスタンダードなレベルのなかにも、ものを発見する楽しさや面白さはいくらでも転がっているではないか、というのが彼らの主張である。彼らが最近出版した＜団地再生計画/みかんぐみのリノベーションカタログ（INAX出版）＞は、正しくそのような日常的アイデア集である。

実現した近作「八代の保育園（2001）」においても突出した表現は一切回避されている。木材は構造材としての梁や柱に、また仕上材としての床にも天井にも露出されているし、ディテールにも格別の抽象化への操作がなされているようには見えない。ものはものとして即物的なレベルを保っている。またプランニングにおいても＜妹島＋西沢＞や＜小嶋一浩＞等のような抽象的操作はない。具体的なレベルで具体的な解決を企てる、つまり作品性を排除する、という方向で、彼らは一貫しているのである。

宇野求の試みも具体性という点では＜みかんぐみ＞と共通している。しかし彼は大学に籍を置くプロフェッサー・アーキテクトであり、実現された作品は多くない。

そのなかで彼の最新作＜VILLA FUJII(2000)＞は自然のなかに建つゲストハウスである。先に述べた建築家の作品と異なり、屋根や梁、壁、開口部等の建築要素は消されることなく、建築要素として表現されている。抽象操作が行われていない、という点では＜みかんぐみ＞と共通しているが、＜みかん＞の表現が素っ気ない程即物的につくられているのに対し、宇野の表現はしっとりとして奥行きのある質感を保とうとしているように見える。それは阿部仁史が試みようとするものの＜もの＞たる性質の表現とも異なる。もっと自然で落ち着いたゆとりの表現とでも言ったらよいであろうか。西欧の＜ヴィラ＞を参照しつつ、彼がこの建築を解説することからも、＜建築＞への彼の信頼をうかがうことができる。

しかしこの実作よりも、宇野求が友人である岡河貢とコラボレートして出版した＜TOKYO 2001（2001）＞に、私はより彼の建築に対する本質的指向を感じとる。ここにはTOKYOという都市の特異性を敷衍させた14のプロジェクトが紹介されている。例えば東京湾岸の高速道路上に計画される＜ハイウェイレジデンス＞、個人やカップル用のワンルーム・アパートメントだけでつくられる＜ワンルームスカイスクレーパー＞、コンビニエンス・ストアとハウジングが溶融した＜コンビニエンスハウジング＞等、ハイパー・アーキテクチュアによる近未来のTOKYOのランドスケープが描かれている。ここに描かれているヴィジョンは部分的には妹島＋西沢の超抽象的建築として既に実現されている、とも言えよう。かくしてここに登場する5組の建築家達は相互に対立し合い、時に接近し、それぞれに異なる位相をテーマとしつつ、どこかでリンクし合う関係にある。拡散する日本の現代建築のひとつの断面から、それを解明する端緒が得られればと期待する次第である。

伊東豊雄

1941年　韓国、ソウルに生まれる
1965年　東京大学工学部建築学科卒業
1965年－1969年　菊竹清訓建築設計事務所に勤務
1971年　株式会社アーバンロボット（URBOT）を東京に設立
1979年　伊東豊雄建築設計事務所に改称
AIA名誉会員
IAAから"Academician"を受賞（2000年）
2001年グッドデザイン賞を仙台メディアテークで受賞
北ロンドン大学名誉教授

Spain
スペイン

Abalos y Herreros
アバロス＆エレロス

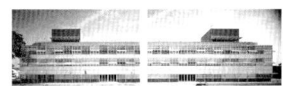
Central administration Building, Universidad de Extremadura, Merida, Spain, 1999-2001
© Bleda & Rosa

El Mirador: Mixed-use tower block, Cadiz, Spain, 1999
© exit lmi

Four Bioclimatic Housing Towers in Salburúa, Vitoria, Spain, 2001-2002
© exit lmi

Wœrman tower in Las Palmas, Canary Island, Spain, 2001-2003
© gestalt

Iñaki Abalos and Juan Herreros have worked together since 1984; they are senior teachers in the Architecture School of Madrid where they were also construction tutors during the period 1984-1988. They are the authors of *Le Corbusier. Skyscrapers*, *Tower and Office*, and *Natural- Artificial*. Their work, which has received several awards, is compiled in a monograph published by Gustavo Gili; it has been reviewed by specialized magazines and has taken part in individual and collective exhibitions such as the one promoted by the MOMA with the motto "Light Construction" (New York, 1995), or "New Trends of Architecture 2002" (Tokyo 2002). In 1997 it was published in *Areas of Impunity*, which compiled texts, work and projects up to that date and in 2000 in *Recycling Madrid* with the same criteria. They have taken part in several workshops and international seminars, being named "Buell Book Fellows" and "Visiting Teachers" of Columbia University, New York, in 1995, and "Diploma Unit Masters" in the Architectural Association of London in 1998, as well as "Professeurs Invités" in the EPF of Architecture of Lausanne. Since 1992 they have directed and coordinated the International Multimedia League (LMI), which is an organization dedicated to contributing to the simplification and intensification of artistic practice.

イニャキ・アバロスとホァン・エレロスは1984年から協同している。マドリッド建築学校で教鞭をとり、1984年から1988年には建設学も教えている。『ル・コルビジェ．超高層建築』、『タワー・アンド・オフィス』、『ナチュラル―アーティフィシャル』の著者である。これまでに受賞している彼らの作品は、ギュスタボ・ジリより出版された作品集に収められ、専門誌にもしばしば紹介されている。また個展やニューヨーク近代美術館が催した「ライト・コンストラクション」（ニューヨーク、1995）、「日本・ヨーロッパ建築の新潮流」（東京、2002）のようなグループ展にも出展されている。1997年にそれまでのテキスト、作品とプロジェクトをまとめた『免責の領域』が編集され、また2000年には『リサイクリング・マドリッド』が同様の方針で編れた。彼らは「ビュエル・ブック・フェローズ」等の国際セミナーやワークショップに参加しており、1995年にはコロンビア大学の客員教授、1998年にはAAスクールのディプロマ・ユニット・マスター、EPFアーキテクチュア・ラウサナの客員教授を務めている。1992年からインターナショナル・マルチメディア・リーグ（LMI）のディレクションとコーディネートを行なっている。これは芸術活動の簡明化と強化に寄与するための組織である。

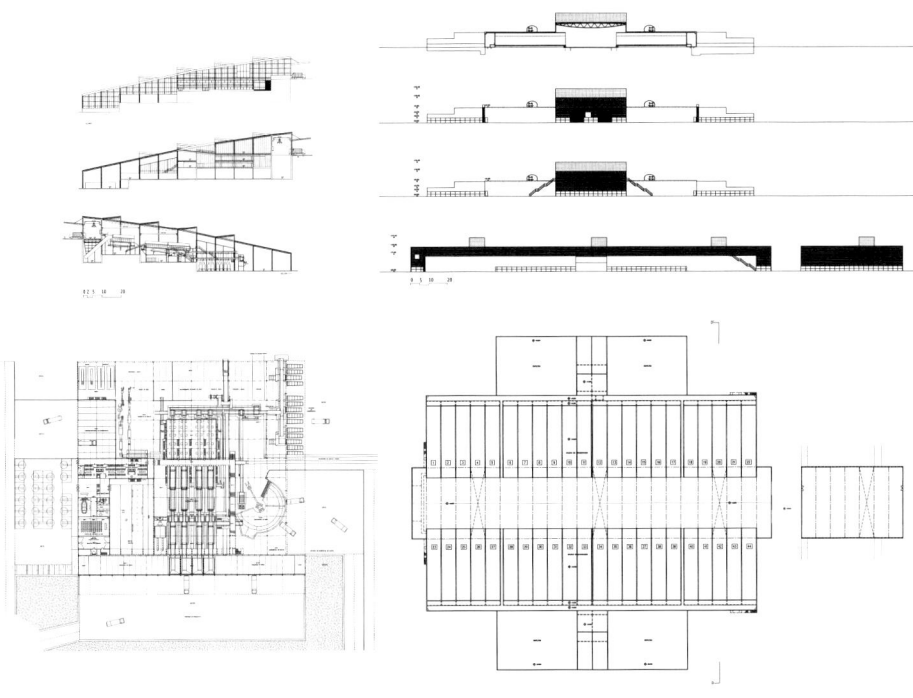
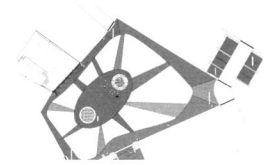
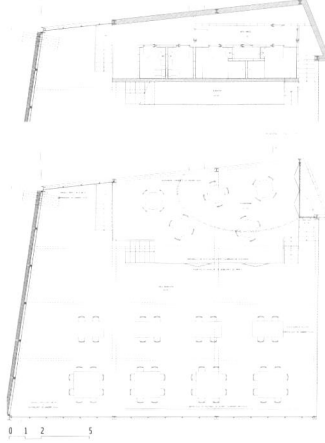
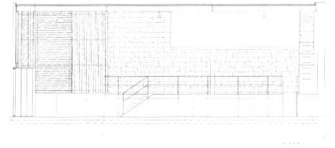

New recycling plant for urban waste
Valdemingómez, Madrid, Spain, 1997-1999

The project is part of a group of projects that were to create a rational system for the treatment and recycling of waste, as well as the transformation and the incorporation of its land into the future Southeast Regional Park, which was one of the city's most attractive projects intended to even out the social and environmental differences that existed between the North and the South. The recycling plant concentrates a heterogeneous group of buildings for the selection and processing of refuse, storage, workshops and offices, all brought together beneath a large, inclined green roof that echoes as much the gravitational character of the process as it does the original hillside upon which it sits, "restored" by taking advantage of the compost that is produced. The building is wrapped with recycled polycarbonate that unifies the various programs and incorporates a museum area that has a route for visitors, aimed at making the public more environmentally aware.
The green roof, the polycarbonate, the light riveted structure and the interior finishes show this spirit, as they demonstrate the best environmental compromise that is currently possible with available techniques.
This building is composed of two complementary constructions: one is dedicated to the production of compost from organic waste, and the second is dedicated to the control and the weighing of the trucks that enter the enclosure. Both have been treated as though they were industrial objects that set up a dialogue with the scale and the singularity of the landscape, built using systems that are analogous to those used in the first building.
The center has a life-span of twenty-five years, after which it will be recycled as a service building for the park or dismantled so that its components themselves may be recycled.

新しい都市廃棄物リサイクルプラント
スペイン、マドリッド、ヴァルデミンゴメス
1997-1999

これは廃棄物を処理、リサイクルするとともに、その土地を変容し、将来の南東地区公園に組みこむための合理的なシステムをつくるという一群のプロジェクトの一環である。それは北部と南部の社会的・環境的格差を均等にするという、マドリッドで最も魅力的なプロジェクトのひとつであった。
リサイクルプラントは多様な建物群の集合である。分別、廃物の処理施設、倉庫、ワークショップ、事務室等の施設がすべて大きな傾斜した緑色の屋根の下に入っている。屋根の傾斜は、重力を利用した工程を反映すると共に、そこで生産されるコンポストを使い、それが位置するのがもとは丘の中腹であったことを"復元"している。建物はリサイクルされたポリカーボネイトで包まれ、プログラムのための様々な施設や、環境問題を多くの人に認識してもらうための展示スペースと見学ルートがその中にはある。
緑の屋根もポリカーボネイトで、軽く鋲止めされてあり、内部も同様である。これが現在可能な技術の中では最も環境的に問題の少ない構法である。
建物はふたつの相補的な建築物からなる。ひとつは有機的な廃棄物から堆肥をつくる施設であり、もうひとつはやって来る収集トラックを監視し、重量をはかる施設である。どちらの建物も周囲のランドスケープのスケールと特異性について対話をかわす工業的なオブジェのように扱われ、最初の建物に使用した建築システムと同様の方法でつくられている。
このセンターは25年の使用期間が決まっているが、それ以降は公園の管理施設となるか、取り壊されて各部材がリサイクルして使われることになる。

Village Hall and Square
Colmenarejo, Madrid, Spain, 1997-1999

The initial intention of paving a small square in a village within the metropolitan area of Madrid caused us to propose that the only available site be occupied with a village hall that was meant to strengthen civic life.
For the square, we proposed an outline that was capable of reorganizing the unorthodox group of elements that were to be preserved, while the hall was thought of as both a covered extension of the square and a tensed enclosure of its incomplete body.
To materialize both ideas, an extremely light and permeable construction system was used, finished with natural or recycled materials that allow continuous changes of image and very different uses of the space. The project changes the hierarchies and the perception of the space, setting up a dialogue between memory and the present with the intention of reflecting the changing condition of these peripheral areas.

コルメナレホ村ホールと広場
スペイン、マドリッド、コルメナレホ
1997-1999

マドリッド首都圏内の村の小さな広場を舗装するという当初の計画を聞いて、市民の生活を豊かにするための村営ホールは、有効利用できる部分だけを占有すべきであると私たちは提案した。広場については、残すべき要素の変則的なグループを再構成できるアウトラインを提案した。一方、ホールは広場の覆われた延長と捉え、不完全な全体の緊張した囲いと考えた。このアイディアを現実化するため、非常に軽量で透過性のある建築システムを用い、イメージの連続的な変化や空間の多様な利用を可能にする天然、あるいはリサイクルされた材料で仕上げている。このプロジェクトは場所のヒエラルキーと知覚を変化させ、記憶と現在の対話をもたらし、周辺エリアの状況の変化を反映させようとする。

New recycling plant for urban waste
Valdemingómez, Madrid, Spain, 1997-1999
© Luis Asín

Village Hall and Square
Colmenarejo, Madrid, Spain, 1997-1999
© Bleda & Rosa

Japan
日本

Atelier Hitoshi Abe
阿部仁史アトリエ

Shirasagi Bridge, Miyagi, Japan, 1994
© Shunichi Atsumi (Studi Shun's)

Miyagi Sekii Ladies Clinic, Hurukawa, Miyagi, Japan, 2001
© Nacasa & Partners

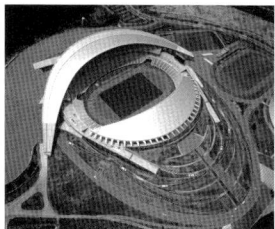

Miyagi Stadium, Rifu, Miyagi, Japan, 2000
© Eiji Kitada

Yomiuri Media Miyagi Guest House, Zaó, Miyagi, Japan, 1998
© Shunichi Atsumi (Studi Shun's)

Hitoshi Abe was born in Sendai, Japan in 1962. He received his master's degree in Architecture in 1989 from the Southern California Institute of Architecture. From 1988 to 1992, he worked for Coop Himmelblau in Los Angeles. In 1992, he received his doctorate in architecture from Tohoku University and established Atelier Hitoshi Abe in Sendai. Since he has been the principal architect at his atelier, as well as the head of Architecture Design Laboratory at Tohoku Institute of Technology. His completed works include the Miyagi Stadium (2000), n-house (2000), Michinoku Folklore Museum (2000), restaurant "Neige Lune Fleur" (1999), Gravel 2 (1998), Yomiuri Media Miyagi Guest House (1997), Miyagi Water Tower and Shirasagi Bridge (1994). He was awarded for the 14th Yoshioka Award for Yomiuri Media Miyagi Guest House (1998), Tohoku Architectural Award for Michinoku Folklore Museum (2001), and the 42nd Building Contractors Society Award for the Miyagi Stadium (2001).

映画のハロルド・ロイドは決して笑わない。彼はただ機械のように淡々と走り続けることによって、さまざまに暴れ回る世界にアクセスするのだ。この映画でわれわれが見ているのは、俳優であるロイドの存在ではない。彼の身体はすでにフィルムの世界に融け込んでしまっており、われわれが楽しんでいるのはそこから生じる波動なのである。
テクノロジーというプログラムが目指しているのは、われわれの身体をどれだけ多様な時空に開くことができるのかということにほかならない。本来、われわれが備えている他への存在へのアクセス能力は、最近のテクノロジーによって圧倒的に加速され、身体はさまざまに結合を始めて、世界に緩やかに融け出し始めているのだ。その先に見え始めているのは差異ある同一性に支持されたボーダーレスな世界観である、どうやらわれわれはテクノロジカルなパラダイスを目指しているらしいという予感である。しかしながら、建築は本来的に身体と世界との間を遮断しようとする反楽園の存在であり、内部しかない世界に外部を生み出すものである。このアダムの葉っぱに類するものは、いまだ楽園からの追放を招いた差異に向かうベクトル上で、融け出そうとする身体をとらえて箱詰めにしているのである。
建築か楽園か？われわれはいずれかのキーを選択しなくてはならない。

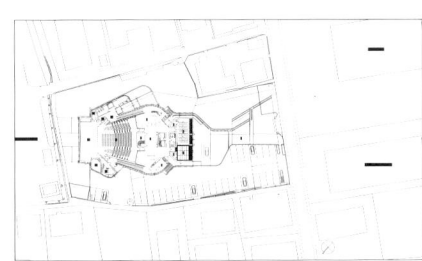

Shiki Community Hall
Reihoku, Kumamoto, Japan, 2000-2002
Atelier Hitoshi Abe + Yasuaki Onoda

Conditions
As one of the projects for the Kumamoto Artpolis, Citizen's Town Development Project, it was necessary to consult with the local inhabitants on the fundamental issue of "what should we make?" rather than simply "how do we make a specific building type?"

Location
The former site of a public office that was moved to alongside a bypass. It is in the central part of the region, and adjoins an elementary school.

Design intent
We began exploring the difficult themes of this project through workshops, to create an outward-oriented base for the support and integration of the varied activities of the local inhabitants. In summary, it appeared that we must build a platform to constantly maintain the activities of this workshop. Sublimating our methods and intentions, a passive "what can be received?" situation began to be transformed into an active "what can be given?" one, and both during and after construction the workshop will continue to question the purpose of this forum. The architects' professional skills were enhanced, and the role of giving meaning to this forum was extended to the local inhabitants. Escaping the limits of architectural "hardware," this process becomes a supple entity.

Concept of the preliminary plan
Network axis x community axis. Performance/meeting functions as network nodes. Public hall functions as community support. Two different axes are linked by the information corner into a facility of new form.

仮称）苓北町民ホール
熊本県天草郡苓北町支岐　2000-2002
阿部仁史アトリエ＋小野田泰明

要求：
「くまもとアートポリス、私たちのまちづくり事業」のひとつであるこのプロジェクトにおいては「特定のビルディングタイプの建物をどうつくるのか？」ではなく「何をつくるべきなのか？」という根本的なことから住民と一緒に考えることが要求された。

敷地：
バイパス沿いに移動した役場の跡地。志岐地区の中心部に位置し、志岐小学校に隣接している。

趣旨：
この難しい課題に対してワークショップを通じて探り出したのは、住民のさまざまな活動を支援し、結びつけ、外に向けて発信する基地をつくること、つまりこのワークショップのアクティビティそのものを恒常的に維持し得るプラットホームをつくるべきであるということであった。手段が目的に昇華したことにより、「何を得られるのか」といった受動的な場が「何を与えられるのか」といった能動的な場に変わりはじめ、ワークショップは建設中も竣工後も継続され、場の意味を問い続ける。建築家の職能は拡張されて、場に意味を与える役割は住民にまで広げられた。建築はハードウェアの束縛から抜け出して、柔らかな運動体になっていく。

基本計画：
ネットワーク軸×コミュニティ軸。ネットワークのノードとしての舞台芸術・集会機能。コミュニティサポートしての公民館機能。異なる二軸が、情報コーナーで連結される新しい型の施設。

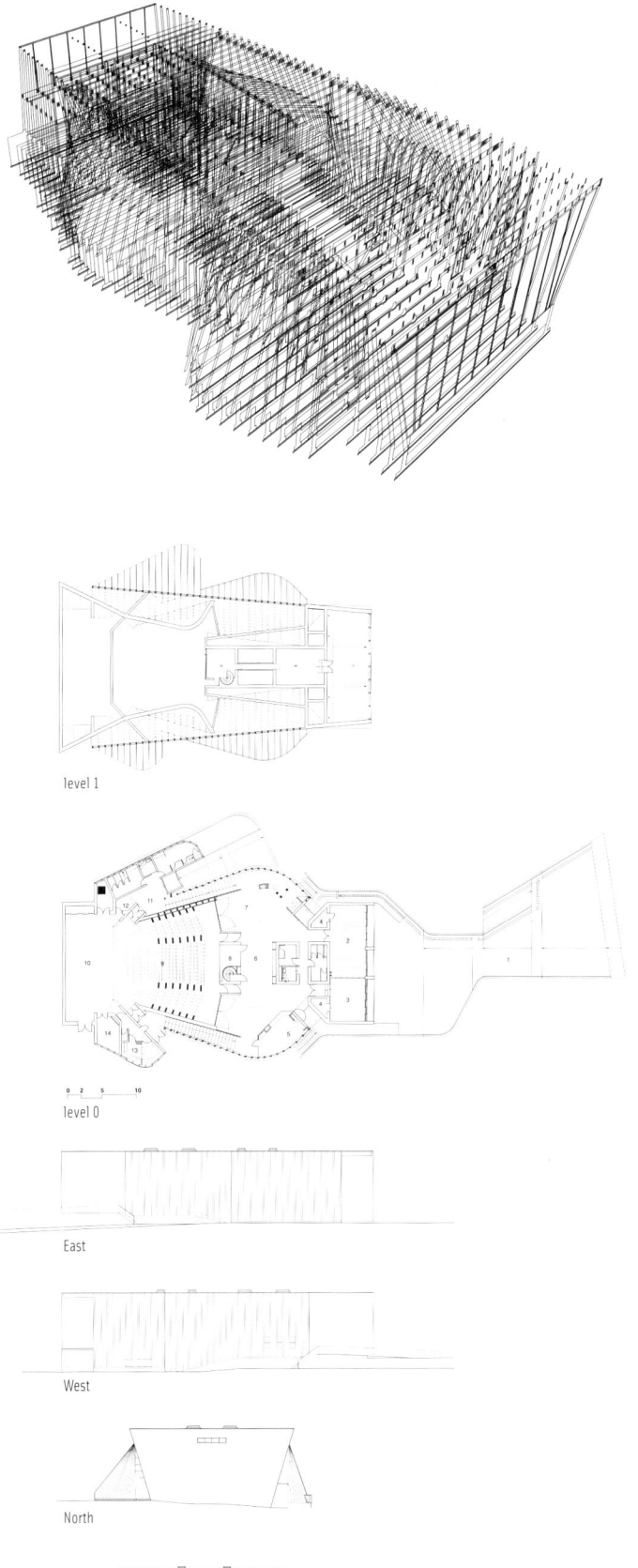

level 1

level 0

East

West

North

Shiki Community Hall
Reihoku, Kumamoto, Japan, 2000-2002
© Daici Ano (Nacasa & Partners)

Greece
ギリシャ

Yannis Aesopos
ヤニス・アエソポス

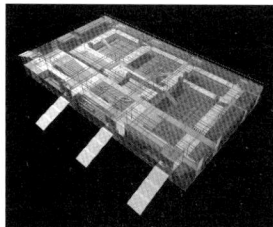

Kansai-kan of the National Diet Library, Japan, 1996 (with Christina Loukopoulou)

Monastiraki Square, Athens, 1998 (with Christina Loukopoulou)

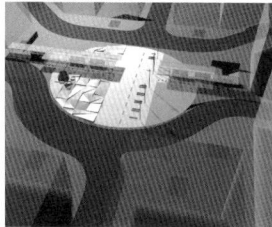

Omonoia Square, Athens, 1998 (with Christina Loukopoulou)

Zefyri Cultural Center, Athens, 1996 (with Christina Loukopoulou)

Conceptual association

Our work views architecture as a discourse of space that supports a multiplicity of activities. We are interested in the prevalence of activity over form, a condition we found to be inherent in the contemporary city shaped through rapid and even paralogical urbanization processes. This is also the case in the contemporary Greek city produced through the infinite repetition of the generic building type of the *polykatoikia* (the privately constructed medium-size apartment building) and its un-designed residues which operate as public space. The contemporary (Greek) city resists easy categorizations and identifications of form, place, public and private; however, programmatic densities develop freely within its banal built mass. Any aesthetic discourse and formalistic ambition is completely subjugated to the everyday flux of activities that are based on the ephemeral, the experiential and the eventful. An association with this 'non-context' has to seek an unveiling of its concealed order and a positive appropriation of its constituent elements in a conceptual and not an iconographic or formal manner. Straightforwardness and simplicity of concept, reduced form, multi-programmatic or un-programmed platforms and containers, soft borders, spatiality of movement and views have become for us the principal elements of architecture.

Yannis Aesopos (1966) studied at the National Technical University of Athens (1989) and at Harvard Graduate School of Design (March 1991). He is the co-editor of Metapolis review of architecture and urban culture in Athens (1997-) and an Assistant Professor of Architecture at the University of Patras, Greece. Aesopos lives and works in Athens.

概念との共存

私たちは、建築とはアクティビティの多様性を可能にする空間の話法だと考えている。急速で時に非論理的なアーバニゼイションの過程を経てつくられた現代の都市に固有の状況である、アクティビティの形態に対する優位について私たちは興味をもっている。ポリカトイキア（民間でつくられた中規模のアパートメント）という一般的な形式の建物が無限に繰り返し建設され、そのデザイン不在の残余空間がパブリック・スペースとして使われる、現代のギリシャの都市にあっても同様である。現代の（ギリシャの）都市を、形態、場所、パブリックとプライベートといった基準で分類したり、同定したりするのは容易ではない。しかしプログラムの密度はこの凡庸な建設物の塊の中で自由に展開しているのである。どんな美学的な会話や形態的な欲望も、エフェメラルなもの、経験的で多事的であることに基づいた日々のアクティビティの流動に全く従属してしまっている。この「コンテクストの不在」と共存してゆくためには、図像的・形態的でない概念的な方法で、その隠された秩序の覆いを取り、その構成要素を積極的に適用することを目指さなくてはならない。概念の率直さと明快さ、単純化された形態、多重のプログラムの／プログラムのないプラットフォームや容器、柔らかな境界、動きと視界の空間性といったものが建築にとって主要な要素となる。

1966年生まれのヤニス・アエソポスは国立アテネ工科大学（1989）とハーバード大学院デザインスクール（修士号1991）で学んだ。建築／都市文化の批評誌「メタポリス」の共同編集者であり（1997-）、パトラス大学建築学科の助教授をつとめる。アテネ在住。

level 3

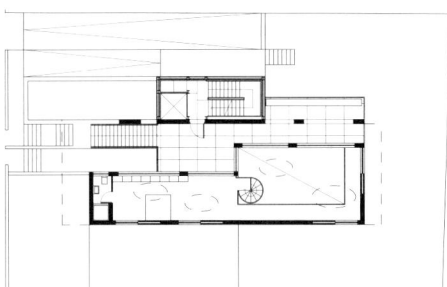
level 2

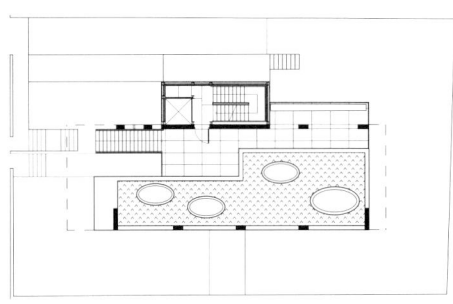
level 1

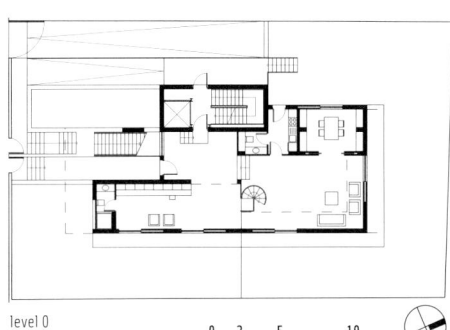
level 0   0 2 5 10

Poly/mono-katoikia
Athens, Greece, 1997-2002

The building is situated in a residential suburb of Athens in which *monokatoikias* (single-family residence houses) freely coexist with *polykatoikias* (multi-residence apartment buildings). The unlikely 'symbiosis' of these two most common building types of the Greek city instigated the design which proposes a hybrid structure combining a two-story suburban *monokatoikia* with the structural frame of a *polykatoikia*.

The monokatoikia is attached to the ground, closes itself to the street and opens up to its surrounding garden; within its double-height living space a metal mezzanine level is used as a bedroom.

The *polykatoikia* is lifted from the ground and offers three floors of identical apartments with large balconies that open up to the view. The apartments are accessed through a free-standing metal and glass structure that contains both staircase and elevator.

The void, ground level entrance space of the generic *polykatoikia* (the 'pilotis') is displaced to the first floor. This empty, 'in-between' space, accessed by a large staircase, is, at the same time, a ground and a roof, an elevated entrance and a pebble - garden. It physically separates the two building types and injects movement and action right into the heart of the building.

ポリ／モノ―カトイキア
ギリシャ、アテネ　1999-2002

モノカトイキア（一家族の住む家）とポリカトイキア（集合住宅ムアパートメント）が自由に共存するアテネ郊外の住宅地に建物はある。ギリシャの都市の最も一般的なこの二つのビルディングタイプの滅多にない'共生'が、ポリカトイキアの構造フレームの中に2階立ての郊外型のモノカトイキアを入れ込むというハイブリッドなデザインを発想させた。

モノカトイキアは地面に接し、通りに対しては閉じて、周囲の庭に向けて開いている。2層分の高さをもつリビングスペースの中に、金属製の中2階があり寝室として使われる。

ポリカトイキアは地面から浮かんで3層の同一なアパートメントとなり、風景の開けた大きなバルコニーを持っている。アパートメントは中に階段室とエレベーターをもつ、自立した金属とガラスの構造物によってアクセスされる。

一般的なポリカトイキアでは地上にあるヴォイドなスペース（ピロティ）は、ここでは2階に置かれている。幅広い階段によってアクセスされるこの空（から）の中間的な空間は、同時にグランドであり屋根であり、空中のエントランスであり小石の敷かれた庭である。それは物理的に二つのビルディングタイプを分け、建物の心臓部に動きと活動を注入する。

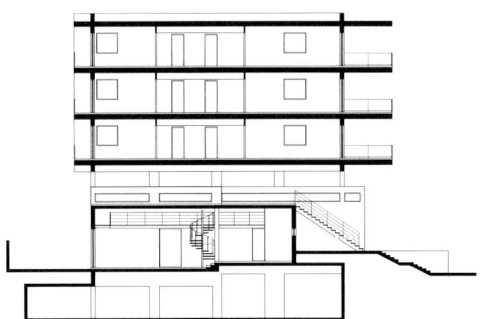

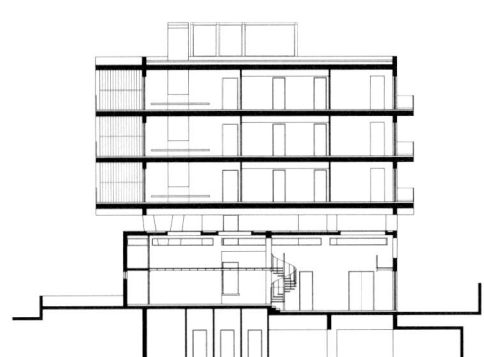

Poly/mono-katoikia
Athens, Greece, 1997-2002
© Eritz Attali

Portugal
ポルトガル

Aires Mateus & Associados LDA
アイレス・マテウス&アソシアードス

House, Alvalade, Portugal, 1999-2000

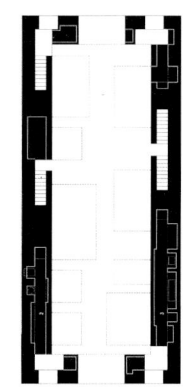

House, Brejos de Azeitão, Setúbal, Portugal, 2000

Manuel Aires Mateus was born in Lisbon, Portugal, in 1963. Graduated in 1986, he was a collaborator of Gonçalo Byrne in 1983. He has been teaching since 1986, having been a visiting professor in Portugal, Spain, Italy, Switzerland, Argentina, England, Brazil, Norway, Mexico and the United States.

Francisco Aires Mateus was born in Lisbon, Portugal, in 1964. Graduated in 1987, he became a collaborator of Gonçalo Byrne in 1987. He has been teaching since 1999, having been a visiting professor in Portugal, Switzerland and Brazil.

The constructed projects have mostly been the result of awarded competitions. Some of the most relevant works are the extension to the engineers guild headquarters in Lisbon, student housing, campus II in Coimbra; canteen, campus university of Aveiro; central pedagogical unit, polo II university of Coimbra; universidade Nova rectory in Lisbon; library, auditorium and arts center of Sines in Sines; the rebuilding of the Trindade college in Coimbra.

For their works they have been awarded with the Architect/ Arkial award (Portugal), Luigi Cosenza award (Italy), II Bienal Ibero / Amerinan of Architecture (México) and the F A D Award of Architecture and Interiorism (Spain).

They aim to maximize the possibilities open to each work in the program and the context, proposing spatial structures that are strongly habitable and identifiable, characterized by the density of the materials used, which settles upon geometries apparently diagrammatical, leading to a clear logic in the development of the project.

マニュエル・アイレス・マテウスはポルトガルのリスボンで1963年に生まれた。1986年に学位を取得し、1983年からゴンサール・ビルヌの協力者を勤めた。1986年から教鞭をとり、ポルトガル、スペイン、イタリア、スイス、アルゼンチン、イングランド、ブラジル、ノルウェー、メキシコ、アメリカで客員教授をつとめている。

フランシスコ・アイレス・マテウスはポルトガルのリスボンで1964年に生まれた。1987年に学位を取得し、1987年からゴンサール・ビルヌの協力者を勤めた。1999年から教鞭をとり、ポルトガル、スイス、ブラジルで客員教授をつとめている。

実現したプロジェクトのほとんどは、設計競技で勝ち得たものである。主要な作品は、リスボンのエンジニア組合本部の増築、コインブラのキャンパスIIの学生宿舎、アベイロ大学キャンパスの学生食堂、コインブラのポロII大学の中央教育学部、リスボンのノバ大学の神父宿舎、シネスのシネスアートセンター、図書館とオーディトリウム、コインブラのトリニダードカレッジの再建等である。

アーキテクト／アルキアル賞（ポルトガル）、ルイジ・コセンツァ賞（イタリア）、IIビエナル・イベロ／アメリナン・オブ・アーキテクチュア（メキシコ）、FAD建築・インテリア賞（スペイン）等の受賞をしている。

私たちが目指すのは、どのプロジェクトのプログラムやコンテクストについてもオープンに考え可能性を最大化し、非常に住みやすい、アイデンティファイできる空間構造、明確に図式的・幾何学的でありかつ密度の高い材料を使うという特徴を持ち、プロジェクトの展開と共に明快な論理へと収束するような空間構造を提案することである。

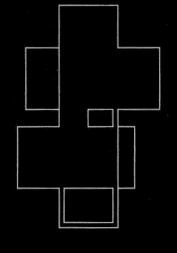
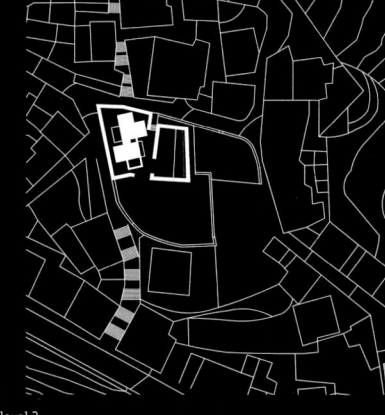
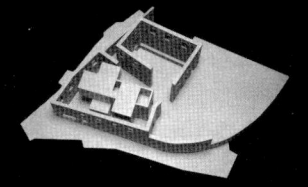

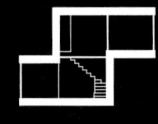

level 2

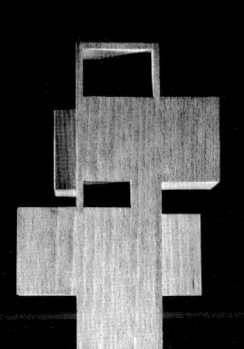
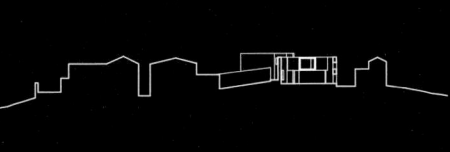
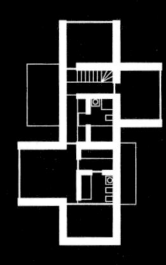

level 1

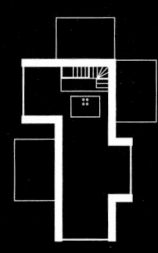

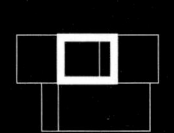

level 0

0   4,5   9 m

House in Alenquer
Alenquer, Portugal, 1999-2002

The existing house had, as its main value, its external walls that, when stripped, revealed themselves. The walls created spaces with a strong identity, given by their weight as well as by the ambiguity of their limits. These internal/external spaces were "furnished." On one side a water tank was excavated in the continuity of the walls. On the other side the enclosed areas. The spaces of this small house ought to be clear. The glass limit creates a precise boundary on the thick walls. Tension is given by the confrontation between a freely redesigned geometry over an existing object, and the object with clear rules that, by the perception of its walls, merged in itself and became autonomous from them.

アレンケルの住宅
ポルトガル、アレンケル　1999-2002

そこにもとあった住宅は、特徴として、引き剥がしても再生できる屋外の壁をもっていた。その壁は、その量感と限界のあいまいさによって、強いアイデンティティをもった空間をつくりだしていた。内部/外部のこの空間は"ファーニッシュ"されていた。片側では、壁の延長線上で水槽が掘り出された。もう一方には囲われたエリアがあった。この小さな家の空間は明確でなくてはならない。ガラスの限界が厚い壁の正確な境界をつくりだす。既存のオブジェの上に自由に描き直された幾何学と、壁を認知することによってそこにあらわれる壁からは自立した明快なルールをもったオブジェとが対峙することによって緊張感が生まれる。

House in Alenquer
Alenquer- Portugal, 1999-2002
© Daniel Malhão

United Kingdom
イギリス

Allford Hall Monaghan Morris
アルフォード・ホール・モナハン・モリス

Barbican Arts Centre, London, England, 2001
© Tim Soar

Monsoon Headquarters, London, England, 2001
© Tim Soar

North Croydon Medical Centre, London, England, 1999 © Tim Soar

Dalston Lane Housing, London, England, 1998
© Tim Soar

Simon Allford, Jonathan Hall, Paul Monaghan and Peter Morris founded the practice in 1989. We shared a view that architecture could be satisfying to use, beautiful to look at, cost effective to build and operate and that the procurement process could itself inform the project.

Each of our projects has different needs, so outwardly our buildings show great diversity but there is an underlying consistency to our designs, which comes from our adherence to these founding principles.

We strive for a pragmatic and clear working method. Pragmatism enables us to optimize a site and a budget for a particular brief. Clarity facilitates discussion of our concepts between the client, the design team, statutory authorities and the public.

Our maxim, "If it can't be drawn it can't be discussed" reminds us constantly that proposals should be strong and logical, and must be presented clearly, so that all these constituencies can contribute to the outcome.

Our working method shapes our aesthetic approach. If a design concept is clear and logical, the resulting building will express its function in a clear and logical way. It will be easy to recognize and enjoyable to use.

In optimizing a budget we do not waste money on expensive disguises; a feature which deserves expense is important and its importance should be apparent.

We are innovative where appropriate, but innovation is as often finding simpler ways of doing things better as it is finding new things to do.

サイモン・アルフォード、ジョナサン・ホール、ポール・モナハンとピーター・モリスにより1989年に事務所が設立された。私たちは、建築とは機能を満たし、美しく、建設と使用の費用対効果があり、そして実現の過程自体がプロジェクトをあらわすという共通の視点をもっている。

私たちのプロジェクトは、それぞれが違った与件をもつため、表面的には建物は多様であるが、こういった基本原則に忠実であるために、その設計には通底する一貫性がある。

私たちは、プラグマティックで明快な作業方法に努めている。プラグマティズムによって敷地と予算を概ね最適化して考えることができる。明快さが、クライアント、設計者、役所と市民の間で、私たちのコンセプトを議論することを容易にする。

これらの異なる立場の人間がすべて成果に寄与できるように、計画案は力強く、論理的で明快に提示されなくてはならない。「描くことができないならば、議論することもできない」は、このことを常に意識するための、私たちの合言葉である。

わたしたちの作業方法が、美学的なアプローチをかたちづくる。もし設計コンセプトが明快で論理的ならば、できあがる建物はその機能を明快に論理的に体現するだろう。それは容易に認知でき、使いやすいものとなるだろう。

予算を最適化するという点では、高価な見せかけに費用はかけない。支出を必要とする部分は重要な部分であり、その重要性が明らかなものである。

私たちはしかるべき場合には斬新なことをするが、イノベーションをいうのは新たに発見するというより、得てしてよりシンプルに物事を解決する方法を見つけることだと考えている。

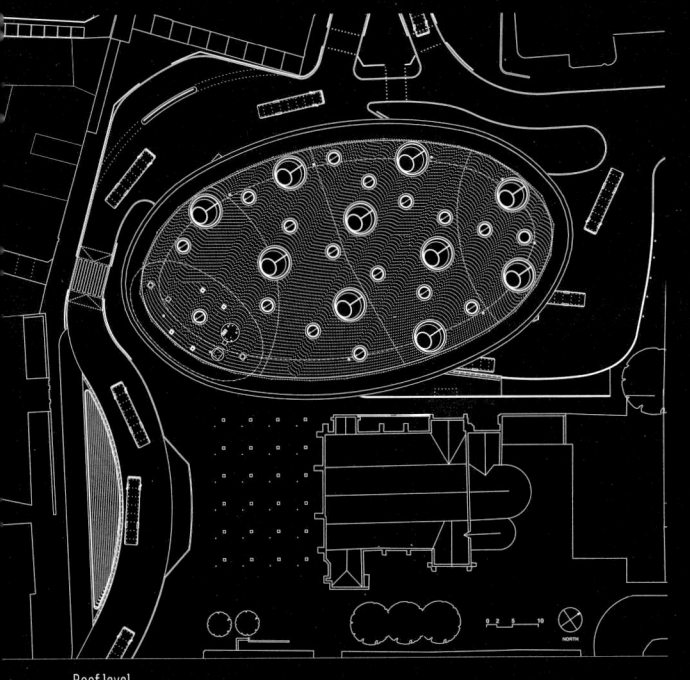

Roof level

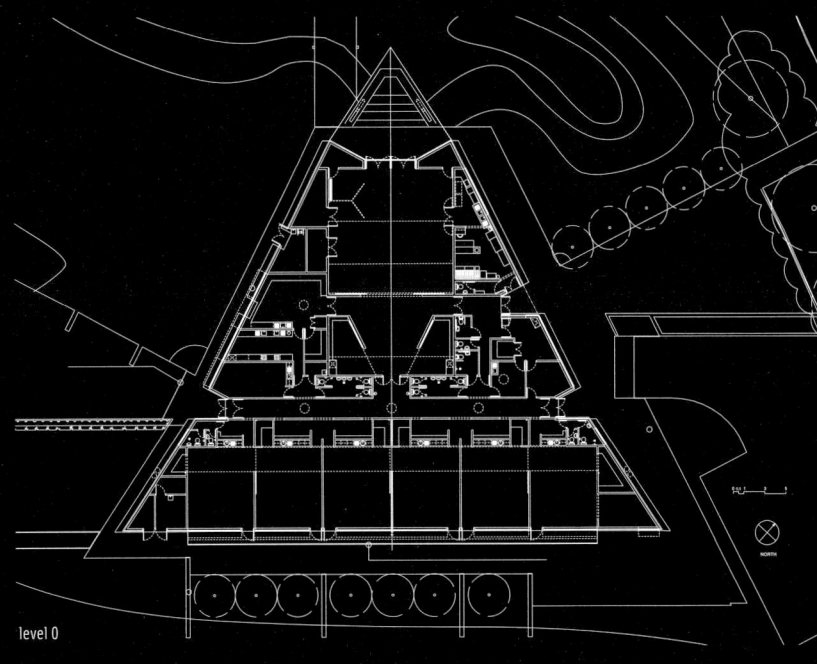

level 0

Saint Paul's Bus Station
Walsall, West Midlands, United Kingdom, 1996-2000

The new bus station – selected in open international competition – is conceived as a 'Room for Walsall' rejecting the brief for a collection of bus shelters. An elliptical canopy, 80m x 45m, hovers 8m above the bus lanes elevated on a combination of steel 'trees' and the concrete shear walls forming the core of the concourse.

Through the re-design of the road layout, the new station has also defined a new town square in front of St Paul's Church. This new civic space along with the elliptical canopy has regenerated a back-lands site.

From outside the canopy's powerful geometry reconciles the fragmented townscape while within it creates panoramic views of the world beyond.

セントポール・バスステーション
英国、ウェスト・ミドランズ、ウォルソール 1996-2000

この新しいバス・ステーションは国際公開コンペティションで選ばれたものであり、バス乗り場を、シェルターの集合という考え方を否定して、"ウォルソールの部屋"だと私たちは捉えている。80m×45mの楕円形のキャノピーが、樹状の鉄骨とコンコースのコアとなるコンクリート壁に支えられて、バスレーンの8m上に浮かんでいる。

道路のレイアウトの変更により、このステーションはセント・ポール教会の前に新しい街の広場を誕生させた。楕円のキャノピーをもった公共のスペースが、裏通りのような場所を再生させた。

外からは、キャノピーの強い幾何学性が、分断された街並みを調停し、キャノピーの中からは、外の世界のパノラマを見ることができる。

Great Notley Primary School
Black Notley, Essex, United Kingdom, 1997-1999

This international competition-winning design for a new prototype sustainable school within a standard government budget is located on a green-field site.

A triangular plan organizes all accommodation around a central internal court. Dedicated circulation space has been limited to a single corridor. The corresponding reduction in area of 10% is reinvested in the sustainable aspects of the building.

The precise geometry is further celebrated in the flared footprint, serrated roof-line and steep roof-lights, which naturally ventilate internal rooms. The cedar cladding is bisected by a dark-stained 'plimsoll line'; a device, which orders the fenestration.

The building has been likened to a 'stealth bomber' landed in rural Essex.

グレイト・ノトリー小学校
英国、エセックス、ブラック・ノトリー 1997-1999

公共建築の標準的なコストで、サステイナブルな学校の新しいプロトタイプをつくるという、国際設計競技で設計者に選ばれたプロジェクトで、緑の草地に立っている。

三角形の平面の中央に屋内の中庭があり、そこを囲んで全ての諸室が置かれている。動線のためのスペースは、1本の廊下に集約されている。そこから生じる10%の面積減は、建物のサステイナブルな側面に活用している。

広がる平面形と、鋸状のルーフライン、室内の自然換気を促す急勾配のトップライト等は、厳密な幾何学によっている。杉板の外装は、濃く着色された"プリムソル ライン"と呼ぶ採光のための装置により二分されている。

建物は、エセックスの田舎に着陸した"ステルス・ボマー"のようだと言われている。

Saint Paul's Bus Station
Walsall, West Midlands, United Kingdom, 1996–2000
© Tim Soar

Germany
ドイツ

b&k+
b&k+

Dwelling and atelier house Geisselstrasse, Cologne, Germany, 1997-2000 (Team b&k+ b,m)
© Michael Reisch

Max, sky-scraper, Frankfurt, Germany, 1999

Dwelling and commercial house Am Stavenhof, Cologne, Germany, 1999-2000
© b&k+

Dwelling house Fabianek - Vaalser Quartier, Aachen, Germany, 1998-2000 (Team b&k+ r)
© b&k+

Since its establishment in the year 1996 the team of b&k+ analyzes cultural systems and structures to apply this research to the architectural process. Architecture, regard less of scale, is from the very beginning a hybrid, an -in between of the concept regarding inside and outside. It is part of a landscape.

Starting from the play of construction and experience, as it is defined in the term Landschaftsbegriff, we develop an interdisciplinary design strategy, in which experimental and pragmatic techniques merge. Ecology, economics and technology are as important as sociocultural and political values. We don't consider planning standards and building codes as a burden to the design process but transform these regulations as well as statistical figures or analyses such as noise calculations into creative potential. In these buildings specialization and flexibility are not contradictions.

Each situation already knows its solution, because it is – like each cell – informed. This information only needs to be found, deciphered and translated. Our work is to collect all information and extract its importance and generative potential. Without any doubt we must incorporate not only technicians, but also artists, musicians, philosophers and scientists into this working method.

In all our projects we seek these forms of collaboration to develop our plus-network. Out of these platforms we produce houses, and also books and exhibitions, or we even found cultural institutions such as an academy in Sindelfingen, Germany. Furthermore it happens, that the product itself becomes inspiration or material, and generates inspiration for musicians that interpret and process these projects again into compositions. A common culture arranges and enriches our active present.

1996年の設立以来、b&k+というチームは文化のシステムと構造を分析し、その成果を建築のプロセスに応用してきた。
建築は原初的に、そのスケールの大小に関わらず、内と外という概念に関してハイブリッドであり中間的である。それはランドスケープの一部なのだ。

建設と経験の戯れから出発して、「風景の概念」という言葉に定義されるように、実験性と実際性が統合された、相互性をもった設計の戦略をたてる。
エコロジー、エコノミクス、テクノロジーは社会文化的・政治的な価値と同様に重要である。私たちは、計画基準や法的規制を設計プロセスの負担だとは考えない。むしろこういった規制を、騒音値のような統計的な数値や分析と共に、創造的なポテンシャルに変容させる。このような建物では、特殊化と柔軟性は矛盾しない。

どのような状況もその解法がわかっている。なぜなら細胞のように情報は与えられているからだ。この情報を見つけだし、解読し、翻訳すればよいのだ。私たちの仕事は様々な情報をすべて集め、その重要性と生成的なポテンシャルを厳密に計ることだ。
このような方式では疑いなく、技術者だけでなく、芸術家、音楽家、哲学者や科学者を巻き込んで行く必要がある。

すべてのプロジェクトで、私たちはこのようなかたちの協同によるプラス＋のネットワークの展開をめざしている。こういった基盤から、私たちは、住宅に始まり出版や展覧会のプロデュース、あるいはドイツのジンデルフィンゲンにおけるアカデミーのような文化組織の設立まで行っている。
さらには、こうして生み出されるものが音楽家のインスピレーションや素材となり、音楽作品の中にこれらのプロジェクトが解釈され、加工されるということがおこるのである。共通の文化が私たちの現在の活動を用意し、豊かにしているのである。

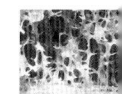

The three projects;- *Telematic Landscape, *New Loft Building Kölner Brett and *BMW Delivery and Event Center, present an example of how b&k+ explores and understands its work.

A project doesn't terminate with its deadline, but gets carried over and further redefined into other projects or buildings. We do not only work with various materials and influences in order to create, but also consider creation as material itself that can inspire and generate other media.

Telematic Landscape

…is an independent, hybrid project. It explores the parameters and schemes of a "telematic" landscape and its experimental construction in reality.

Information is used as a building material and placed in the "Landscape" as a constituent element of our culture. Out of simple clusters a complex framework is generated where space doesn't stop at the surface of the projection-screen or the defined limits of a building.

Real space merges into virtual space. In front of, between or behind are applied to virtual as well as real spatial structures. We use the term telematic for the networking of those techno-cultural instruments that are able to connect all adjacent and distant spaces, as well as our eventful Now into a synchronous and shared space.

三つのプロジェクト、「テレマティク・ランドスケープ」、「ニュー・ロフト・ビルディング、ケルナー・ブレット」、「BMWデリバリー&イベントセンター」は、b&k+がどのように仕事を探求し、理解しているかを例示する。

プロジェクトは締め切りで完結するものではなく、継続されて他のプロジェクトや建物の中で問い直される。私たちは創造するために様々な素材や影響と取り組んでいるだけでなく、創造することを他のメディアを刺激し何かを誘起するような素材そのものとして考えている。

テレマティク・ランドスケープ

…は独立した、ハイブリッドなプロジェクトである。これはテレマティク・ランドスケープのパラメータと方法、そして現実での実験的建設を探求するものである。

情報が建設材料のように扱われ、"ランドスケープ"の中に我々の文化の構成要素として置かれる。単純な集合から複雑な組織が生成され、そこでは空間が映写スクリーンの表面や建物の境界にとどまらない。

現実の空間が仮想空間になる。仮想空間でも、現実の空間構造と同じように前、間、後ろ、という概念があてはまるのだ。テレマティクという用語は、出来事に満ちた現在を同期の共有される空間に結びつけるとともに、隣接する、あるいは離れてある空間を結びつけることを可能とするテクノカルチュラルな道具のネットワークだと考えている。

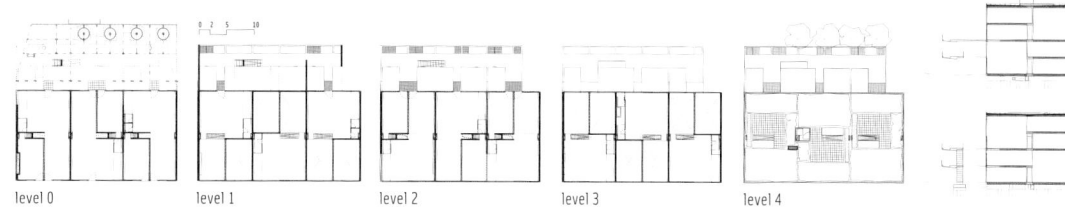

level 0　　level 1　　level 2　　level 3　　level 4

New Loft Building, Kölner Brett
Köln, Germany, 1997-2000
© Michael Reisch

Telematic Landscape
Hanover Expo 2000, Germany, 1998
© b&k+

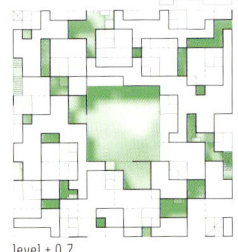

level + 0.7

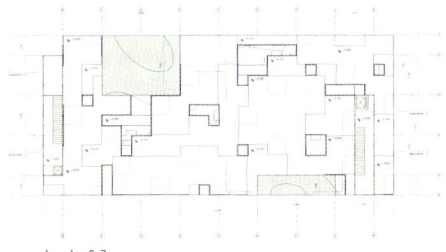

level + 0.7

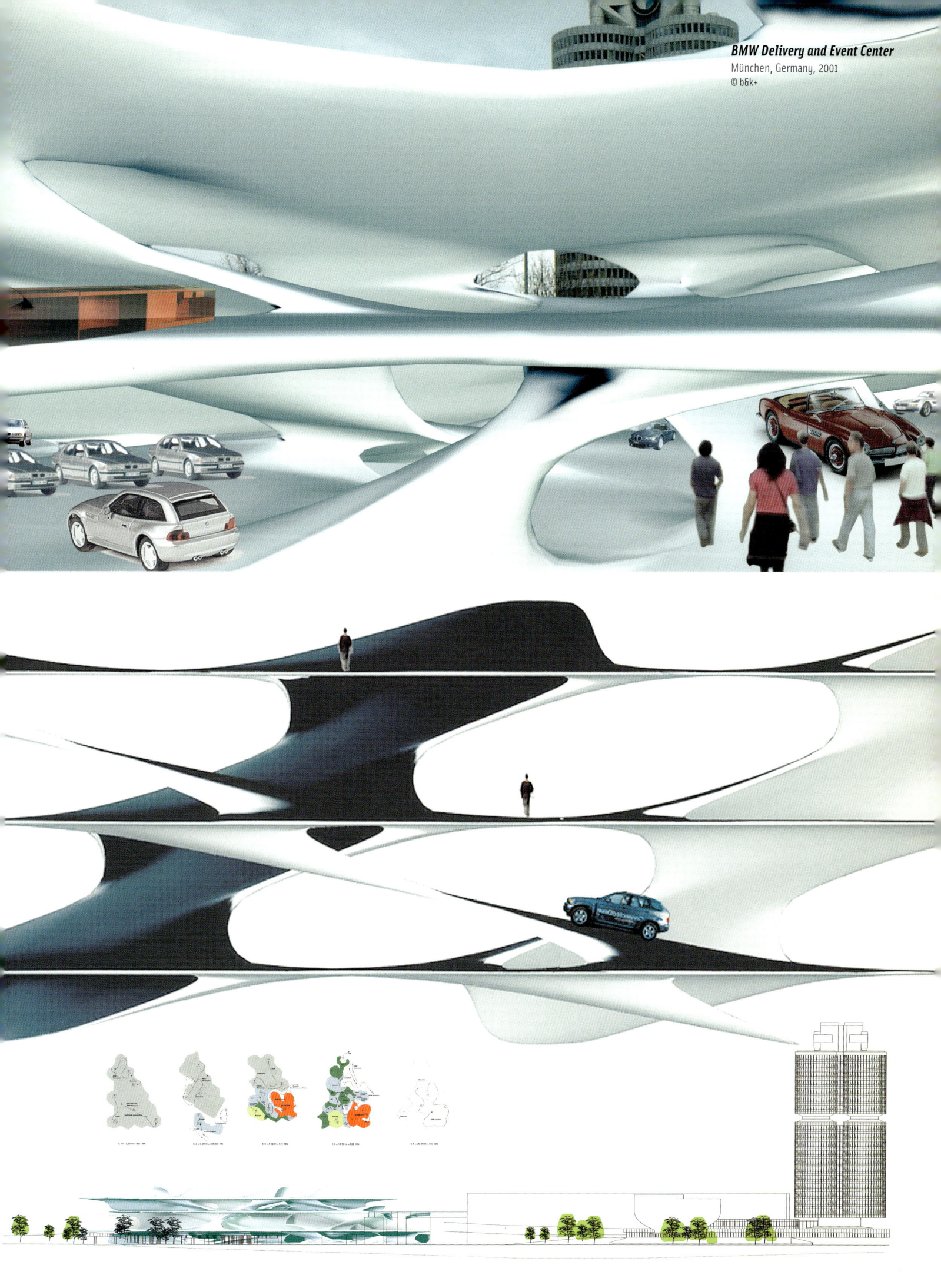

BMW Delivery and Event Center
München, Germany, 2001
© b&k+

The Netherlands
オランダ

Architect Agency Cepezed B.V.
アーキテクト・エージェンシーCEPEZED

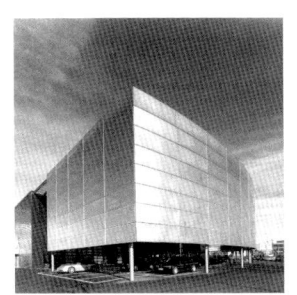

Porsche Showroom in Zuffenhausen,
Stuttgart, Germany, 1999
© Faz Keuzenkamp

Office Building, Cepezed,
Delft, The Netherlands, 1998-1999
© Faz Keuzenkamp

During its development, CEPEZED has realized a wide spectrum of projects, varying from residential projects and offices to factories, sports buildings and urban schemes.
The architectural language developed in the office bears much resemblance with what critics often wrongly refer to as "High-Tech - Architecture." It would be more appropriate to call it "an architecture that applies project-specific building technologies and materials." Of course this requires a thorough participation in the process of development and realization, and a more extensive knowledge of production technologies, which is reflected in our detail design. Usually CEPEZED carries out the projects through all design stages from inception to completion. The office currently has 32 employees. The internal office structure is horizontal and the educational level of the employees is very high. Most employees have the status of project architect and carry project responsibility, which enables flexibility and growth without loss of quality. The office is led by Michiel Cohen and Jan Pesman. Projects are developed in a team (matrix structure), which enables a relatively accurate prediction of the amount of work required.
The diverse knowledge of individual employees is usually extended with the input of specialist consultants. Often building components are developed for the building industry as a spin-off from the design process.
CEPEZED uses the appropriate techniques and materials for its buildings as much as possible. The construction, for instance, is often a light steel construction, which results in an open and flexible building. Aspects such as maintenance, recycling, and energy saving are taken into account when selecting materials. Technical installations are kept to a minimum and integrated into the concept. New developments are quickly used and new products are developed.

This all leads to buildings, which stand out in:
- A high level of iQ/kg
- Very good value for money
- Great durability
- Perfectly suited installation

CEPEZEDはその発展の過程で、多様な種類のプロジェクトを実現してきた。それは住宅から、オフィス、工場、運動施設、そして都市計画にも及ぶ。
私たちのオフィスで育ててきた建築言語は、批評家がよく誤って言及する"ハイテクアーキテクチュア"というものによく似ている。しかしそれは"プロジェクトに適した建築技術と素材を用いる建築家"と呼ぶのがよりふさわしい。
そのためにはもちろん、プロジェクトの展開と実現の過程に、徹底的に参加すること、そして生産技術に関して通常以上に広範な知識を有することが必要になる。このことは私たちのディテールのデザインにあらわれている。CEPEZEDは通常、プロジェクトの第一歩からすべての設計段階、そして完成にいたるまでプロジェクトに関与する。
私たちのオフィスには現在、32人の所員がいる。オフィス内の構造は横並びであり、所員の教育レベルは極めて高い。ほとんどの所員がプロジェクト・アーキテクトの地位にあり、プロジェクトの責務を負っている。このような構造が、質を損なうことなく、柔軟性と成長をもつことを、可能にしている。ミシェル・コーヘンとヤン・ペスマンが、オフィスのリーダーである。
各プロジェクトは（マトリクスの編成の）チームにより実施され、そこで必要とされる作業量の比較的正確な予測をすることができる。所員個々が豊富な知識をもつと同時に、専門的なコンサルタントと共同することで更にそれを広げる。しばしば、デザインプロセスの二次的な産物として、建築部品として製品化されることがある。
CEPEZEDは建物に可能な限り適切な技術と材料を使用する。例えば、軽量鉄骨を構造とすることが多く、建物はオープンでフレキシビリティをもったものになる。材料を選ぶ際には、メンテナンス、リサイクル、省エネルギーをいった側面を良く検討する。設備装置類は最小限とし、コンセプトと一体化したものとする。最新の技術をもちい、新たな製品がつくられる。
これらの方針は、以下のような点ですぐれた建物となる。

・ 単位重量あたりのIQの高レベル
・ 金銭的に極めて高い価値
・ 長い耐用年数
・ 完全に適合した建築設備

Indoor Carting Track
Delft, The Netherlands, 1997-2000

Project Description
Most of the indoor carting tracks in the Netherlands are located in reused storage or production buildings. The opportunity to design an indoor carting track from scratch is quite exceptional. The novel program has led to a new type of indoor carting track. The space concept is that of a huge container (50 x 60 x 12 m) made of glass. Inside, different entangled carting tracks are located on four different levels, supplemented with an office area and a restaurant. In daylight it forms a very open and brightly lit space. At night the building is lit artificially and functions as an enormous neon light, showing off the racing activities to its surroundings and especially to the passing drivers on the nearby motorway.

Location
The building is adjacent to one of the busiest highways in the Netherlands, the A13 between Rotterdam and The Hague (exit Delft North).

Design
Inside the glass container are four levels with tracks. These levels are connected by ramps, forming three-dimensional tracks. The racing tracks are interlocking over the different levels and they can be used either simultaneously or connected as one track with a total length of 1300m (3900 ft). This makes it Europe's longest three-dimensional carting track.
The permanently occupied areas are located in a separate volume inside the glass container. This building-in-a-building consists of two parts connected by a transparent staircase: On one side of the staircase are the offices, on the other side there are bars and a restaurant where the guests can enjoy a spectacular view of the various tracks.

Construction
By opting for a steel construction, the entire building could be left open. The steel construction has been left exposed throughout the building. The main load bearing structure consists of facade columns at 3.6m intervals. The columns inside the building are placed at 14.4m intervals. The floors of the carting tracks are made out of reinforced concrete. In order to create an intermediate support for the glazing in between the facade columns, very slender vertical trusses have been applied.
The outside glass facade is attached to the construction with stainless steel brackets. The 3.6 x 0.75m glass panes are made of toughened glass and have been fixed lap sided. The box-in-a-box that contains the permanently occupied areas is made of concrete-filled steel profiles with THQ beams with hollow beam floors in. A steel beam runs on the outside, on which the insulated wall has been placed, consisting of metal panels and glass.

屋内カーティングトラック
オランダ、デルフト 1997-2000

プロジェクトの概要
オランダの屋内カーティングトラックは、ほとんど倉庫や工場だった建物を再利用している。屋内カーティングトラックをゼロから設計するというのは、極めて例外的なことである。この珍しいプログラムは、新たなタイプの屋内カーティングトラックを生むこととなった。空間のコンセプトはガラスでできた大きな（50x60x12m）コンテナである。この中に、カーティングトラックが4層にわかれてもつれあって敷かれる。オフィスのエリアとレストランが付属する。日中はとてもオープンで明るく照らされたスペースがそこにはある。夜には建物は人工的に照らされて、レースが行われていることを周囲、特に近くの高速道路を走るドライバーたちに示す、巨大な広告灯となる。

場所
建物は、オランダで最も交通量の多いハイウェイのひとつ、ロッテルダムとハーグを結ぶA13（デルフト北出口）に隣接してある。

設計
ガラスのコンテナの中に、4層のトラックがある。各階は斜路で結ばれることで、3次元のトラックをつくりだしている。各階のトラックを独立して同時に使うことも可能だし、レース用トラックが他の階とつながり、全長1300mの1本のコースにすることもできる。こうするとヨーロッパで最長の立体的なカーティングトラックとなる。
ガラスのコンテナの中に、別個のボリュームとして占有部分がある。この建物内建物は、透明な階段室によって結ばれた二つの部分からなる。階段室の片方にはオフィス、もう一方にはバーとレストランがあり、来場者はそこから様々なトラックのスペクタクルな光景を楽しむことができる。

建設
鉄骨造とすることで、建物全体をオープンなものにすることができた。鉄骨部材は建物のあらゆる場所で露出している。主な耐力構造は3.6m間隔で立つファサードの柱であり、建物内部の柱は14.4mスパンである。カーティングトラックの床は鉄筋コンクリートである。ファサードの柱間のガラス支持のため、非常に細い垂直のトラスが用いられている。外側のガラスのファサードは、ステンレスのブラケットで構造体に取り付けられている。3.6x0.75mのガラス板は四周磨かれた強化ガラスである。箱の中の箱となる占有部分は、コンクリートを打込んだ鋼材とTHQ梁からなり、中にボイドスラブが架かる。外側には鉄骨梁が走り、金属板とガラスからなる、断熱壁がとりつけられている。

Austrian Academy of Science
Graz, Austria, 1997-2000

The design
The research building would have to consist of a large number of small units/work spaces (12-36 sq m). This, and the desire to create a very flexible Building, led to the concept of slabs that could be freely arranged.
The competition site did not offer the context or the surroundings for the building to relate to. As a design on a green field site, the building creates its own context. The disposition of the slabs seems only at first sight arbitrary, outside areas are created with different atmospheres - the patio, the bright garden, the lawn, the paved front area, with an indentation with the surrounding green area.
The slabs are grouped around a central area, the atrium, and seem to curiously extend their feelers out to the different directions of the world.
This reflects a bit the idea of modern science, in which the exchange of thoughts about new research findings with other disciplines has become an important characteristic.
Where the different building edges offer the possibility to retreat, the atrium is the true heart, the center to which everything else is attached, and where the scientific exchange of thoughts takes place.
Here is the main entrance, and all galleries end in this zone.
The lowest atrium level is at basement level, in which the main common areas like the library and canteen are, and the seminar rooms with ancillary spaces.
Together with the outside patio, it forms a triangular space with an introvert character, which becomes an ideal meeting point for all staff members, inside as well as outside. The special character of the atrium is emphasized by the fact that the actual entrance is at ground floor level. Consequently, there are a few common areas at ground floor level as well, like garages, guest rooms and the caretaker's residence, of which the last two have separate entrances.
Altogether, an attempt was made in the design process to optimize all of these concepts in a building and create a stimulating work environment for scientists.

Construction and choice of materials
The main load bearing construction consists of a light steel frame in the facade areas, with concrete floor slabs spanning them. The closed facade areas consist of sandwich panels, which have a stainless steel skin on the outside. The glazed bands in the facade are equipped with a stainless steel panel that can be used as a sunscreen when opened and as a black-out when closed. The freely modular partition walls can be normal closed slabs, or they can be glazed if required.
The facades on the gallery-sides of the slabs are relatively more open, having more glass elements, in order to give views of the various outdoor spaces and improve the orientation.

Expansion
In case of a future desire for expansion, two options are given: The slabs can be extended towards the East and the West, and also another floor can be added with the same construction principle without problems.

オーストリア科学アカデミー
オーストリア、グラーツ 1997-2000

設計
研究施設は、数多くの小さな（12-36㎡）ユニット／ワークスペースからなる。このことと、フレキシブルな建物をつくりたいという欲求が、自由に設定できるスラブというコンセプトにつながった。設計競技の敷地はコンテクストのない、建物を連関させるべきもののない環境にあった。緑の草地に立つ建物は、自らコンテクストをつくらなくてはならない。スラブの配置は、一目見ると無原則のようだが、外部に異なる雰囲気をもった場所を生じさせるようにできている―パティオ、明るい庭、芝生、舗装された前面等が、周囲の緑地に凹凸をつくる。
スラブは中心の領域、アトリウムを囲んで集まっている。そしてその触角を世界の異なる方角に、興味深くのばしているようである。これは近代科学の考え方を少々反映している。そこでは新たな研究上の発見を他の分野とやりとりすることが、重要な特徴である。
建物のエッジは後退する可能性をもつが、アトリウムは真の心臓部であり、他のすべての部分が帰属する中心であり、科学的な思考の交流が行われる場所である。ここに主エントランスがあり、すべての回廊がこのゾーンで留まる。アトリウムの底部は地下階にあたり、そこには図書室や食堂、セミナー室や予備スペースなどの共用施設がある。
外のパティオと共に、そこに内向的な性質をもった三角形のスペースをつくり、内外共にスタッフの格好の出会いの場所となる。アトリウムの特別な性格は、実質的なエントランスが1階レベルにあるということによって、強調される。結果として、1階にもいくつかの共用部分、ガレージ、来客室、管理人の住居があり、来客室と管理人の住居は独立したエントランスをもっている。
全体として、これらのコンセプトを最適化して建物に取り入れ、科学者たちにとって刺激的な研究環境をつくるために、設計の過程で努力がなされた。

建設と材料の選択
主要構造部は、ファサード面の軽量鉄骨のフレームと、その間に架かるコンクリートの床スラブである。閉じたファサードの領域は、サンドイッチ状のパネルからなり、外側はステンレスの皮膜が覆っている。帯状の開口部分はステンレス製のパネルで、開放時には日除けとなり、閉めることによって室内を暗室化できる。自由に設定できる間仕切壁は、普通の閉じたスラブでも良いし、必要ならばガラススクリーンとすることもできる。回廊側のファサードは、相対的によりオープンであり、ガラスの割合が多い。これは様々な屋外空間の景色を眺め、また建物内の位置を把握しやすくするためである。

増築
将来の増築の必要が生じたときのため、二つの選択肢が用意されている。東西それぞれに、スラブ状の建物を延長することも可能であるし、またもう一層、同様の構法で階をふやすことも問題がない。

Indoor Carting Track
Delft, The Netherlands, 1997-2000
© Faz Kezenkamp

Austrian Academy of Science
Graz, Austria, 1997–2000
© Cepezed

Belgium
ベルギー

evr. Architecten
evr.アーシテクテン

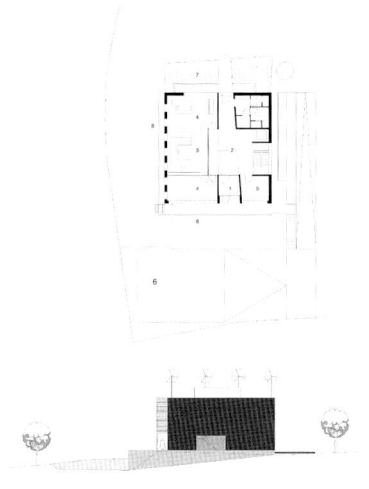

Animal Centraal Besturingsgebouw
Dijlevallei, Leuven, Belgium, 2000-2003

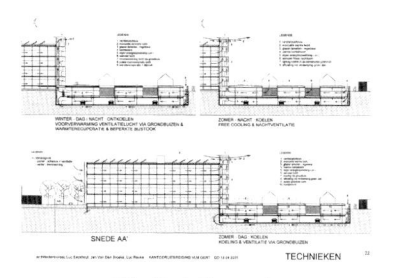

VLM - office building extension,
Gent, Belgium, 2001-2004

Sustainable building and looking forward are the basic goals of our office, founded in 1994 when Luc Reuse, Luc Eeckhout and Jan Van Den Broeke started to work together.

Mostly we did urban conversions and private housing projects, experimenting with passive and renewable energy systems. We designed Belgium's first zero-energy house in 1996 and won several awards in national and international bio-climatic building competitions.

In 1998 we designed the new office building of Oxfam in Ghent. Since then we have been commissioned to do larger projects, mainly office buildings for the public sector.

The construction of any new building affects our environment for decades to come. Any significant building should therefore be a smart building: treating the environment with care, creating living or working conditions that are best for the users but also for the planet itself. For us Westerners, that means: restricting our destructive need to consume and pollute, making frugal use of natural resources, reducing the area of our "ecological footprint." We aim to design buildings that are more respectful and less pretentious.

Our concepts are always based on:
• taking advantage of environmental characteristics
• a clear architectural language
• passive concepts to reduce the energy demand
• the use of materials with a limited energy content optimum technology

サステイナブルな建物と、常に前向きであることが、リュック・リューセ、リュック・エークハウトとヤン・ヴァンデンブルッケが協同して1994年に設立したオフィスの基本的な目標である。

私たちはパッシブで再生可能なエネルギーシステムを実験的に用いながら、主に都市の改造や住宅プロジェクトをおこなってきた。1996年にベルギー初のゼロエネルギーハウスを設計し、国内外の生気候学的な建築物のコンペティションでいくつかの受賞をした。1998年にはゲントのオックスファムに新しいオフィスビルを設計した。それ以降、私たちは大きな建物、主に公的機関のオフィスビルを手がけるようになった。

どんな建物であれ、新しく建築するものは我々の環境に何十年か影響を及ぼす。重要な建物はそれ故、よくできた建物—環境に配慮し、建物の利用者だけでなく地球全体に対して最適な生活や労働条件を与えるもの—でなくてはならない。私たち西欧人にとって、このことは消費や汚染をもたらす破壊的な必要を制限し、天然資源の利用をできるだけ制約し、私たちの"生態学的影響範囲"を減らすことを意味する。私たちは、より敬意に値し思い上がりのない建物を設計することを目指している。

私たちのコンセプトは常に以下のようなことを基本としている：
・環境の特徴を生かす
・明確な建築言語
・エネルギー需要を抑制するパッシブなコンセプト
・限定されたエネルギー含量をもった材料の使用
・最適化された技術

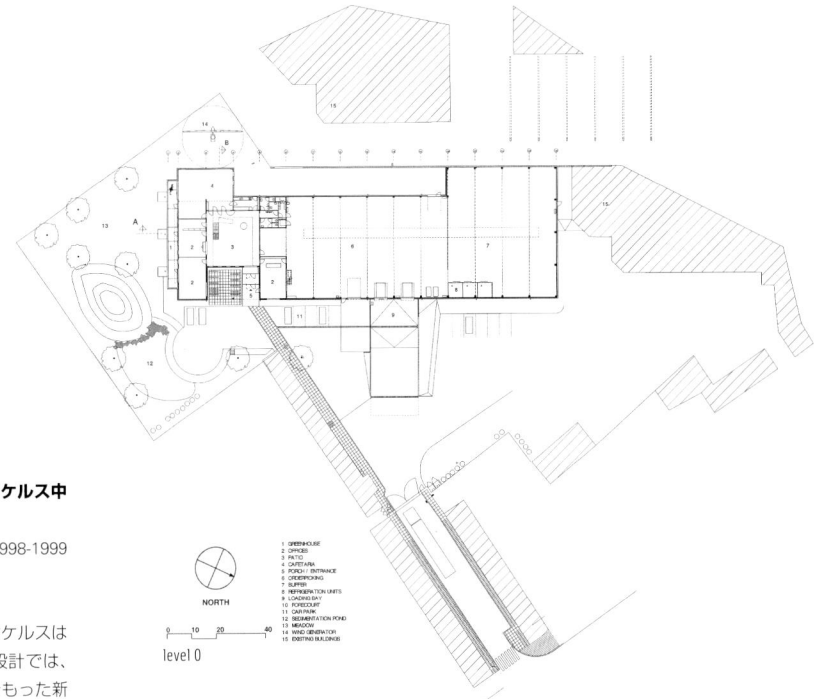

National secretariat & distribution centre for Oxfam Wereldwinkels

Gent, Flanders, Belgium, 1998-1999

Building a fair world
Oxfam – Wereldwinkels is a fair-trade organization in Belgium.
The commission consisted of the construction of a new low-budget building with offices, meeting rooms and a warehouse with a loading bay. For Oxfam, sustainable building was an obvious requirement, in line with its global social commitment. This building respects people and the environment through its location, design and construction, its hospitality and its integrated technologies.

Urban planning
The building does not encroach upon any of the very scarce open space, but is a sensible replacement for a disused industrial urban site.

Architecture
The design shows a simple, barn-shaped volume with the warehouse on the north side and the offices on the south side. Inside, all the functions are arranged around the central "patio," as an expression of the receptive, communicative and non-hierarchical structure of this movement. The most important ingredients of the spatial expression are functional logic, visible structures, internal vistas, ample daylight and the sensuality of natural materials.

Energy
An ecological building is a minimum-energy project. By combining compactness and good zoning with new insulation techniques, the use of passive solar energy and advanced technology, the energy requirement for heating is less than 40 kWh/m² net office area per year.

Materials
Only recyclable or recycled materials with a low energy content were used, the choice was based on their life-cycle analysis.

Water
Rainwater and water-saving appliances and taps are used. The surplus rainwater from the roof is returned via a perforated pipe system and a sedimentation pond in the garden.

オックスファム・ウェレルトウィンケルス中央事務・配送センター

ベルギー、フランダース、ゲント　1998-1999

公正な世界の建設
オックスファム - ウェレルトウィンケルスはベルギーの公正取引機関である。設計では、オフィス、会議室、倉庫と荷捌場をもった新しい建物を低予算でつくることが要請された。
オックスファム（国際的非政府組織）にとって、サステイナブルな建物をつくることは、そのグローバルな社会活動内容からして自明の要請であった。建物はその配置、デザイン、建設、ホスピタリティとテクノロジーに関して、人々と環境に敬意を払ったものでなくてはならない。

都市計画
建物はかつての工場としてあった建物の跡を注意深くなぞり、乏しいオープンスペースを奪うことのないように置いた。

建築
建物のデザインは、単純な小屋型のヴォリュームであり、倉庫部が北、オフィスが南側にある。内側ではすべての施設が中央の"パティオ"のまわりに置かれ、この活動の受容力、コミュニケーションの尊重、ヒエラルキーのない構造をあらわしている。

エネルギー
エコロジカルな建物とは、最小限エネルギーのプロジェクトである。建物のコンパクトさと適切なゾーニング、新たなインシュレーション方法、パッシブ・ソーラー・エネルギーや最先端技術の使用により、オフィス部分の暖房に必要なエネルギーは、ネットで40kWh/m²以下である。

材料
低エネルギー含量の、リサイクル可能かリサイクルされた材料だけが使用された。その選択はライフサイクルの分析に基づいている。

水
雨水を利用、節水型の機器や蛇口を使用している。余剰の雨水は、多孔管のシステムと庭の沈殿池により還元される。

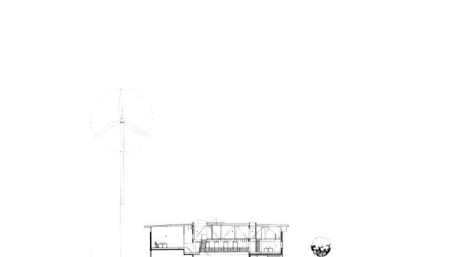

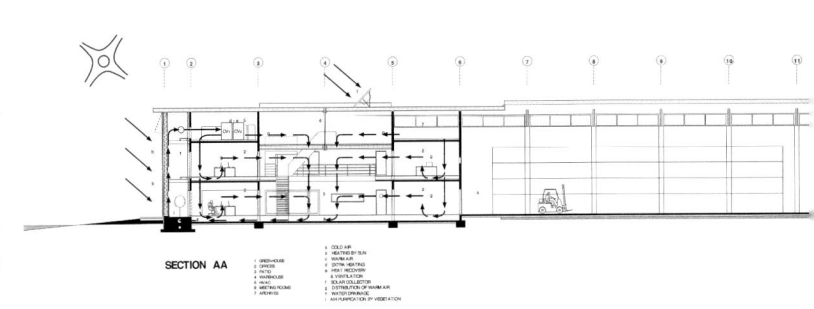

National secretariat & distribution centre for Oxfam Wereldwinkels
Gent, Flanders, Belgium, 1998 – 1999
© evr.Architecten (left page)
© Patrick Hanssens, © Hilde D'Haegere, © evr.Architecten, © Koen van Dame (right page)

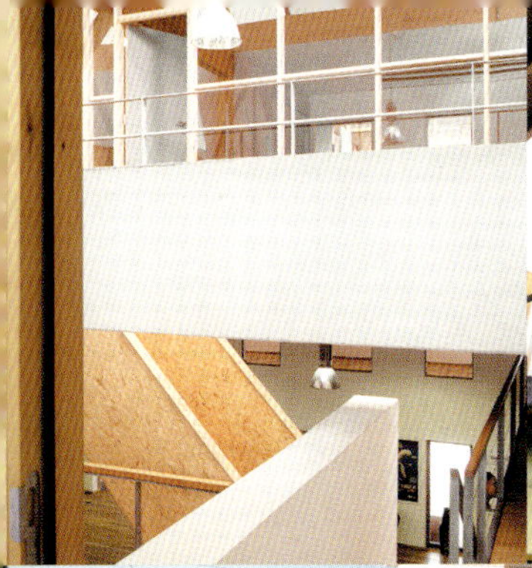
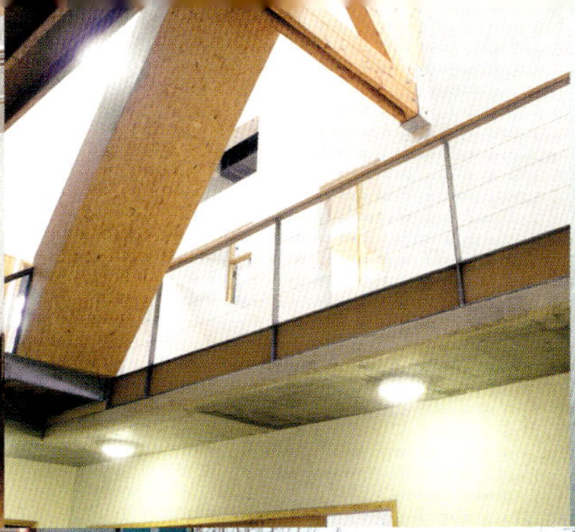
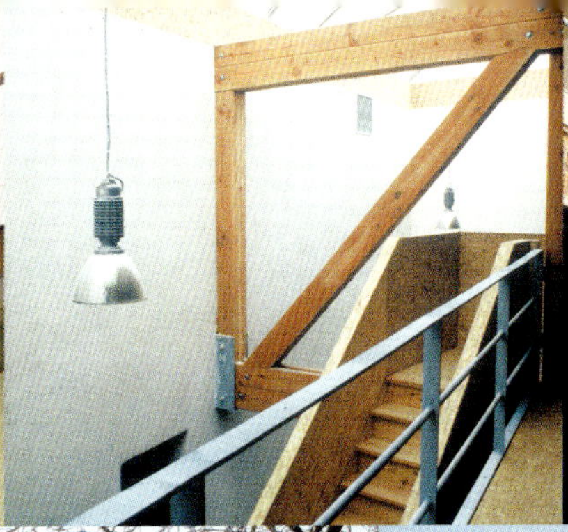
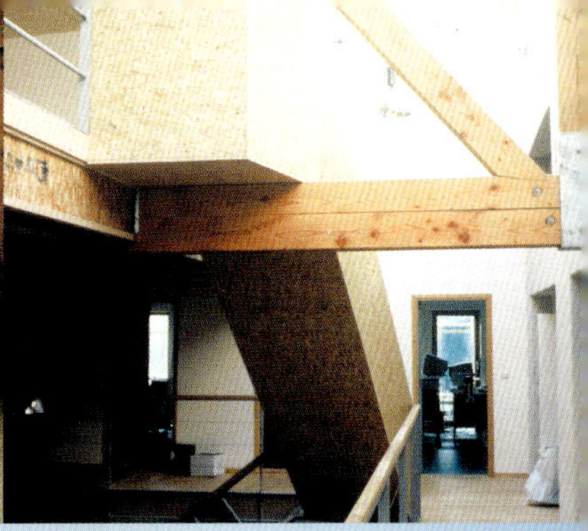
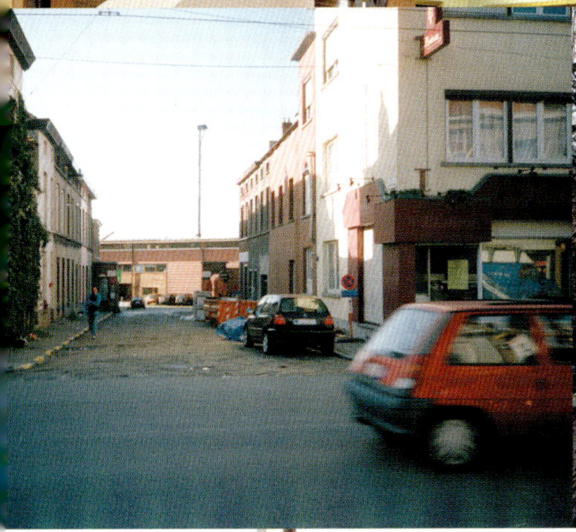
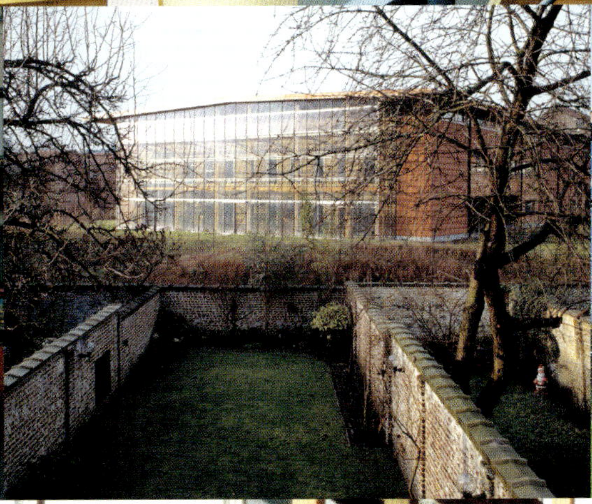
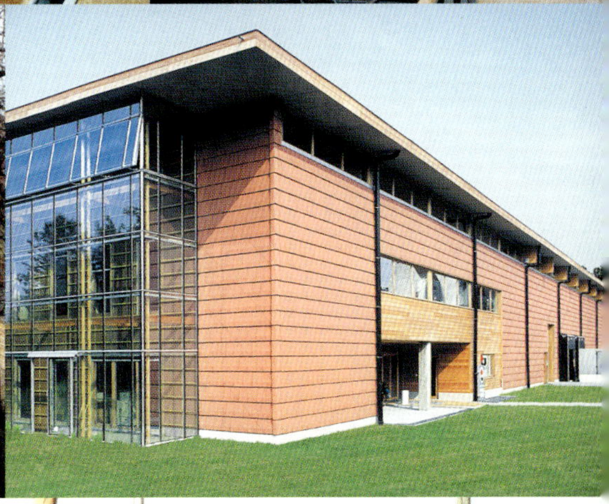
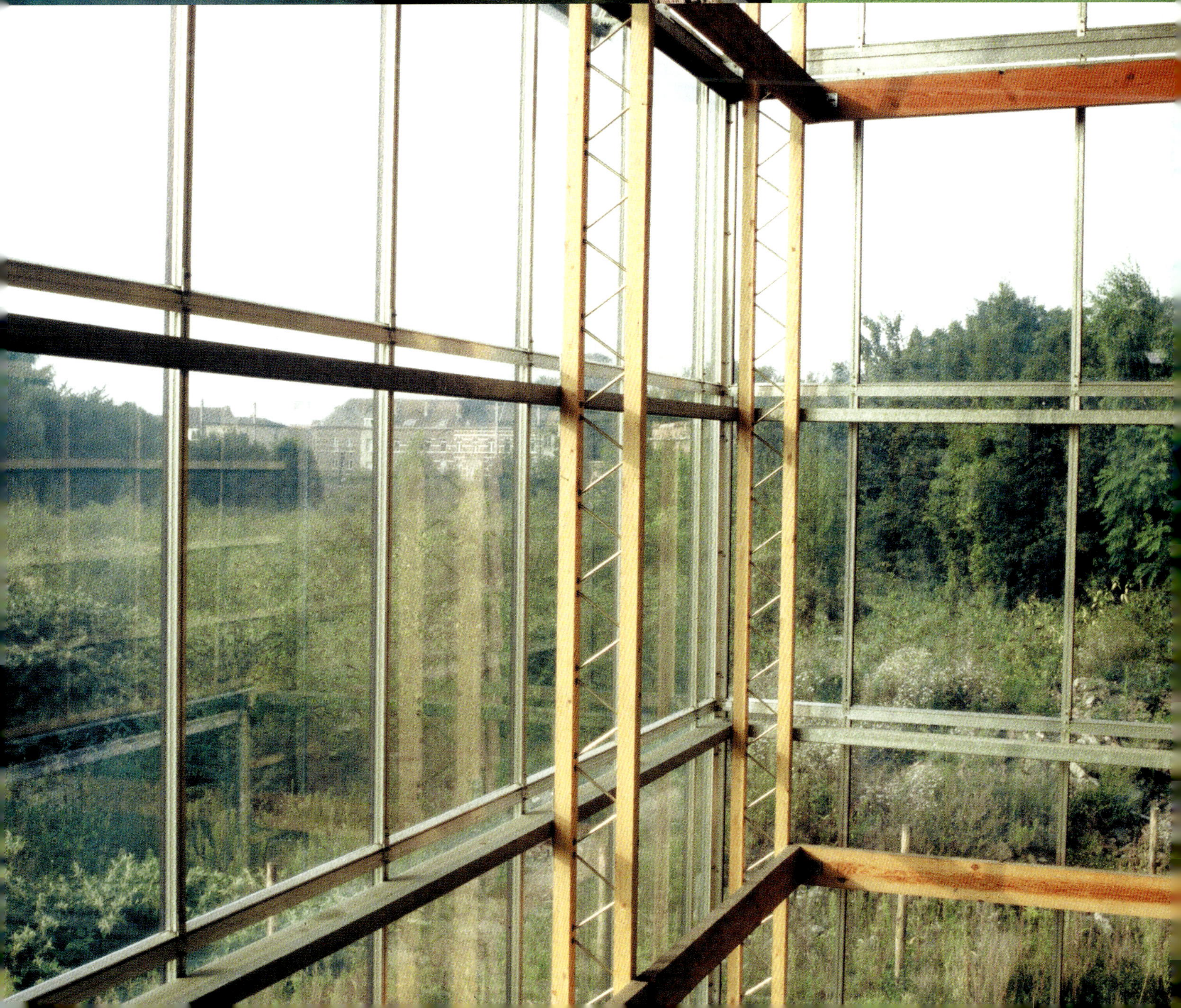

Sweden
スウェーデン

Studio Grön arkitekter ab
スタジオ・グレーン建築事務所

Skärhamn Hotel, Skärhamn, Sueden, 2001
© Studio Grön

Aquarium and Science Center,
Gottebörg, Sueden, competition 2001
© Studio Grön

Swedish Post Headquarter,
Stockholm, Sueden, competion 2002
© Studio Grön

Teachers Collage,
Malmö, Sueden, competion 1999
© Studio Grön

Studio grön (studio green) is a cooperation platform for three Nordic architects: Fredrik Lund from Norway, Martin Forsby from Sweden and Mika Määttä from Finland. The three principal partners met at the school of architecture at Chalmers in Gothenburg and have collaborated in a large number of Nordic and international competitions since 1992.

After winning the open international competition for the new restaurant Trädgårn in Gothenburg in 1996 we were commissioned to realize the building. We have also designed a conversion of a former gymnasium into a faculty for media production and some smaller projects such as villas and summer houses.

Parallel with the design of buildings we explore the field of architecture by producing architectural projects, making lectures and educational projects at different schools both in Scandinavia and abroad.

We stress integration between the disciplines of landscape design, urban design and architecture and we regard architecture as a form of public art. In most of our projects we try to strengthen the urban qualities by creating durable spaces for public life.

As our name indicates, we are interested in exploring the relationship between architecture and nature. Inspired by the masters of Nordic modernism, such as Aalto and Asplund, we search for architecture of quiet intensity, simplicity and tectonic sensitivity.

スタジオ・グレーン（スタジオ・グリーン）は3人の北欧建築家の協同基盤である。ノルウェー人のフレデリック・ルンド、スウェーデン人のマッティン・フォッシュビュー、フィンランド人のミカ・マータの3人である。3人はイェーテボリのシャルマーズ工科大学で出会い、1992年から数多くの北欧や国際的な設計競技で協同してきた。

1996年にイェーテボリの新しいレストラン、トレードゴーンの設計競技で優賞し、実施設計をすることになった。また、ギムナジウムであった建物のメディア・プロダクション学部への改装のデザイン、ヴィッラやサマーハウスといった小規模のプロジェクトも行っている。

実際の設計活動と併行して、私たちは建築プロジェクトのプロデュース、講義や教育的なプロジェクトを、北欧及び国外で行っている。

私たちは、ランドスケープデザイン、都市計画、建築の分野が統合されていくことの重要性を大事にしている。また、建築はある種のパブリックアートだと考えている。私たちのプロジェクトでは常に、パブリックな生活のためのパーマネントなスペースをつくることにより都市の質を高めることを目指している。

グループの名前が示す通り、私たちは建築と自然の関係を探求することに興味をもっている。アアルトやアスプルンドのような北欧モダニズムの巨匠たちに刺激を受けて、私たちは静謐な強靭さ、簡明さと構造的感性をもった建築を模索している。

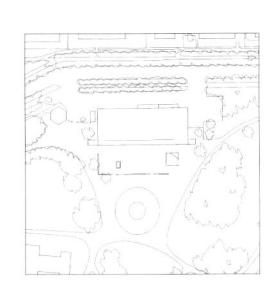

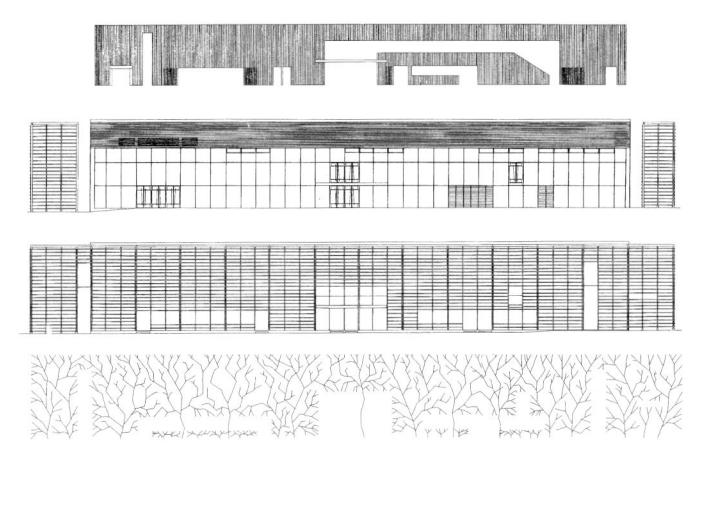

Restaurant Trädgårn
Gothenburg, Sweden, 1996-1998

On the border between the busy inner city ring and the tranquillity of "Trädgårdsföreningen" central public park, this restaurant and nightclub was built as a result of a first prize in an international competition.

The contrasts of this border inspired us to form a simple building with large open public spaces towards the park and closed volumes containing service facilities towards the street. Along the window facade facing the park there is a 3.5-meter-wide and 80-meter-long veranda with a screen of seasonally changing climbers. Flowers and green leaves blossom in spring and summer and then fall off after a colorful autumn to allow the low light into the restaurant in the winter.

The timber slats in the veranda and the exterior walls are of untreated Siberian larch-wood, which over time has weathered silver-gray to hold some of the dignity of old traditional Scandinavian farming buildings. In contrast to the rough exteriors, the interiors are dominated by gently oiled and sophistically mounted birch.

The attention to details, clarity of form and the use of sensual materials in this project demonstrate our ambition to create a silent and tactile architecture in the transition between the natural qualities of the site and the public life of the city.

レストラン・トレードゴーン
スウェーデン、イェーテボリ　1996-1998

活気のある都市中心部のリングと、中央公園トレードゴードフォレーニンゲンの静けさの境界線上に、このレストラン／ナイトクラブは国際設計競技に優賞してつくられた。

この境界のもつコントラストは、公園側に広い開かれたパブリックな空間をもち、道路側にサービス諸室の閉じた領域をもつ、明快な建物を着想させた。公園に面したガラスのファサードの前には、3.5m幅で80mの長さのベランダがあり、季節によってスクリーンに囲まれる。春から夏には花や緑が咲き乱れ、極彩色の秋をすぎると木の葉も落ちて、冬の低い陽光をレストラン内に招き入れる。

ベランダと外壁の木材は処理をしていないシベリア唐松で、時が経つとともに銀灰色になり北欧の伝統的な農家のような威厳を獲得することを願っている。荒々しい外部と対照的に、内部は丁寧にオイルを塗り複雑に重ねられたかばの木が主である。

ディテールへのこだわり、形態の明快さ、繊細な素材の使用は、自然に恵まれた敷地と、都市のパブリックな生活の間の移行点に、静かで触感のある建築をつくりたいという私たちの願いによる。

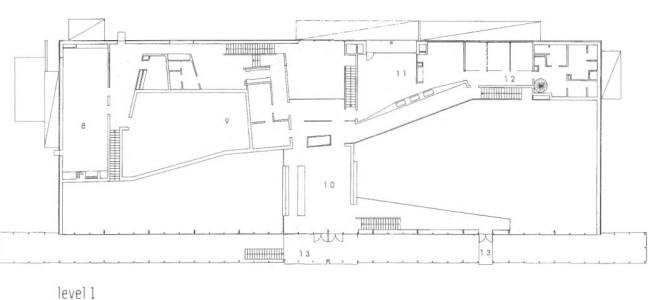

level 1

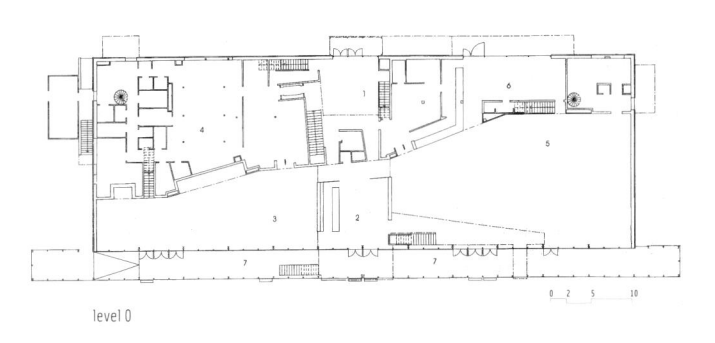

level 0

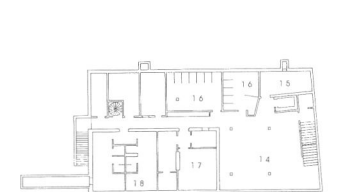

level -1

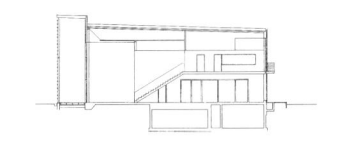

Restaurant Trädgårn
Gothenburg, Sweden, 1996-1998
© Åhe E: Son Lindman AB, © Hans Wretting (left page)
© Hans Wretting (right page)

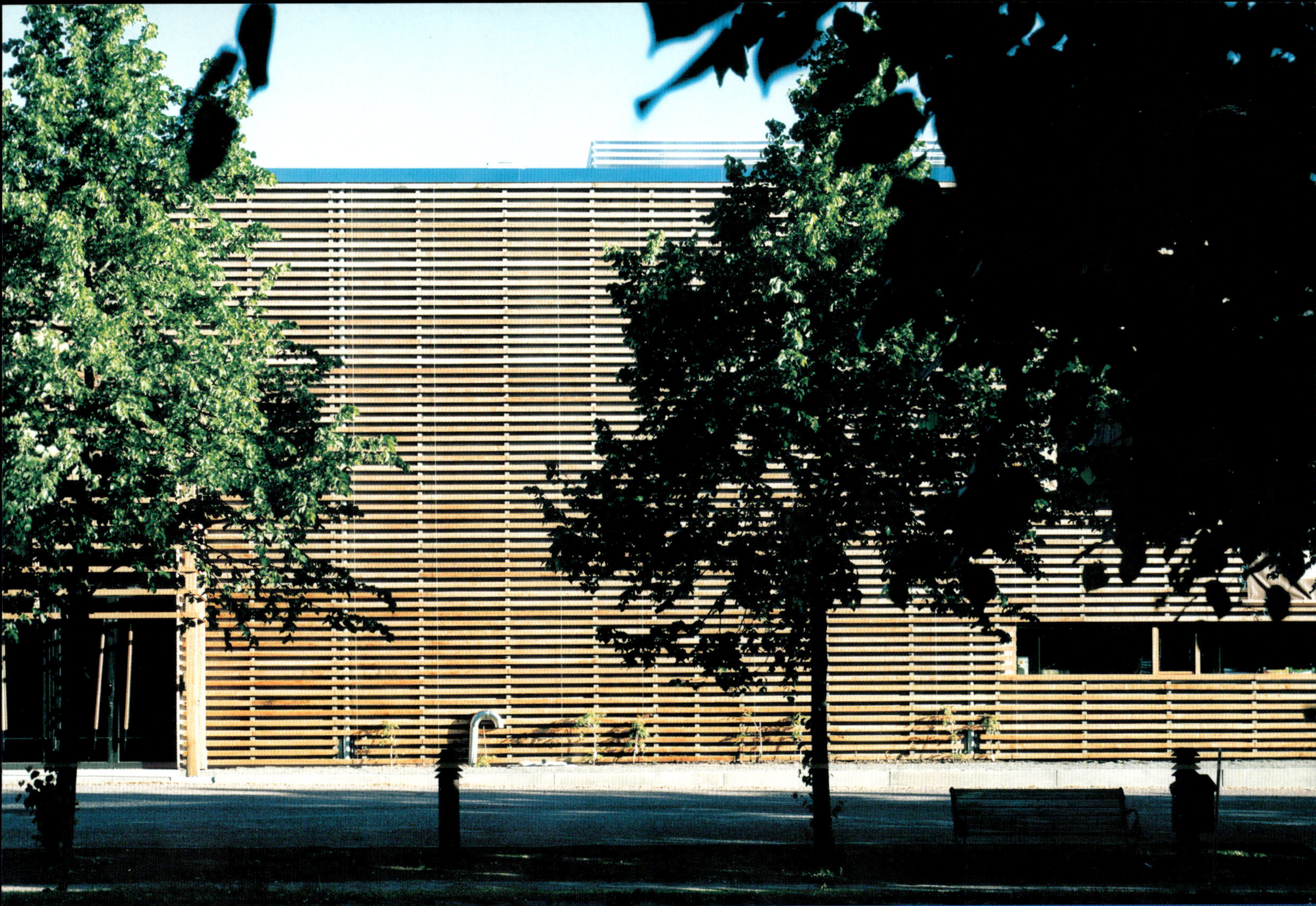
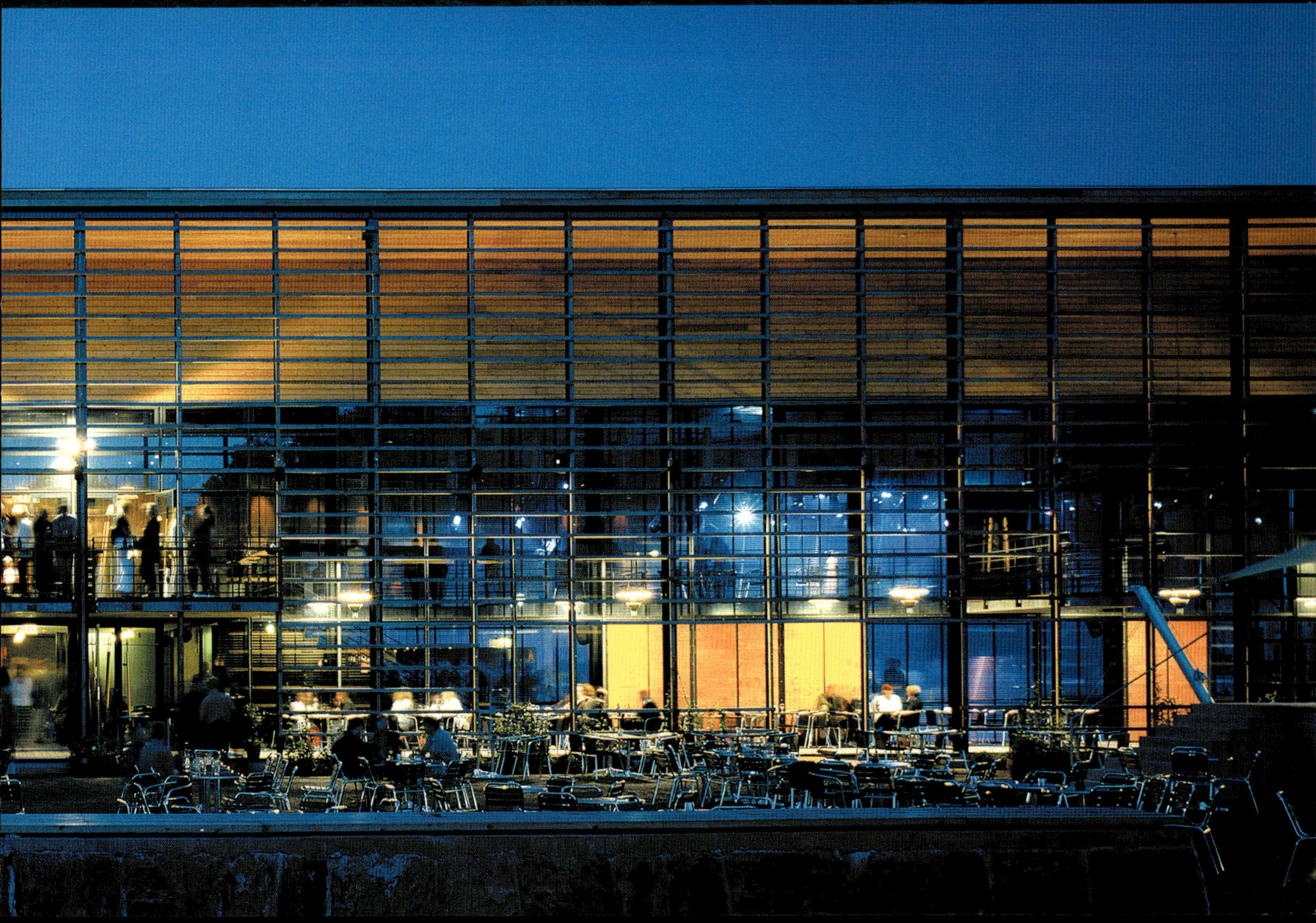

日本 Japan

Kazuhiro Kojima / C+A
小嶋一浩／C+A

I was still doing my master course under the supervision of Professor Hiroshi Hara, when I, together with friends, organized Coelacanth, to start our careers as architects.
I made my auspicious debut in the field of architecture with the "Himuro Apartment" (Osaka, 1987), which received the "Kashima Award" in 1985, when I was 26.

The first chance to design a public building came in 1990, when I won the first prize at the international open competition for "Osaka International Peace Center." What I was trying to realize in my work at that time was the free feeling that is embraced by Tokyo, the chaotic city.

The relationships between "activities" and "space" had become another theme for me when I designed "Utase Elementary School" (Chiba, 1995), where I intended to encourage the activities of over seven hundred students. This theme, highly appreciated in the Japanese educational field, was developed and carried on in "Kibikogentoshi Elementary School" (Okayama, 1996), "Hakuou Comprehensive High School" (Miyagi, 2001), "Art & Science College" (Qatar, 2001-), etc.

My concern for "activity" has survived, to blossom into another theme, "Black and White," as will be described.
I developed a new method of design while working on "Space Blocks Kami-shinjo" (Osaka, 1998); I tried to perceive architecture in three dimensions from the very first stage by adopting combinations of several cubes which I called "space blocks."
This method is currently continuing in the form of eco-conscious and porous space as can be seen in "Hanoi Model" (Hanoi Vietnam, 2002) which also employs these "blocks."

In 1998 I set up a laboratory at Tokyo University of Science as Associate Professor, while acting as a partner of C+A.

Himuro Apartment, Osaka, Japan, 1987
© C+A

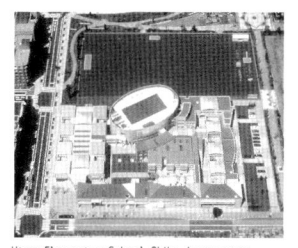

Utase Elementary School, Chiba, Japan, 1995
© Urban Arts

Kibikogentoshi Elementary School, Okayama, Japan, 1996
© Hiroyuki Hirai

Space Blocks Kami-shinjo, Osaka, Japan, 1998
© C+A

大学院時代を東京大学原広司研究室の下ですごした私は、大学院在学中に仲間とシーラカンスという設計チームを立ち上げていきなり実務のキャリアをスタートさせた。1985年、26歳で設計した「氷室アパートメント」で鹿島賞（SD REVIEW '85）を受賞したのがデビューである。1990年には「大阪国際平和センター」の国際公開コンペ1等ではじめての公共建築を実現する機会を得た。この頃までのテーマは、混沌とした東京の都市の様相が持つ自由な気分を建築化することだった。次に「打瀬小学校」では、アクティビティと空間の関わりをテーマに700人を超える子供たちのアクティビティを喚起する建築を設計した。この方法は日本の教育の世界で評価されて「吉備高原小学校」「迫桜高校」「ART & SCIENCE COLLEGE, QATAR」などに発展する。アクティビティへの関心は後に述べるような「黒と白」という方法へと進化した。また、「スペースブロック」と呼ぶキューブを3〜5個組み合わせて始めから立体で建築を考える設計のツールを開発し、「スペースブロック上新庄」というアパートを実現した。この方法は現在設計中の「ハノイモデル」などの環境コンシャスなポーラスな空間へとつながっている。1998年以降はC＋Aのパートナーとして活動する一方、東京理科大学で研究室を主宰している

Hakuou Comprehensive High School + Art & Science College, Qatar

Up North, some two hours on the bullet train, lies this rural area whose population has been decreasing. Two existing high schools have been integrated here, to be reincarnated as Hakuou Comprehensive High School.

Normal schools in Japan consist only of rooms with their own functions and corridors to combine those rooms. We call this kind of space "black," where "a space" has only one corresponding "usage." On the other hand, "white" is a space that can hold various "activities;" a "white" space changes its name in concert with its different usages. Thus the given status for school can be said to be "jet-black."

Even though it is seemingly functional, a "black" space often turns out to be tight and inconvenient, for its usage is quite limited and has no flexibility. Here in this school, a "white" space was attained by installing F.L.A (Flexible Learning Area,) which plays several roles such as a circulation space, a room for students' self studies, meetings and exhibitions etc..

The total size was reduced from the initial design, for the F.L.A. was obtained by combining the area of laboratories that had been used only in one specific way. A solar collector laid over the large square roof of 120 meters on each-side allowed to cut down the maintenance expenses even in this cold region.

On the other hand Art & Science College, Qatar, is planned to be built in a desert area. Here I am trying to develop the theme "black and white" which I identified through the design of "Hakuou Comprehensive High School," while emphasizing Islamic culture. Rather lively activities by large numbers of people have been arranged on the lower floor, laying out calm and small-group activities on the upper. In deciding the façade and daylighting, I actively adopted traditional Islamic geometry and daylighting, to interpret them in modern ways.

迫桜高校＋アーツ＆サイエンス・カレッジ、カタール

「迫桜高校」は東京から新幹線で北へ2時間のルーラルで人口が減少しつつある場所に既存校を統合して新設された総合学科高校である。従来の日本の学校のプログラムは諸機能を持った部屋とそれをつなぐ廊下だけでできている。私たちは、こうした「使われ方」と「空間」が一対一対応している空間を「黒」、逆に使われ方によってその場所の呼び方が変化するようないろいろなアクティビティに応答できる空間を「白」と呼んでいる。学校の与条件は「真っ黒」である。「黒」は一見機能的なようでも、使用頻度が少なく、自由度もないことから窮屈で不自由なことが多い。ここでは、F.L.A.(Flexible Learning Area)と呼ぶサーキュレーションでもあり自発的な学習やミーティング、展示などができる空間を導入することで「白」を獲得した。これは与条件を分析し、特定用途にしか使われない教室を統合することで得たものであり、全体規模は当初より縮小している。寒い地方であるが120m角の広大な屋根に載せた太陽熱集熱面により維持費を軽減している。
「Art & Science College, Qatar」は、ドーハ近郊の砂漠エリアに建設予定である。イスラムの文化を尊重しながら、「迫桜高校」で発見した「黒と白」の方法を発展させている。下階に多人数の活動、上階に少人数でカームな活動を配置した。ファサードや光の扱いではイスラムの幾何学と自然光の扱い方を現代的に解釈した。曇ることさえほとんどないこの土地の強い光の中でファサード、内部のシェードが太陽の動きに応答して表情を変え続ける。

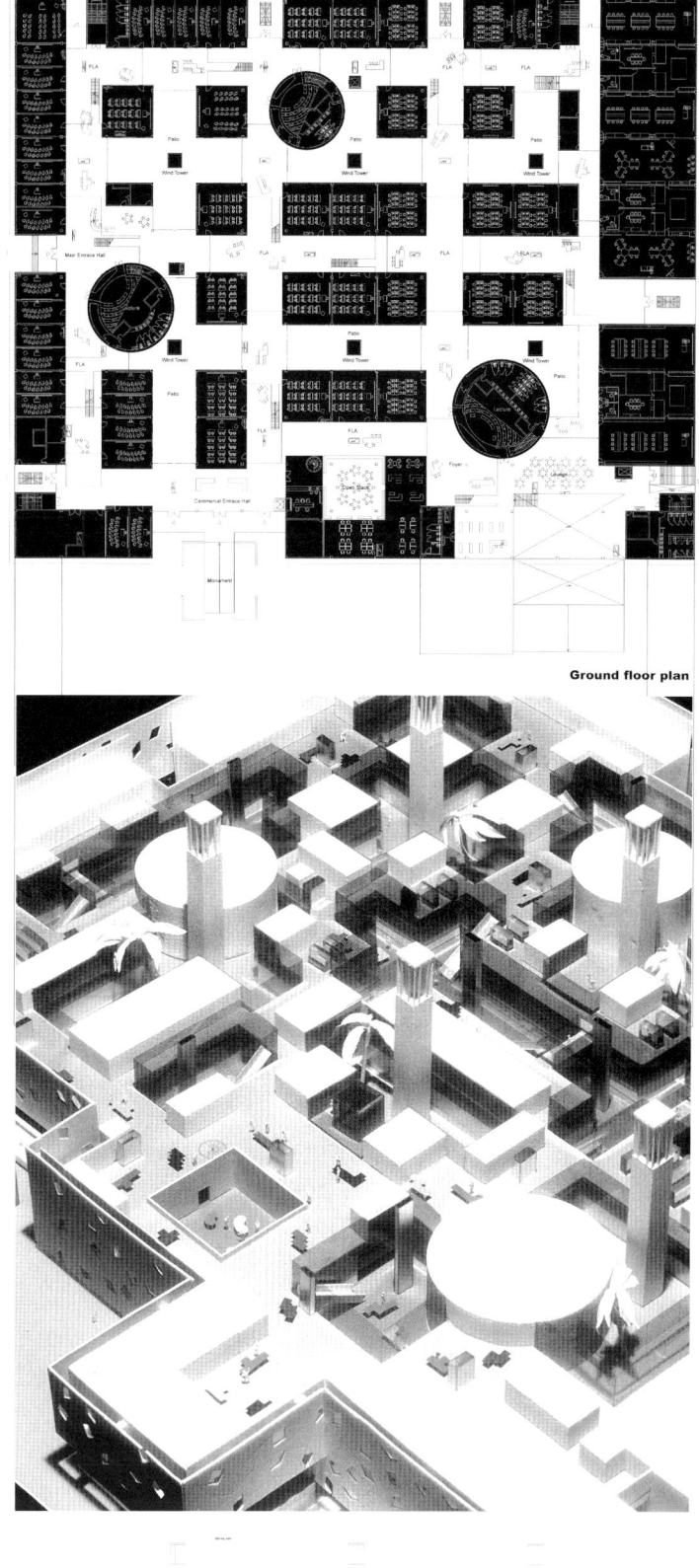

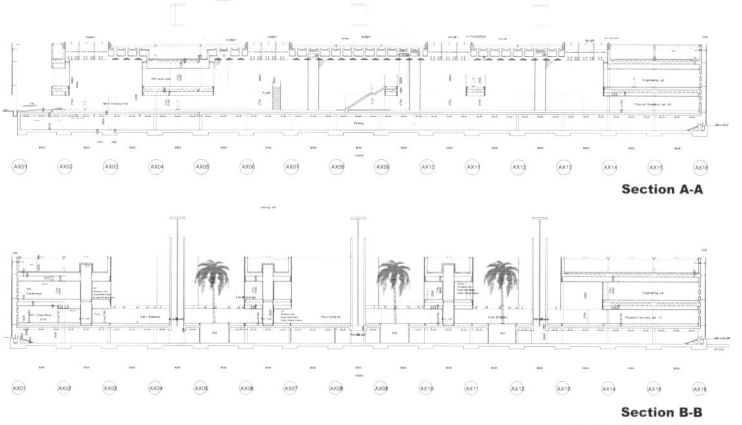

Ground floor plan

Section A-A

Section B-B

Arts & Science College / Qatar Education City
Qatar, Doha, 2001-2003
© Tomohiro Sakashita / GA Photographers

Hakuou Comprehensive High School
Kurihara-gun, Miyagi Prefecture, Japan, 1997-2001
© Hiroyuki Hirz

Ground floor plan

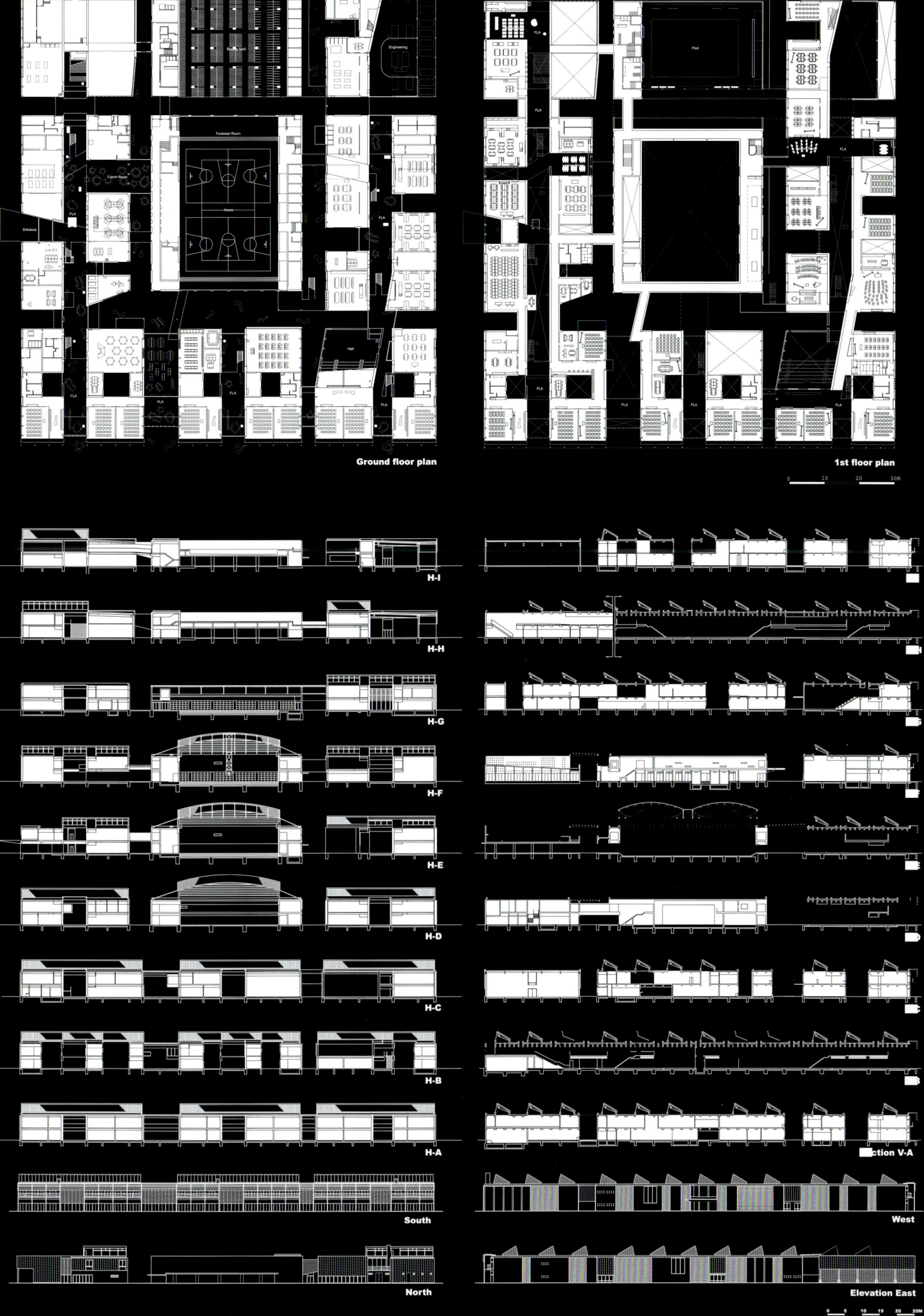

1st floor plan

H-I
H-H
H-G
H-F
H-E
H-D
H-C
H-B
H-A

Section V-A

South

West

North

Elevation East

フランス France

Anne Lacaton & Jean Philippe Vassal
アンヌ・ラカトン&ジャン・フィリップ・ヴァッサル

The Latapie house, Bordeaux, Floirac, France, 1993
© Philippe Ruault

University of Arts & Human Sciences, Grenoble, France, 1995-2000
© Philippe Ruault

Immeuble de Bureau, Nantes, France, 2002
© Philippe Ruault

Palais de Tokyo, Site for contemporary arts, Paris, France, 2000
© Philippe Ruault

After graduating from the Bordeaux School of Architecture in 1980, we worked and lived in Niger (Africa) for five years.
In 1987, we opened our own firm in Bordeaux. We have worked and lived in Paris since 2000. We have designed and built several private homes in the Southwest of France : the Latapie home at Floirac-Bordeaux, a house in the trees on Arcachon Bay, a country house in the Dordogne and another one in Coutras, the Arts and Sciences college at the University Pierre Mendès France in Grenoble and recently an office building in Nantes, the Café for the Architektur Zentrum in Vienna and the Palais de Tokyo, Site for contemporary arts, in Paris.

Our approach to architecture:
• Raising good questions and making rigorous replies to them, one after the other
• Always raising the issue of the necessary, the sufficient, what is important, and what isn't
• Avoiding accumulations, looking for simplicity and readability
• Shedding the idea of form other than architectonic or stemming from the context
• Constructing from the interior

Use: shifts, sensations, inner perception, appropriation
Sense: the evocation of a building, its contents, its life
Cost: economy, the right means, as inexpensive as possible to build more

Architecture should be straightforward, useful, precise, cheap, free, jovial, poetic and cosmopolitan.

1980年にボルドー建築学校を出た後、私たちはニジェール（アフリカ）に5年間住み、働いた。1987年にボルドーに事務所を開いた。2000年からは、パリに住み働いている。
いくつかの住宅をフランスの南西部に設計し、つくった。ボルドーのフロアラックのラタピ邸、アルカション湾の林の中の家、ドルドーニュとクートラのカントリーハウス等である。またグルノーブルのピエール・メンデス大学の人文科学学部、近年にはナントのオフィスビル、ウィーンの建築センターのカフェ、パレ・ド・トーキョウの現代美術スペースを手がけている。

建築へのアプローチ：
・それはよい問題を提起し、それに順次厳密な答えを与えること。
・必要であるか、十分であるかという問題、何が重要で何がそうでないのか。
・ものごとが積み重なることを避け、単純さと読みとりやすさを求めること。
・建築的な、あるいはコンテクストに起因する以外の、かたちに関するアイデアを放棄すること。
・インテリアからつくること。

用途：変移、センセーション、内的な知覚、適切さ
感覚：建物の喚起、その内容、その生命
コスト：経済性、正しい方法、より多くつくるため可能な限り安価なこと

建築は率直な、使いやすい、厳密な、安価な、自由な、愉快な、詩的でコスモポリタンでなければならない。

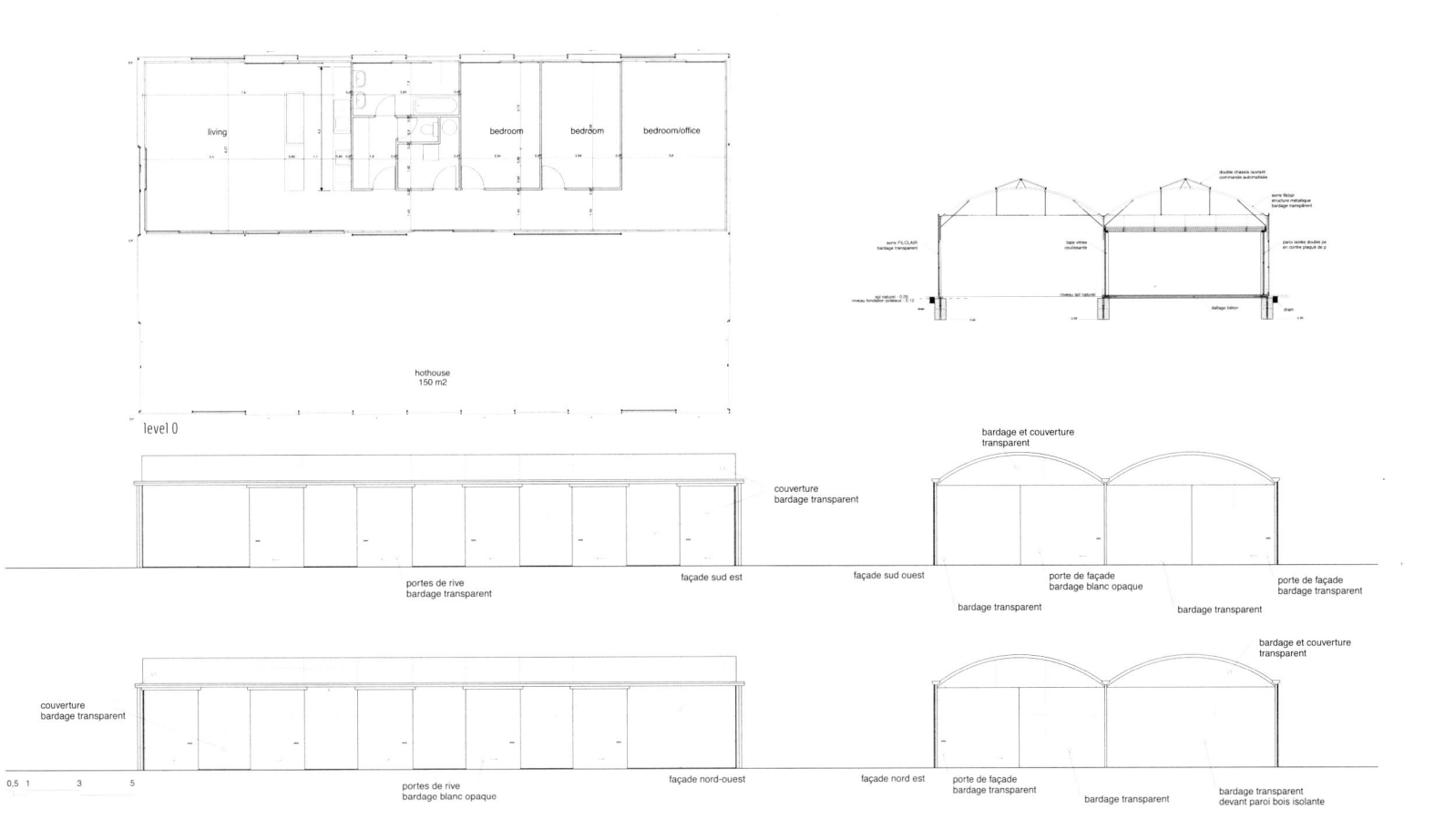

House

Coutras, France, 1999-2000

The construction site is located 50 km West of Bordeaux near the village of Coutras. The plot has an oblong shape. Its 33-meters-wide short end borders on a communal driveway. Part of the ground is classified as agricultural zone restricting building activities on that particular area.
The environment is composed of scattered housing and agriculturally cultivated land with greenhouses and occasional groups of bushes or trees. The low density of vegetation and buildings results in the absence of any profile. This allows an all encompassing view of the landscape that seems to be dominated by the sky.
The position of the house is back from the road and the neighboring houses. With a distance of 30 meters, from the driveway, it is located at the limit of the constructible zone.
Single-level on the ground floor it consists of two identical juxtaposed greenhouses. These are standard greenhouses built of a steel structure and a rigid transparent cover. The greenhouses are provided with automatic ventilation equipment (e.g. automatic opening of roof-elements) necessary for climate regulation. The facade can be opened up at either side to 50% with sliding doors. The plan forms a rectangle along the lot.
It is divided into two parts:
At the eastern side the living-area consisting of living-room, kitchen, bedrooms, is integrated into the greenhouse.
At the western side the conservatory forms the second part of the house.
The rooms of the living-area open towards the fruit garden and the conservatory simultaneously.

住宅

フランス、クートラ 1999-2000

建設場所はボルドーの西50km、クートラの村の近くにある。敷地は長方形であり、33mの長さの短辺が村道に面している。土地の一部は農業用地と定められ、そこへの建設は制限されている。
このあたりは家が点在する農地であり、温室や所々に茂みや木立がある。植生や建物の密度が低いため、特徴的な性格がない。それゆえランドスケープ的には空が支配的だと見ることが可能である。
家の位置は道路と近隣の家から距離を置いている。道路から30mのところにあり、建設可能な部分のぎりぎりの位置にある。
地上に平屋で立つ建物は、併置された二つの同じ温室でできている。これらは鉄の構造体と堅牢で透明なカバーからなる一般的な温室である。また内部気候の調節のための自動換気設備（例えば自動開閉屋根部）を備えている。側面は、どちら側もスライド式ドアで50%開放することが可能である。
平面的には敷地に沿って長方形をなし、二つの部分に分かれる。
東側は居住スペースで、リビングルーム、キッチン、ベッドルームが温室の中につくり込まれている。
西側はサンルームが建物のもうひとつの部分をなしている。
居住スペースの部屋は外部の果樹園とサンルームの双方に対して開かれている。

House
Coutras, France, 1999-2000
© Philippe Ruault

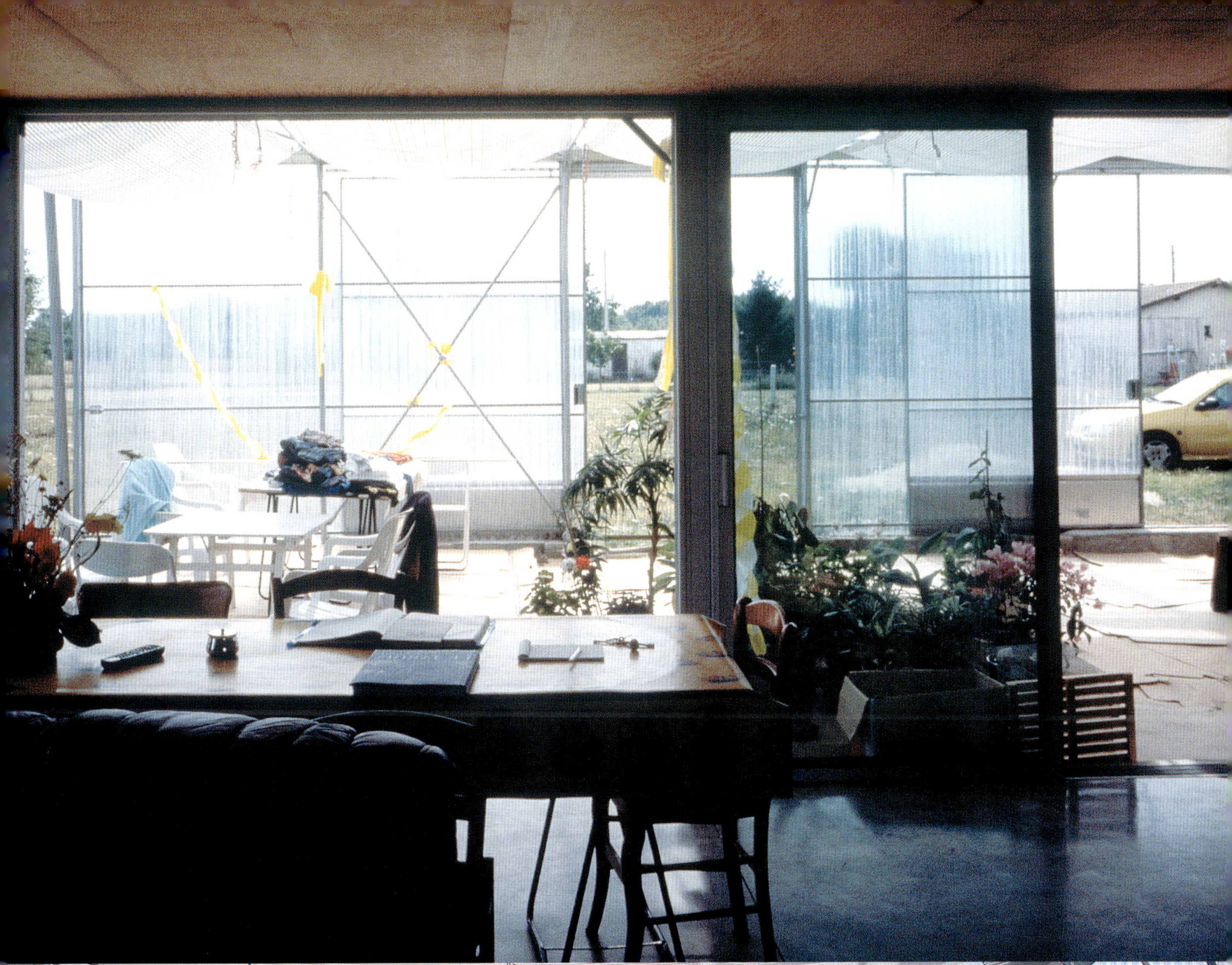

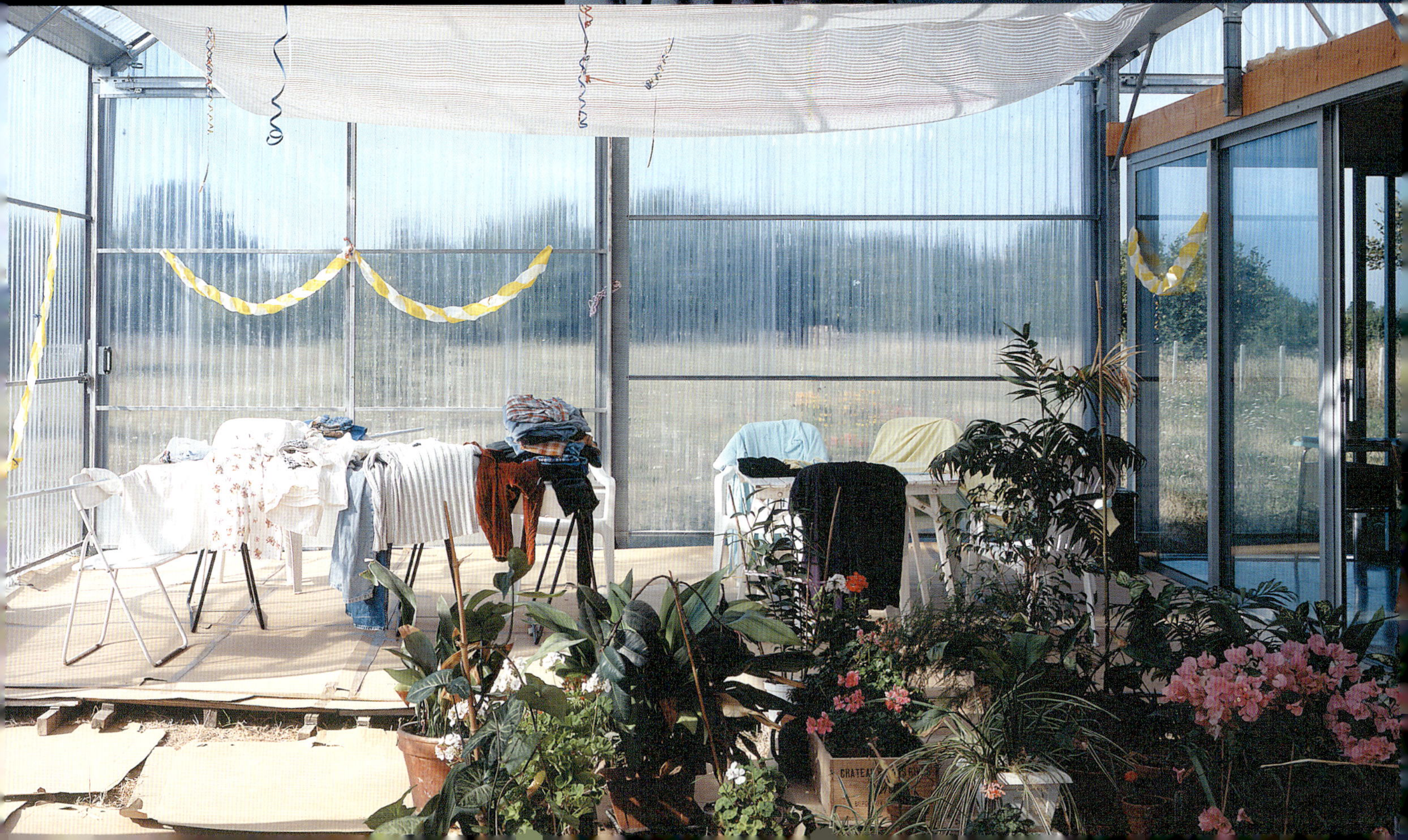

Denmark
デンマーク

Dorte Mandrup Architekter
ドーテ・マンドルップ・アーキテクテー

Antvorskov Church, Slagelse, Denmark, 1997
© Torbeu Eskerod

Taarnby Courthouse, Taarnby, Denmark, 1999
© Torbeu Eskerod

Home For The Future, exhibition 1:1,
Copenhagen, Denmark, 1999
© Jens Lindhe

Daycare Center Naestvedgade,
Copenhagen, Denmark, 2002
© Dorte Mandrup-Poulsen

Born in 1961 in Denmark, Dorte Mandrup-Poulsen graduated from the Aarhus school of architecture in 1991. After working at Henning Larsens office from 1992 to 1995, she founded Fuglsang & Mandrup-Poulsen Architects with Niels Fuglsang.
She established her own office, Dorte Mandrup Architects in 1999. She has been a part-time professor at the Royal Danish Academy of Art, and has received work grants from the National Foundation for the Arts (in 1998, 1999 and 2000)

In 1999 she finished Taarnby Court House outside Copenhagen with Niels Fuglsang. The work was nominated for the Mies Van Der Rohe Award in 2000.

In 2001 she was awarded the National Wood Association Annual Award for Outstanding Architecture for two main works: conversion of Seaplane Hangar H53 for Cell Network DK Headquarters, and Neighborhood Center Holmbladsgade, both situated in Copenhagen.

Rethinking the program requirements initiates every design process and the development of each project aims at enhancing reality as we experience it in terms of the surroundings, the landscape and the climate as well as the functional and economic preconditions.

The office has a pragmatic approach and considers the priorities of the given resources as a necessity, which positively may lead to a fruitful development of alternative solutions. The idiom of the office has its roots in the Scandinavian modern tradition. We attempt to develop a poetic sensuality along with a narrative and symbolic structure.

1961年にデンマークに生まれ、オルフス建築学校を1991年に卒業して学位を取得した。1992年から1995年までヘニング・ラーセンのオフィスで働き、1995年から1999年まではニルス・フールサングと共にフールサング＆マンドルップ＝プルセン・アーキテクツをつくって活動し、1999年には　ドーテ・マンドルップ・アーキテクツを設立した。
デンマーク王立美術アカデミーの非常勤教授であり、国立美術基金から助成金を得ている（1998-99-2000年）。

1999年にコペンハーゲン郊外にニルス・フールサングと協同して設計した トーンビュ・コートハウスをつくり、この住宅は2000年のミース・ファン・デル・ローエ賞の候補となった。

2001年にはふたつの作品で、国立木材協会年間優秀建築賞を受賞した。水上飛行機格納庫H53のセル・ネットワーク・デンマーク本社への改装と、ホルムブラーズガーデ地区センターであり、いずれもコペンハーゲンにある。

どの設計においてもプログラム上の要請をまず考え直してみる。そしてどのプロジェクトでも、機能的・経済的な前提条件と同様に、周辺の環境、ランドスケープ、気候といった私たちが経験する現実を高めてゆくことが、デザインの展開の発端となる。

私たちのアプローチはプラグマティックであり、与えられた条件の優位性を必要事項と捉え、それが実りの多い新たな解法に導いてくれるとポジティブに考えている。
私たちオフィスのイディオムは、北欧の近代建築に根ざしている。これを展開させて、物語性とシンボリズムと共に、詩的な官能を取り入れていこうとしている。

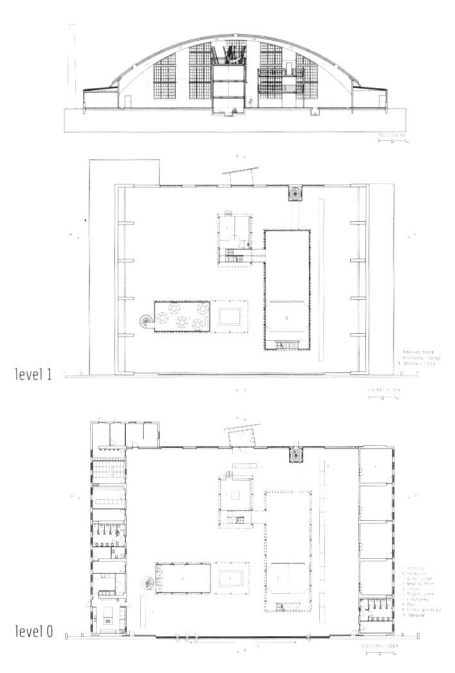

Seaplane Hangar H53, Cell Network DK Headquarters
Margretheholm, Holmen, Copenhagen, Denmark, 2000-2001

The H53 Seaplane hangar, built in 1921, is one of the first pre-stressed concrete structures of its size in Denmark. The goal of the design program was to create a workplace where the entire staff could work in the same space, while still respecting their individual needs, and the opportunity for recreation and contemplation was given a high priority. The goal was not to restore the landmark building to its original condition, but to allow its continuous history to be expressed in peaceful coexistence with the new additions. Three fireproof steel constructions, called the tower, platform and pool, form a spatial framework to support split-level decks, clad in birch plywood, like the floor.
In the uppermost steel elements of the structure, parachute fabric curtains are hung to enable rapid changes in the spatial context. The curtains can also be used as projection screens. The former lube pit has been covered with a glass floor, lit from below by blue fluorescent lighting to signal that the hangar is located on new landfill.
Above the meeting rooms lies the "hammock-tree," which is a staff lounge dedicated to peace and reflection. The staff and guests can lie and look out at the surroundings and still find seclusion from the outside world. Above the meeting room there is a staff lounge, which is furnished with large two- and three-seat sack chairs and low-placed lighting fixtures.
The canteen/café is located toward the building's West end. The canteen seats seventy guests in a calm "slow" seating group as well as a "fast" seating group with high tables and bar stools.
When the seaplane hangar functioned as originally planned, it could be opened in its entire width by large wooden sliding doors. This possibility has been re-established as double, glass sliding doors that open onto a large wooden terrace deck and grill/bonfire area. In this way the hangar space can be opened to the outdoors on warm summer days.

水上飛行機格納庫 H53、セル・ネットワーク・デンマーク本社
デンマーク、ホルメン、マーグレーテホルム 2000-2001

H53水上飛行機格納庫は1921年につくられた、プレストレス・コンクリートの建造物で、この大きさではデンマークでは初めてつくられたもののひとつである。設計の目標は社員全員がこの場所で働きながら、個々の必要を尊重し、レクリエーションや静かに考える機会を重要視したワークスペースをつくることだった。
ランドマークであるこの建物をもとの状態に改修することが目的ではなく、新しい増築部と穏やかに共存しつつ、歴史の連続性を表現することがテーマであった。
三つの耐火性のあるスチールの構造物:タワー、プラットフォームとプールが、空間の枠組みをつくり、床のように樺の合板で覆われたレベルの分かれるデッキを支えている。
構造物の最上部の鉄骨にはパラシュート布のカーテンが吊され、空間の文脈を直ちに変化させることを可能にしている。このカーテンはプロジェクターのスクリーンとしても利用することができる。
ピットであったところはガラスの床で覆われ、下部から青い蛍光灯で照らされて、格納庫が埋立地にあることを示してる。
会議室の上には"ハンモック・ツリー"と呼ぶ、静けさと内省のためのスタッフのラウンジがある。スタッフや来客は横になって周囲を見渡し、外界から隠遁することができる。
会議室の上には別のスタッフラウンジがあり、大きな二人掛け、三人掛けのソファと低く置かれた照明器具がある。食堂/カフェは建物の西端にある。食堂は落ち着いた"ゆっくり"組のために70席があり、別に高テーブルとスツールの"急ぎ"組のためのスペースがある。水上飛行機の格納庫が機能していた当初には、幅一杯の大きな木製のスライドドアが開くようになっていた。この仕組みはバーベキュー/たき火のできる木製テラスに開かれる二重ガラスのスライドドアとして再生されている。暖かい夏の日には、格納庫は外に向かって開くことができる。

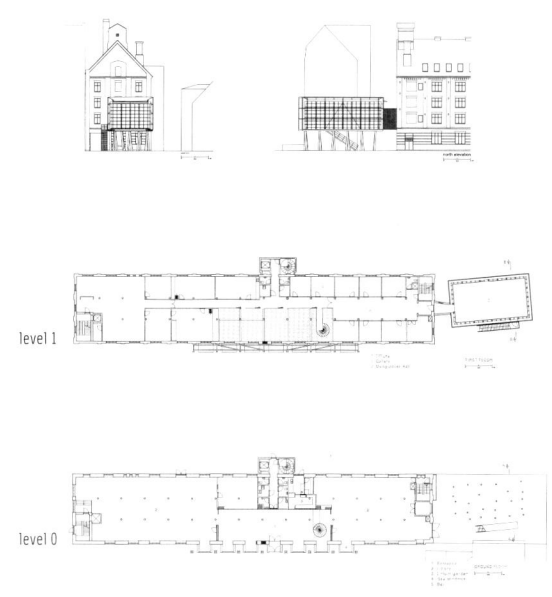

Neighborhood Center
Holmbladsgadequarter, Amager, Copenhagen, Denmark, 1999-2001

The project is part of a larger program initiated by the municipality to improve the somewhat rundown neighborhood. It was carried out on a very low budget. The aim was to create a dynamic correlation between the many different functions in the building and establish a great degree of openness and accessibility to the public. It has been a wish to keep the rather robust and used character of the structure and simultaneously add new spatial qualities.
New elements have been made in simple robust materials. Plywood and white larch are typical materials defining warm and unpretentious surfaces. The conversion of the existing structure is concentrated in a new triple high foyer established in the length of the building. The foyer is used as a library space during the day, and as a café and auditorium in the evening. By removal of the existing decks the structure of the house is exposed. The horizontal stabilization is re-established by an exterior steel frame structure supported by double wooden columns. Bays have been added to the existing window openings.
The inner walls in the foyer are made of maple veneer panels that, by folding, close the library desk area and entrances.

The addition
The addition containing a multipurpose hall, is conceived as a "lair in the treetops" placed at first floor level supported by a "forest" of concrete columns. The load-carrying structure is a visible frame construction in plywood, covered with glass panels The building is slightly turned, and sits between two high house ends, which will be overgrown with vines and ivy. The structure defines the space and at the same time establishes a soft transition between inside and outside.

地区センター
デンマーク、コペンハーゲン、アマー、ホルムブラーズガーデクワティア 1999-2001

この改築プロジェクトは、やや荒廃した地区を整備するための自治体による大規模プログラムの一環であり、非常に低予算でおこなわれている。建物内の異なる機能にダイナミックな相関関係を与え、住民に十分に開かれたアクセスし易い施設をつくることが目的であった。ある種丈夫で使い込まれた既存建物の雰囲気を残して、同時に新しい空間的な特質を付加することができればと考えていた。
新しい要素はシンプルで頑丈な素材でつくられた。白色の合板とカラ松は、暖かく飾らないファサードをつくるのにふさわしい材料である。既存の構造の改築は、建物長手の断面にあらわれる新しい3層吹抜のホワイエに集中している。このホワイエは昼間は図書館とカフェとして使われ、夜にはオーディトリウムになる。古いデッキは取り除いて建物の構造が露出している。水平面の安定は、木造のダブルコラムに支えられた外部の鉄骨のフレームで再構築されている。既存の窓の開口には、出窓が加えられている。ホワイエの内壁は、カエデの化粧合板のパネルで、折り畳むことで図書カウンターのエリアと入口を閉めることができる。

増築部
多目的ホールの増築部は、コンクリート柱の"森"に支えられて2階にあり、"樹状の巣"のように考えられた。この部分の構造は木材による露出したフレームであり、ガラス板で覆われている。建物は二つの高い家型の間に、若干斜めに振られて置かれていて、家型は将来にはつるや蔦で覆われる筈である。この構造物は空間を特徴づけるとともに、内部と外部の間の柔らかな移行をもたらしている。

Seaplane Hangar H53, Cell Network DK Headquarters
Margretheholm, Holmen, Copenhagen, Denmark, 2000-2001
© Jens Lindhe

Neighborhood Center
Holmbladsgadequarter, Amager, Copenhagen, Denmark, 1999-2001
© Jens Lindhe

日本 Japan

Mikan
みかんぐみ

NHK Nagano Broadcasting station, Nagano, Japan, 1998
© Shigeru Hiraga

Tokyo Shibuya AX, Tokyo, Japan, 2001
© Mikan

Tokyo KH, Tokyo, Japan, 2001
© Covi

Tokyo KH, Tokyo, Japan, 2001
© Covi

1 – A *mikan* is a tangerine. Our real name in Japanese is Mikan Gumi which means the class, the gang or the company of the tangerine.

2 – The complexity of the creative process is paired with a search for simplicity.

3 – Banality as an alternative to the extroverted, nearly expressionist character of the eighties in Japan. This apparent banality is mainly on account of multiple parameters. It implies a Platonic vision of space which is controlled by all kinds of happenings.

4 – A shaping process with an anti-formal attitude, the shape is conceived as the result of a process. The result remains open to appropriation as wished, avoiding the dilemma between container and contents, which is often strong in Japan.

5 – Going beyond the limits of disciplines, architecture, interior, furniture, etc. are seen as a whole. We therefore often work in partnership.

6 – Group Work / Think Tank, this allows us to avoid dogmatism. Projects are long kept open to all influences and controversies.

7 – Our approach being non-formal, there is no recurrence in our work, although some unvarying principles appear: a symbiosis with the natural conditions, a fluidity of space and a rational functionality.

1　みかんは柑橘類のくだものの総称である。みかんぐみは保育園のクラスの名前からとられた。

2　ものを創り出すプロセスの複雑さは、つくられるものの単純さとペアである。

3　日本の80年代の表現主義的な派手なかたちと比べると私たちの空間ははるかにシンプルである。しかし、そのシンプルさは様々なパラメータを検討した結果であり、そこで起こるさまざまな出来事のためのものである。

4　わたしたちは形態を表現するためにつくっているのではない。形態は設計のプロセスの結果としてあらわれる。あらわれた空間はオープンエンドで、その空間のためだけではなく、そこでの生活のためだけでもない。

5　建築、インテリア、家具、その他すべてのものに及ぶ。だからいろいろなパートナーと組む。

6　グループワーク／シンクタンク。独断的にならないため、またさまざまな影響や反対意見を受け容られるように、プロジェクトはぎりぎりまでフィックスされない。

7　私たちは形態のためにアプローチはしないので、あらわれる形態はその度にちがう。それでも、いくつかの重要な共通点を見つけられる。それらは自然の条件に対する合理性、空間の流動性、合理的な機能性である。

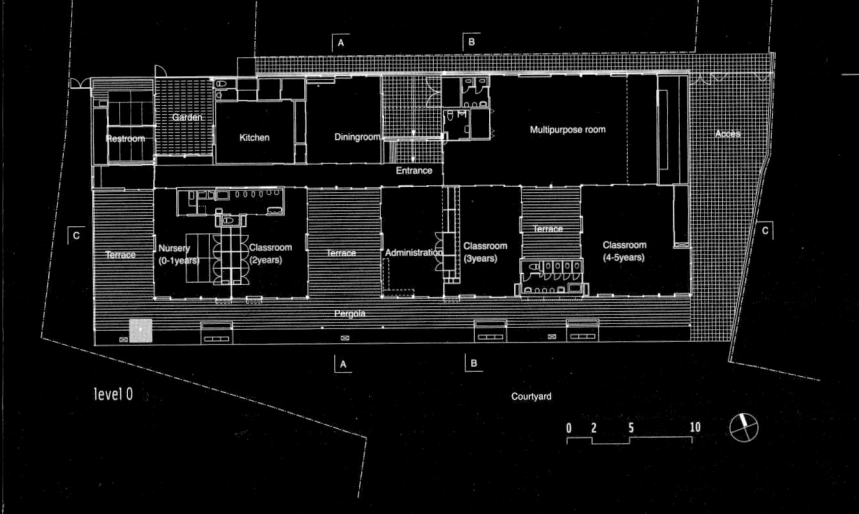

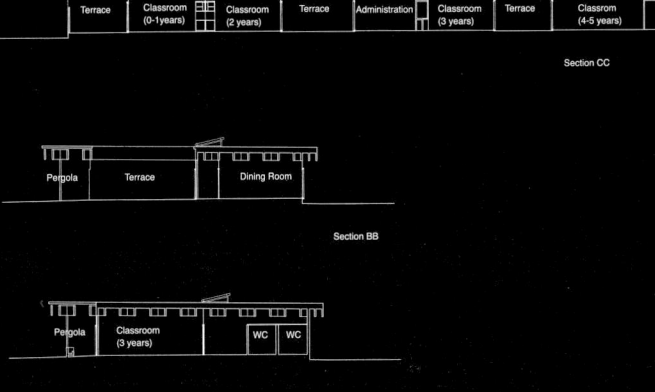

Kindergarten in Yatsushiro
City of Yatsushiro, Prefecture of Kumamoto, Japan, 1999-2001

The overall conception of the project is the result of a process of participation which helped to define the relation between the education of young children and the space.

Participation allowed a useful way to create harmonious relationships between the architects, the users and the various people involved in the project. It also enlightened the process of creation of the building.
The teachers helped both to investigate the ambiguous relation between a well-defined separation of rooms according to ages and a will to create an open and fluent space. They also helped defined the principles of the furniture which became partitions at the same time. Eventually the kids and their parents, through an open workshop under the direction of the architects and two artists, helped design the games and the frescos of the storage area located in the courtyard.

Working with the structural engineer allowed us to emphasize the open character of the school. Actually the whole building is covered by a wooden frame looking like a coffered ceiling, leaving large rooms free of columns.

In general, a series of dialectical spatial relations was born from these various collaborations. The school is a restrained wooden box with an easily recognizable unique volume, although its limits towards the courtyard are ambiguous. Its strict internal distribution is counterbalanced by the fluid and loose relation between the juxtaposed rooms. The ceiling is unusually high although the furniture and the window parts are in accordance to the small size of the children, thus providing an intercourse of different scales.

八代の保育園
熊本県八代市、1999-2001

この計画は一般の人たちが参加して設計された公共施設である。それは、子どもの保育と空間の関わりを考察し関係させることを決定する要因であった。
ワークショップ方式は、建築家が建物のデザインをするとき、そこを使う側の人たちとの間に調和をもたらす上で有意義であると考える。それはまた、建物をつくるためのプロセスを明らかにするものでもある。今回の場合、保母の方達の話は、子どもの年齢による空間が分節することを重視し、同時に、異年齢の子ども達が交流する時間や多目的に利用される場合に対応できるオープンで流動的な空間構成という、この建物のコンセプトの主因となった。子ども達の空間を家具によって可動的につくることとしたことも、現状の使われ方の様子や保母の方からのアドバイスによるものである。さらに、私たちと2人のアーティストの呼びかけに、八代市のバックアップのおかげで子ども達とその両親の参加によって、園庭の倉庫の壁画がみごとにペイントされできあがった。

構造設計者とのコラボレーションによって、この保育園の開放的な性格をより強調する構造システムを持つこととなった。事実、建物全体は木造の斜交格子梁によっておおらかに覆われ、無柱の広い空間となっている。

つまり弁証法的な空間の関係性は、このいくつかのコラボレーションによって生まれたものである。この保育園は単純な単一のボリュームによる木箱であるが、そこに挿入されたいくつかの中庭によって内外部が流動的である。並列された、各年齢別の保育室は、はっきりとした構成を持つが、中庭や建具、そして全体に連続する天井によって流動的で緩やかな繋がりとバランスを保つ。この天井は高いが、家具や木製窓の腰はめ板よって、小さい子どもの身体にあわせられ、空間内に違うスケールが共存する。

Kindergarten in Yatsushiro
City of Yatsushiro, Prefecture of Kumamoto, Japan, 1999-2001
© Shin Kenchiku (left page)
© Coui, © Shin Kenchiku (right page)

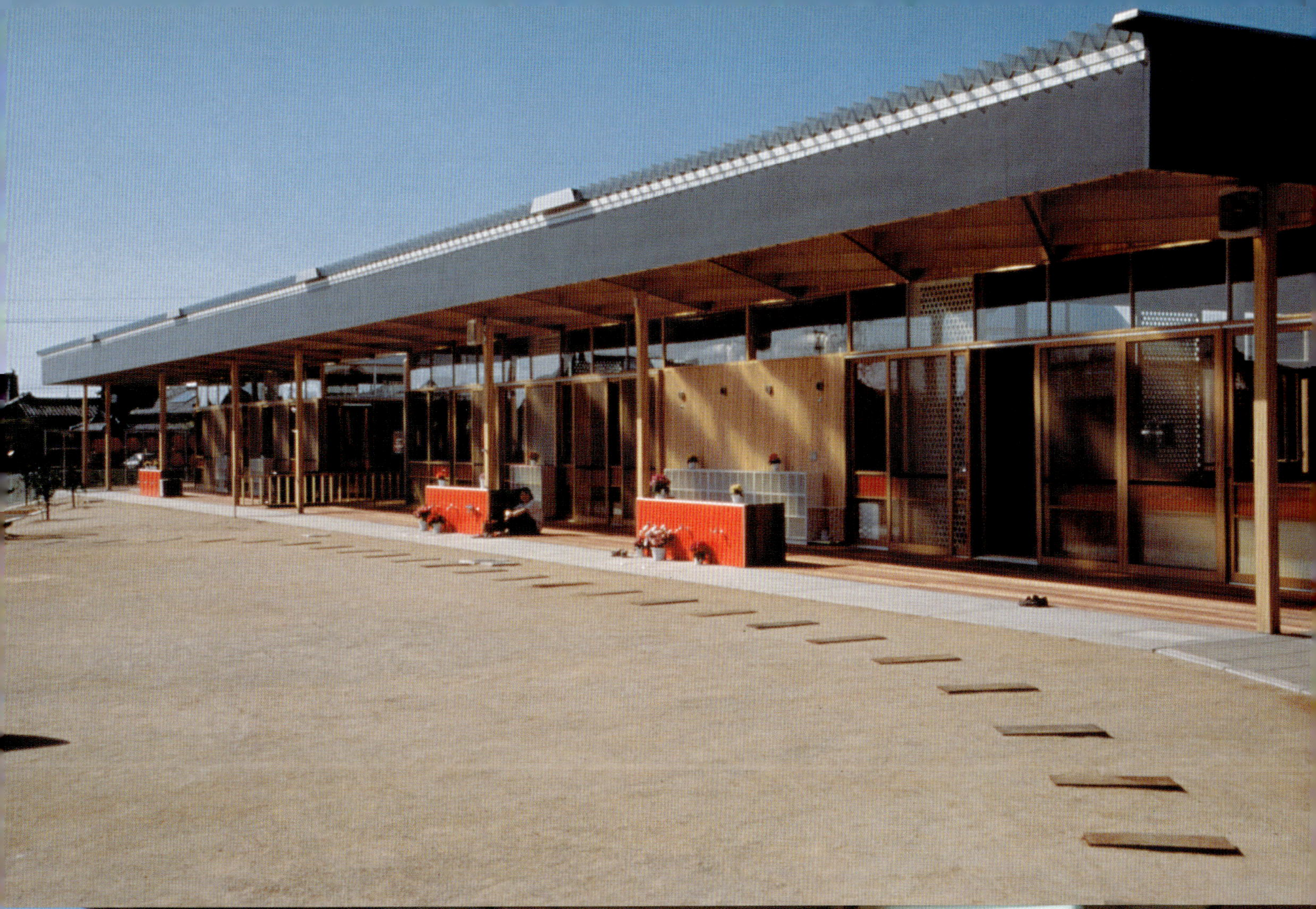
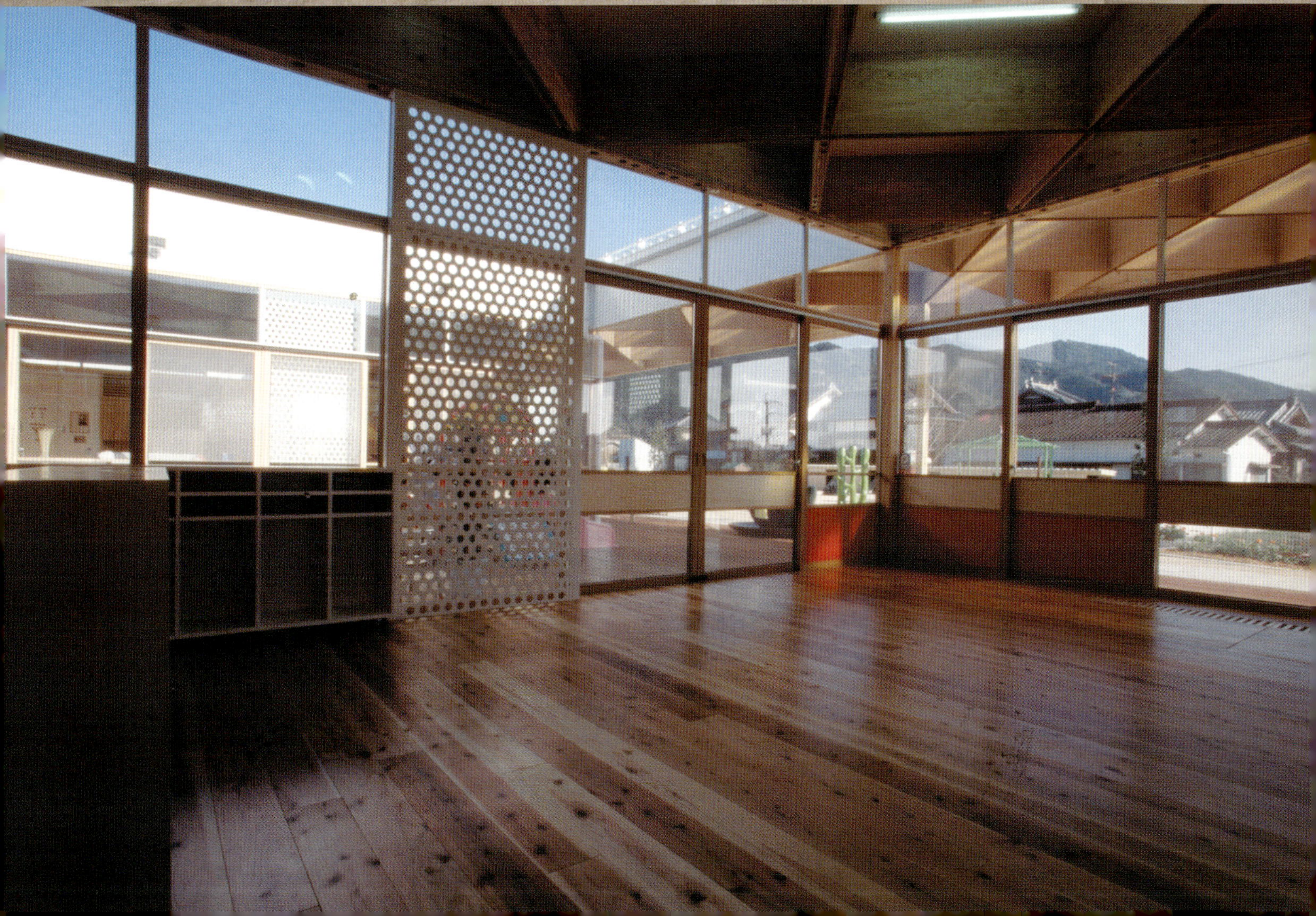

Luxembourg
ルクセンブルク

Ney & Partners sarl
ネイ＆パートナーズ

Tervuren bridge, Brussels, Belgium, 1998-2001
© Daylight

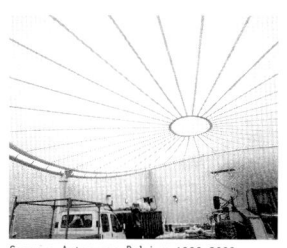

Canopys, Antwerpen, Belgium, 1999-2000
© Daylight

Canopys, Antwerpen, Belgium, 1999-2000
© Daylight

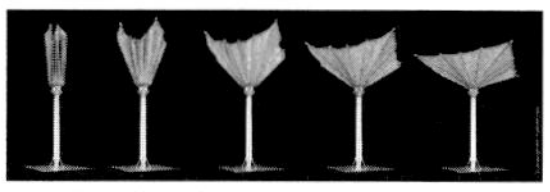

Umbrellas, Alden Biesen, Belgium, 2001-2002
© Daylight

Laurent Ney, a citizen of Luxembourg, was born in 1964 in Thionville (France). He graduated as a civil engineer in 1989 in Liège (Belgium) and collaborated until 1996 in the office of René Greisch in Liège. He received in 2001 the prize of Sint-Lukas archief in Brussels.

Born 1965 in Luxembourg, Nathalie Ries, as an Erasmus exchange student, studied at the Polytecnico Milano from 1991 to 1992. In 1992 she received her graduate diploma in architecture at the Institut Supérieur d'Architecture d'Etat La Cambre in Brussels. From 1993 to 1997 she worked as an architectural collaborator in the office 'Artau' in Malmédy, Belgium.

In 1996 Laurent Ney and Nathalie Ries co-founded T6, in Luxemburg and Ney and Partners, in Belgium.
T6 and Ney and Partners have completed a number of projects, transformations, extensions and new buildings in Luxembourg and Belgium. Ney and Partners deals mainly with highly structural projects.
The integration of new materials and structural reflection in the projects takes an important part in the design process.
In 2002 the Elena building in Brussels received The Belgian Architecture Award in the new construction category.

ルクセンブルグ人のローラン・ネイはフランスのティオンヴィルに1964年に生まれた。1989年にリエージュで土木工学の学位を取り、ルネ・グレッシュのオフィスに1996年まで勤めた。2001年にシント・リュカス・アーカイヴ賞をブリュッセルで受賞した。

ナタリー・リースはルクセンブルグで1965年に生まれ、エラスムス交換学生としてミラノ工科大学で1991年から1992年まで学んだ。1992年にブリュッセルのラ・カンブル国立建築高等学院から建築の学位を取得した。1993年から1997年までベルギーのマルメディにあるアルトー事務所で設計に協同した。

1996年にローラン・ネイとナタリー・リースはT6 sàrlをルクセンブルグに、またネイ＆パートナーズをベルギーに設立した。
T6とネイ＆パートナーズはルクセンブルグとベルギーに数々のプロジェクト、改築、増築、新築を実現してきている。ネイ＆パートナーズは主に高度な構造プロジェクトに取り組んでいる。設計のプロセスでは、新しい素材と構造計画の対応を一体的に考えて行くことを重視している。
2002年にブリュッセルのエレナ・ビルディングで、ベルギー建築賞を新築建物部門で受賞した。

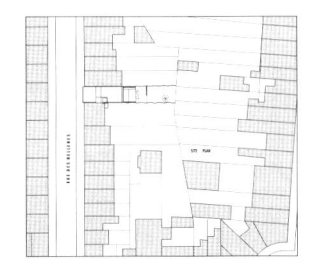

Elena Building
Brussels, Belgium, 1998-2001

The building is situated within a lively residential area, adjacent to the university in Ixelles, Brussels.
It is composed of a duplex office, a duplex apartment, and two studio apartments.

The ground, sandwiched between two buildings, is 6.7 meters by 40 meters. With a construction depth of 17 meters, importance was given to achieving maximum natural light in the center of the building. This was achieved with a subtle play on the alignment of the floor levels and the interior volumes and the incorporation of large glazed facades to the front and back.
The rear façade of the duplex has a glazed panel of 7 x 7 meters. With the orientation being Northeast, no requirements for solar protection are needed, thus offering splendid, unrestricted views of the garden.
The front façade, orientated to the Southeast, required some form of solar protection. This has been achieved with adjustable cedar wood blinds mounted externally 60 centimeters in front of the glazed façade. The mobility of these blinds allows for the regulation of incoming natural light in the offices. The space between the blinds and the façade allow for maintenance access.
The same cedar wood has been used as the finishing material on other parts of the façade to create a coherent whole.
At the top of the building the roof garden offers to the users of the building a place of contemplation and a 360° view over the urban space.
Interior wall enclosures and fixed furniture are constructed to the height of 2.05 meters and completed above this height with glazed panels, allowing the passage of natural light.

エレナ・ビルディング
ベルギー、ブリュッセル　1998-2001

建物はブリュッセルのイクセル大学に隣接した、活気のある居住地区の中にある。メゾネットのオフィス、メゾネットのアパートメント、2つのスタジオ形式のアパートメントからなる。

二つの建物に挟まれた地面は、6.7m幅で40mの長さをもつ。17mの深さとなる建造物であり、建物の内部に最大限の自然光を取り込むことが課題であった。それはフロアレベルと室容積の注意深い取扱いと、正面と背面のガラスファサードによって実現している。
背面は複層ガラスパネルの7m×7mのファサードだが、北東を向いて太陽光の負荷が生じないので、庭の景色を存分に堪能できる。
正面のファサードは南東を向いて、何らかの日除けが必要となる。そのため、ガラス面の60cm外側に、調整可能な杉板のブラインドを設けている。可動のブラインドにより、オフィスに入り込む自然光を調整することができる。ガラス面とブラインド面の間はメンテナンスを可能とする空間があいている。
他の外壁面にもこの杉板を仕上材として用いており、全体に一貫性をもたせている。
頂部には屋上庭園があり、建物の利用者が休憩をし都市景観を360°眺めることができる。
屋内の間仕切と造付けの家具は2.05mの高さに統一してあり、天井との間はガラスにして自然光の通り道としている。

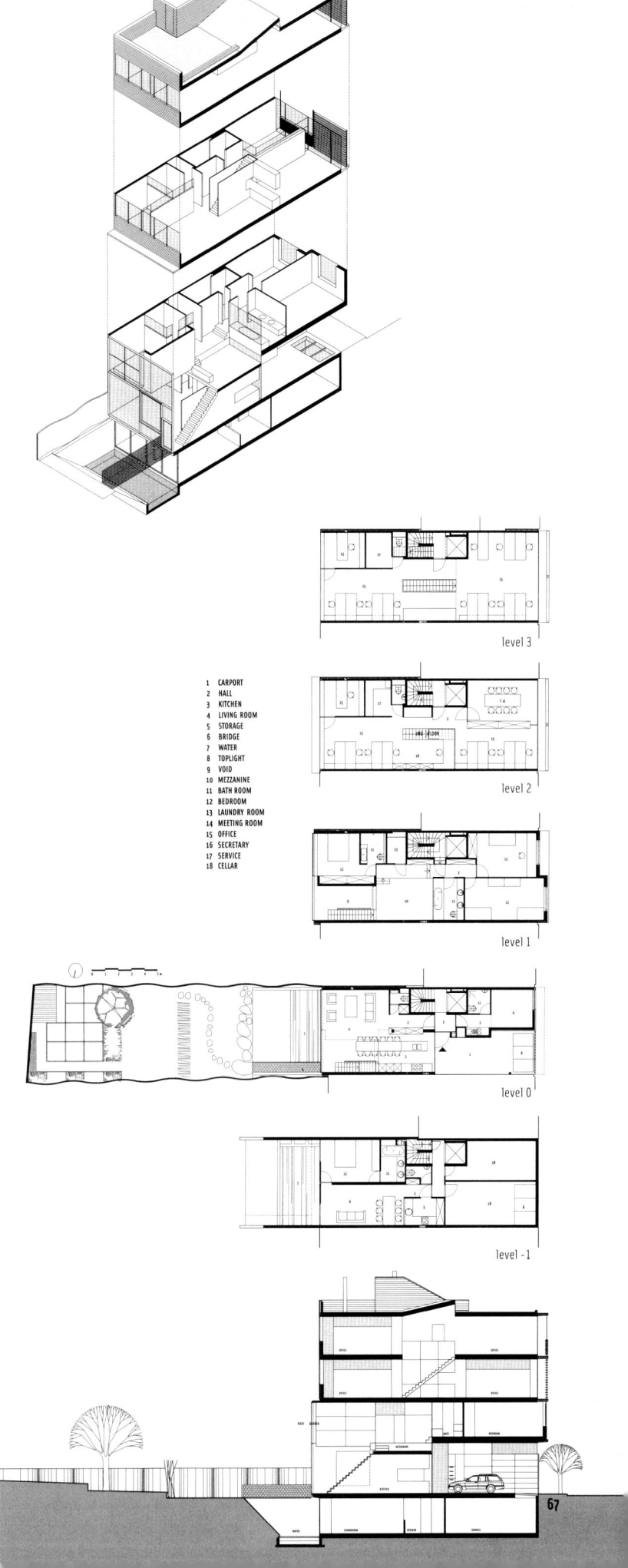

1　CARPORT
2　HALL
3　KITCHEN
4　LIVING ROOM
5　STORAGE
6　BRIDGE
7　WATER
8　TOPLIGHT
9　VOID
10　MEZZANINE
11　BATH ROOM
12　BEDROOM
13　LAUNDRY ROOM
14　MEETING ROOM
15　OFFICE
16　SECRETARY
17　SERVICE
18　CELLAR

Elena Building
Brussels, Belgium, 1998–2001
© Daylight

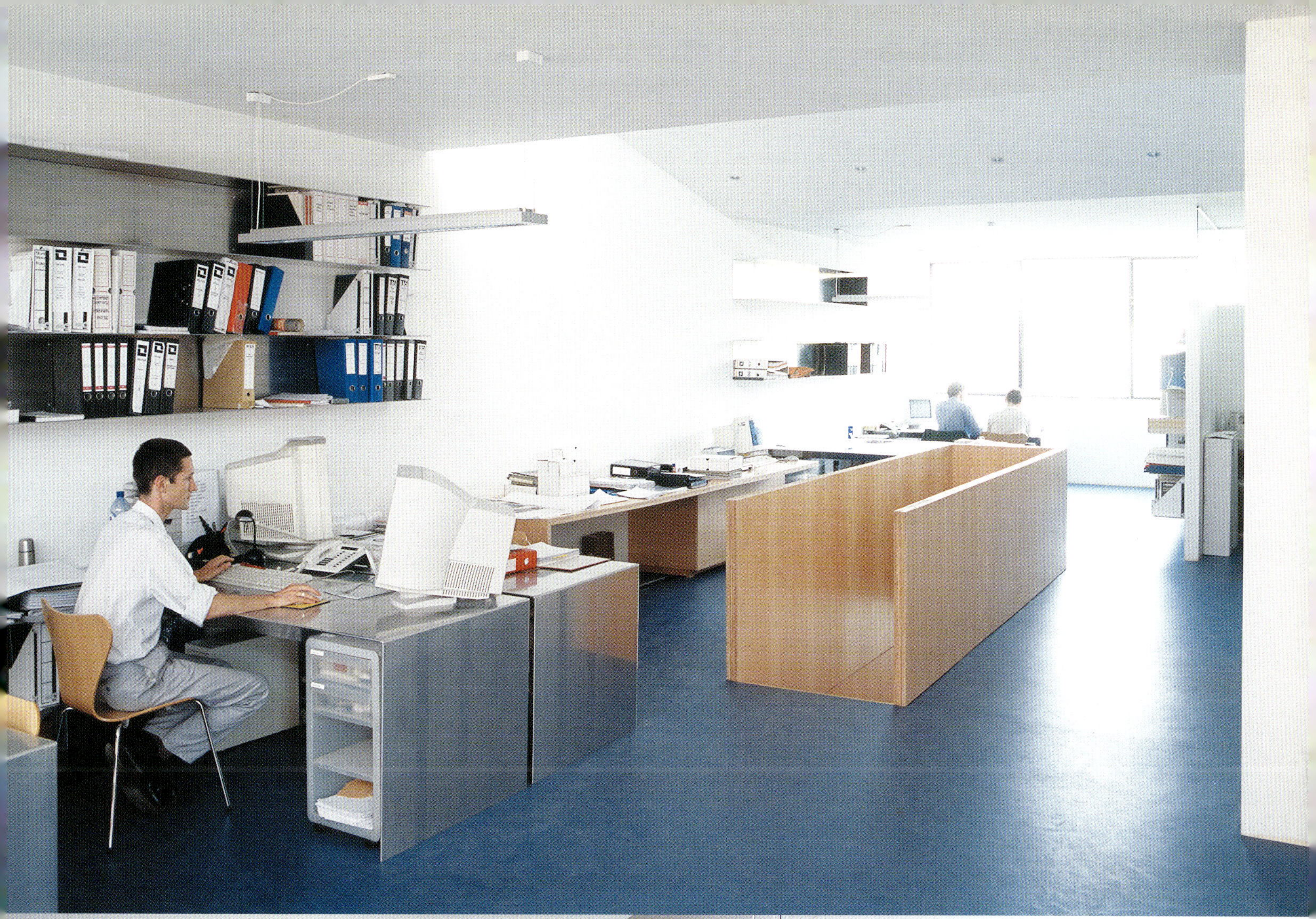

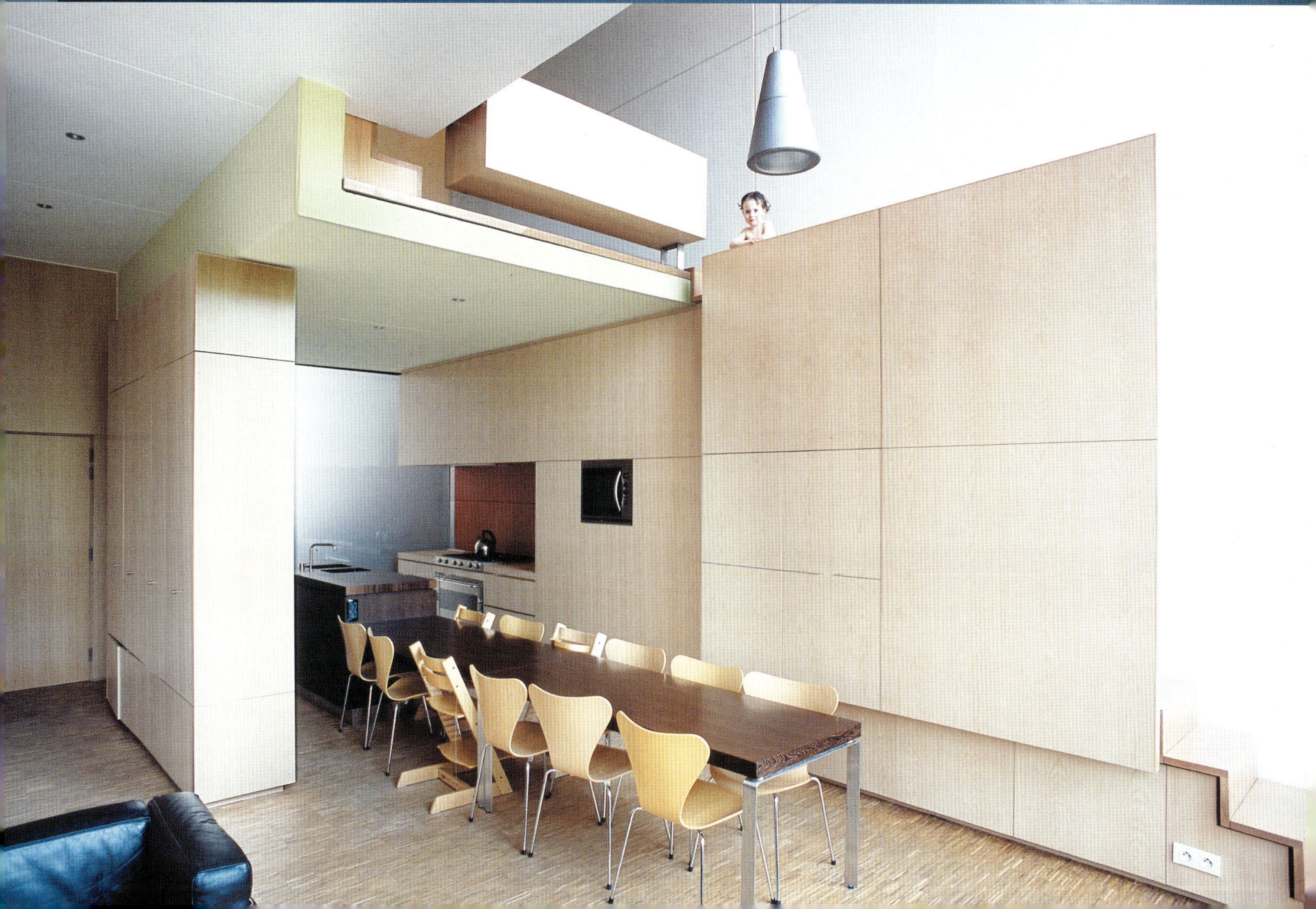

Ireland
アイルランド

O'Donnell + Tuomey Architects
オードネル＆トゥミ・アーキテクツ

Sheila O'Donnell and John Tuomey founded O'Donnell + Tuomey in 1988. They have completed a number of cultural and educational buildings in Dublin including the Irish Film Centre, National Photography Centre and Ranelagh Multi Denominational School. They are currently engaged in the design and construction of university buildings, schools, housing and mixed-use buildings in Ireland and the Netherlands. They have been involved in urban design projects including the Temple Bar regeneration in Dublin and the Zuid Poort masterplan in Delft. Both partners are studio lecturers in University College Dublin and have taught at a number of schools of architecture in UK and the USA including AA, Cambridge, Princeton, Harvard and Syracuse Universities.

シェイラ・オードネルとジョン・トゥミは1988年にオードネル＋トゥミを設立した。彼らがダブリンで手がけた文化施設や教育施設の中には、アイリッシュ・フィルム・センター、国立写真センター、ラネラ多宗派学校などが含まれる。現在、大学建物、学校、住宅、多目的建物の設計や建設がアイルランドとオランダで進行している。ダブリンのテンプル・バーの再生や、デルフトのザウト・ポートのマスタープラン等の都市計画プロジェクトにも関わっている。
パートナーが共に、ダブリンのユニバーシティ・カレッジの講師であり、ＡＡ、ケンブリッジ大、プリンストン、シラキューズ大学等、イギリスとアメリカの建築学科で教えている。

Ranelagh School, Dublin, Ireland, 1998
© Dennis Gilbert / View Photography

Hudson House, Navan, Ireland, 1997
© John Seirle

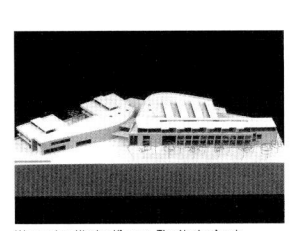

Waterwing Kinder Kluster, The Netherlands, 2002-2003

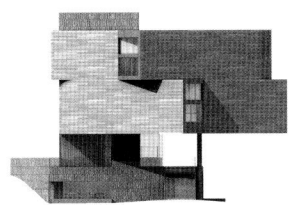

Art Gallery / Restaurant, University College, Cork, Ireland, 2002-2003

The Furniture College Letterfrack
Connemara, County Galway, Ireland, 1995-2001

The project is a rethinking of a former industrial school to accommodate a furniture college, workshops, a furniture restoration unit, student facilities and administrative headquarters for a wide range of community-led activities. A phased construction strategy allows the college to remain in operation while the new buildings are being built.

New buildings and old share a series of social and communal external spaces in an arrangement which reinforces the sense of connection with the village. A new forecourt shifts the axis of entry from its former centralized symmetry; realized in a diagonal relationship with an academic garden which replaces the exercise yard of the former penal institution, the entrance achieves a compositional balance between the existing and the new. A new café with a library above opens onto the garden. Two new machine halls are built between the boggy ground to the South and the landfill foundation of the existing building; a North-lit bench room links new and old buildings together. Heavy delivery traffic has been separated from pedestrians and cars, yet a sense of openness remains.

Climate has been a strong motivating factor; given the location of the site on the western seaboard of Connemara. Wind shelter is created by planting and earth banking and building form.

The structural systems of the various buildings have been designed in response to their contrasting functional requirements and their place in the sequence of construction.

The goal of the project is to transform an obsolete, 19th century institution into an open educational resource for the 21st century.

レターフラック家具学校
アイルランド、ガルウェー州コネマラ　1995-2001

このプロジェクトは、実業学校であった建物を再検討して、そこに家具カレッジ、ワークショップ、家具修復のユニット、学生センター、事務棟といった施設を、コミュニティが主導するさまざまなアクティビティのためにつくるものである。工程計画を工夫することで、カレッジを運営しながら新しい建設を併行して行っている。

新しい建物も古くからのものも、連続する社会的・公共的屋外空間をもち、村との関係を強化するような仕方で連続している。新しい前庭は、以前のシンメトリーのもつ中心性から動線の軸をずらすようにつくられている。かつての刑務所の運動広場にかわってできた、アカデミックな庭と前庭は対角線状の関係をもつことで、入口は古くからの建物と新しい建物の構成のバランスを実現している。
庭に開くかたちでカフェがあり、その上部には図書館がある。二つの機械室棟が、南側の沼地と既存建物の埋立基礎の間に新たにつくられた。北側が照らされたベンチの空間が新しい建物と古い建物を結びつけている。配送用車の交通は、一般の歩行者および車の動線と分離されているが、開放感は残されている。

コネマラの西海岸沿いという敷地ゆえに、気候は特に重要な与件であった。植樹と堤防と建物の形状で、防風のシェルターができている。

それぞれの建物の構造システムは、相対的な機能上の必要性と建設の順序から考えられている。

プロジェクトの目的は、時代遅れとなった19世紀の施設を21世紀の開放的な教育資産に生まれ変わらせることである。

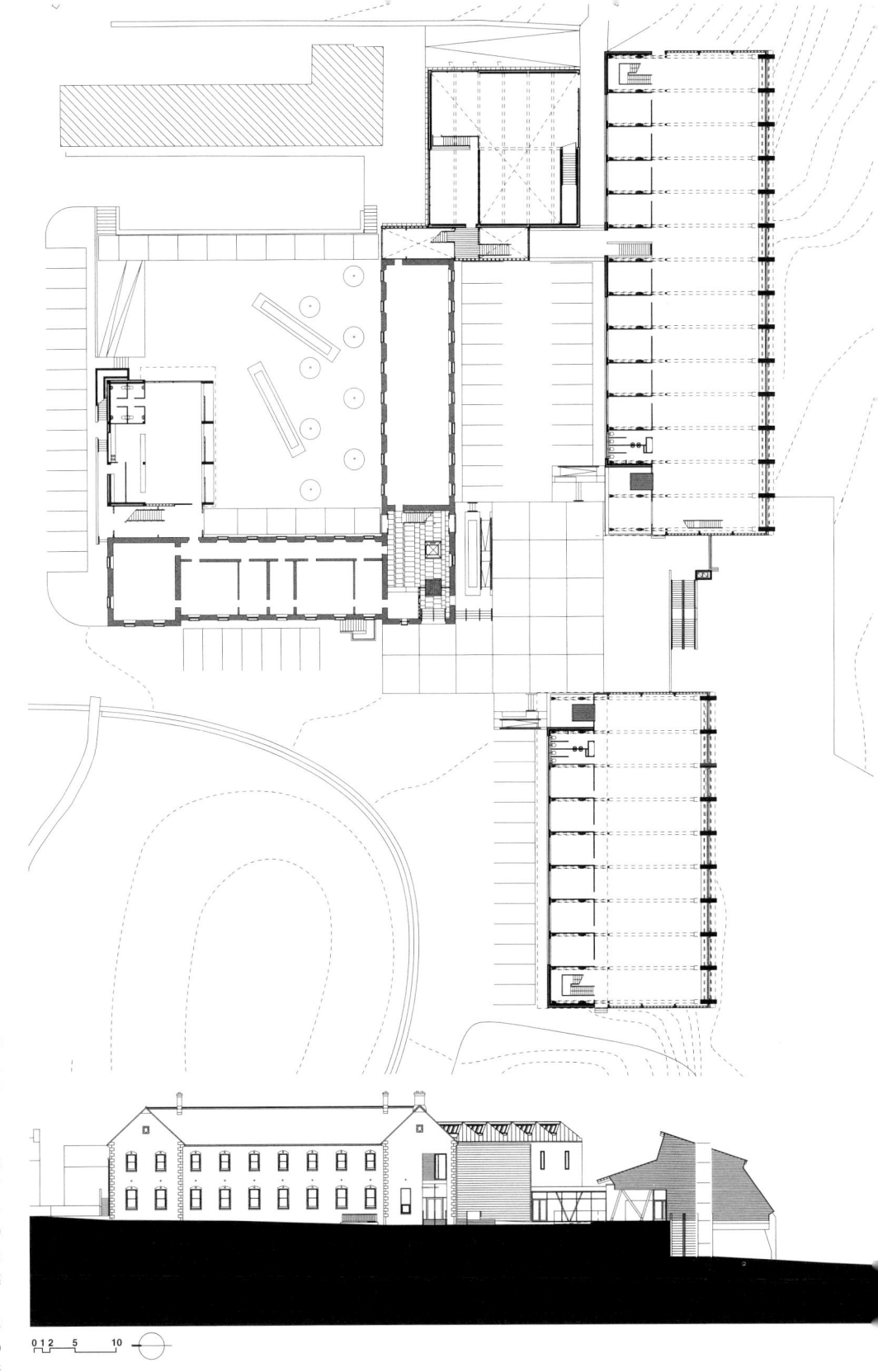

The Furniture College Letterfrack
Connemara, County Galway, Ireland, 1995-2001
© Dennis Gilbert / View Photography

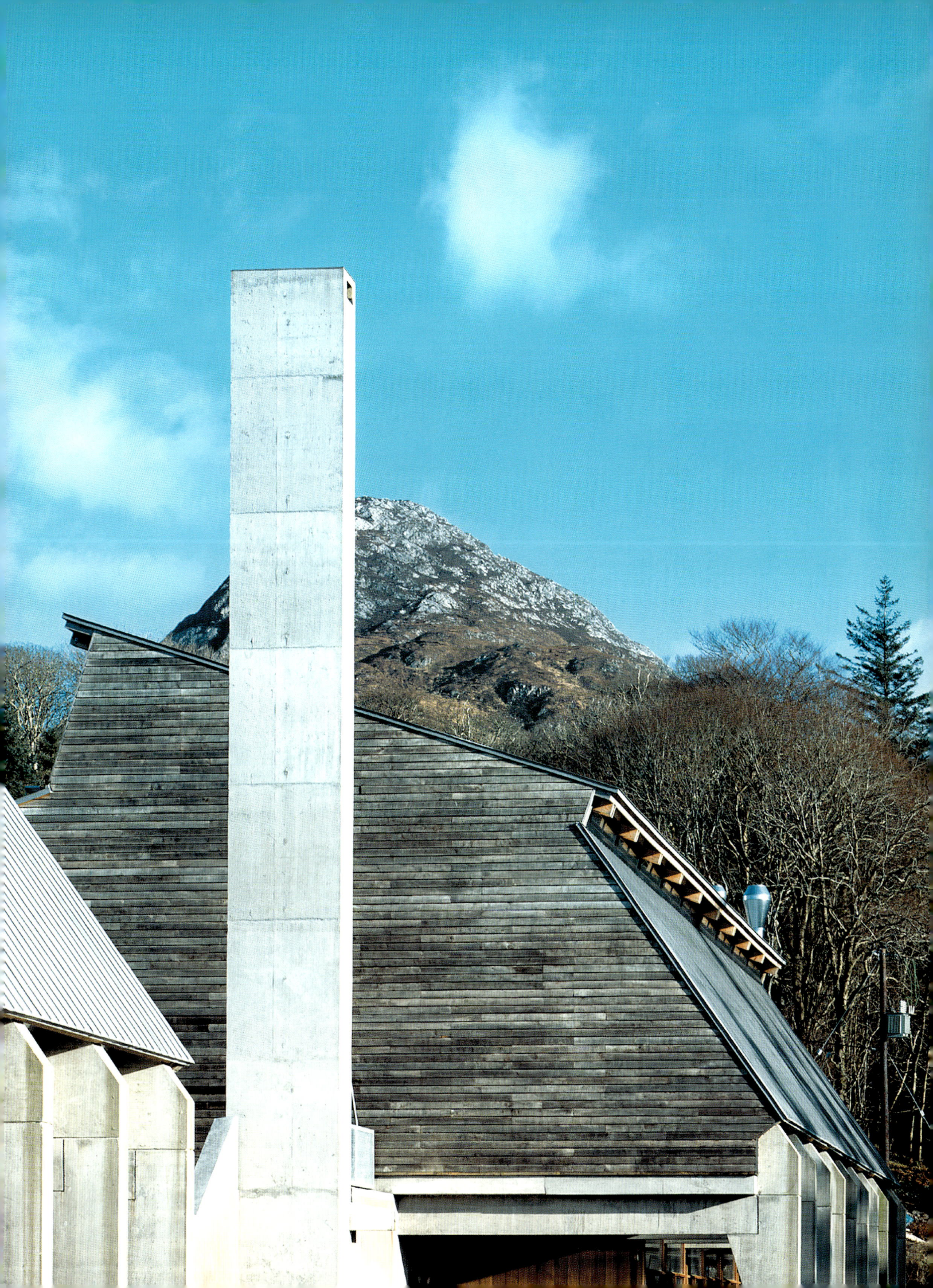

Austria
オーストリア

Riegler Riewe Architects Pty. Ltd.
リーグラー・リーヴェ・アーキテクツ

Federal Institute for Social Pedagogy, Baden, Austria, 1995-1998
© Paul Ott

Housing Graz-Stassgang, Graz, Austria, 1992-1994
© Margheritta Spiluttini

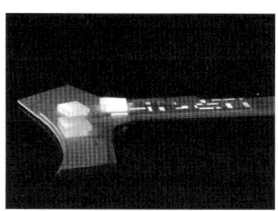

Saleggi Project, Hotel, Casino, Theater Locarno, Switzerland, competition 1999
© Paul Ott

Main Railway station Innsbruck, Tyrol, Austria, 1999-2003
© Paul Ott

Riegler Riewe first think of the design strategically at abstract and analytical levels. Despite the great difficulty of thought related to this stance, the results have little to do with cold creativity. By filtering their thoughts and reducing them to structural considerations, by asking precise questions without formulating answers immediately, they create a design that develops a crystalline quality. Nonetheless, it is not the search for minimalist solutions or a definite and therefore often pathetic reduction that guides them. Instead, their concept is orientated by the functioning pragmatism of everyday life and the task of giving it new space. In a certain sense Riegler Riewe work with the poetics of realism. They try to lead architecture back to a sense of normalcy without reducing it to banality or idolizing everyday life. Even though Riegler Riewe´s thinking takes detours, their approach makes their demand for the further development of architecture clear.

Arno Ritter

The architects Florian Riegler and Roger Riewe founded in 1987 the Architekturbüro Riegler Riewe, in Graz.
In 1996 the Riegler Riewe Architects Pty. Ltd. based in Graz was set up and in 1997 a branch office of the Architekturbüro Riegler Riewe was opened in Cologne.
Several projects have been worked on and executed in the past, of which the Information Technology and Electronics Institutes of the Technical University of Graz, the Federal Institute for Social Pedagogy in Baden and the airport of Graz are the most important.
At present Riegler Riewe Architects are working on the projects for the new railway station in Innsbruck, the House of Literature in Graz and the railway station in Bruck/Mur.

リーグラー・リーヴェはまず抽象的・分析的レベルで戦略的にデザインを考える。こうした思考の姿勢は非常にタフでありながら、そこから生みだされるのは冷たい創造性とはほぼ無縁のものである。思考をフィルターにかけ、構造的な考察に還元し、答えを性急に求めることなく緻密に疑問を投ずることによって、結晶化した特性のなかに輝く要素があらわれるようなデザインを作りあげるのである。しかしながらそれはミニマリスティックな解答を求めたり、限定的なゆえしばしば哀れをさそうような還元に向かうのではない。むしろ彼らのコンセプトが志向するのは、日常生活で機能するプラグマティズムであり、そこに新たな空間を与えることである。ある意味でリーグラー・リーヴェはリアリズムの詩学と共に活動する。彼らは建築を陳腐さに還元したり日々の生活を理想化することなしに、ある種の正常化に回帰させようとしている。たとえリーグラー・リーヴェの思考が迂回路をとったとしても、彼らのアプローチは建築のさらなる展開への欲求を明確化するものである。

アルノー・リッター

フローリアン・リーグラーとロジャー・リーヴェは、1987年にリーグラー・リーヴェ建築事務所をグラーツに設立した。1996年にリーグラー・リーヴェ・アーキテクツがグラーツにつくられ、リーグラー・リーヴェ建築事務所の支所がケルンにオープンした。
今日まで多くの作品がつくられており、代表作にグラーツ工科大学情報電子工学研究所、バーデンの連邦社会教育学研究所、グラーツ空港などがある。現在はインスブルックの新駅舎、グラーツの文学館、ブルック/ムールの駅舎等のプロジェクトが進行中である。

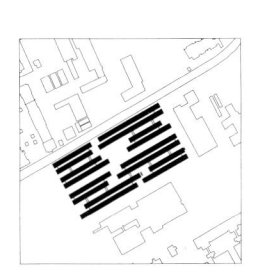

Information Technology and Electronics Institutes

Technical University, Graz, Styria, Austria, 1993-2000

Visiting the new buildings, there is clearly a marked contrast between the sides and the ends of each institute. The solid, tower-like terminations to the run of spaces on each side of the central arcade communicate the basic organization of the interior and reveal the position of the entrances.

Within each institute, the depth of the section on either side of the central space is six meters and this can be utilized to its full depth, for teaching spaces, or to a depth of four meters, for offices and workrooms leaving two meters for circulation.

In drawing attention to the contrast between the material and surface qualities of the concrete which is used throughout the section, Riegler Riewe provides a basis on which the scale of such an interior can be differentiated from that of the exterior.

Much of the ground surface is covered with a gray-white gravel which is intended to encourage the growth of moss where it remains undisturbed.

A lack of interest in traditional hierarchies is reflected in internal layouts which are linear and repetitive while incorporating the possibility of variation and transition.

Peter Allison

情報電子工学研究所

オーストリア、グラーツ工科大学　1993-2000

この新しい建物を訪れると、それぞれの研究棟の側面と端部の明確なコントラストに気づく。中央のアーケードの両側での、空間の流れの堅固な砦のような停止の仕方が、内部の基本的な構成と呼応し、エントランスの位置を明らかにする。

いずれの研究棟でも中央の廊下の両側には奥行き6mのスペースがあり、そこは教室のように全幅を使ってもよいし、オフィスや研究室に4mを使って2mを動線とすることも可能である。

建物全体に使われるコンクリートの材質と表面の特質のコントラストに注意をむけるため、リーグラー・リーヴェはこのような室内におけるスケールと、屋外のスケールの差異が明確化されるような基準を提示している。

外部の地表面は灰色―白色の砂利がしかれ、人の通行しない部分には苔生すことを想定している。

伝統的なヒエラルキーへの無関心は、バリエーションと変更の可能性を保持しつつ、リニアーで反復的な室内のレイアウトに示されている。

ピーター・アリソン

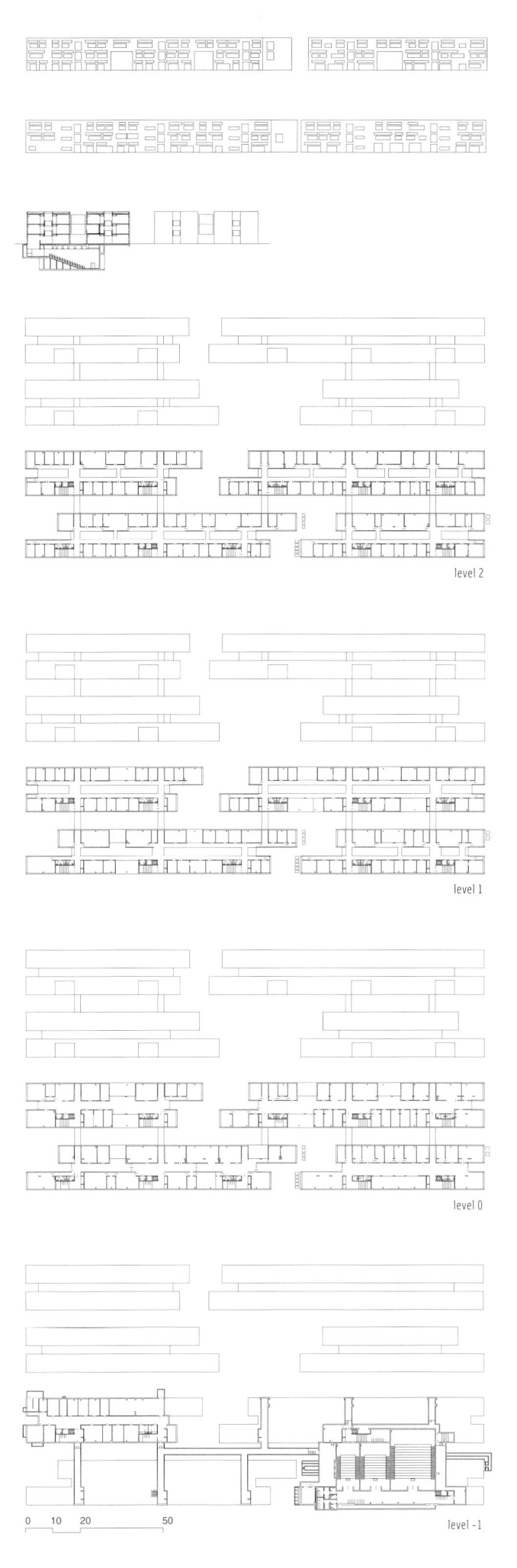

level 2

level 1

level 0

0　10　20　　　50

level -1

Information Technology and Electronics Institutes
Technical University, Graz, Styria, Austria, 1993–2000
© Paul Ott (top), © Thomas Jantsher (back)

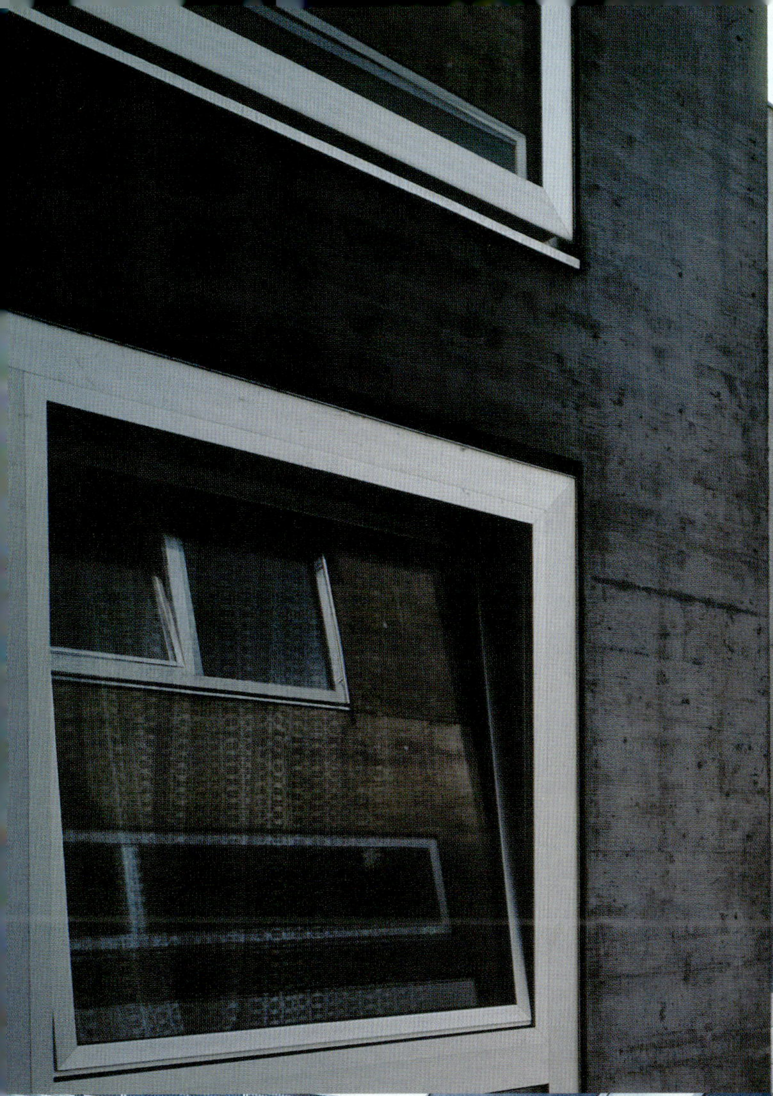
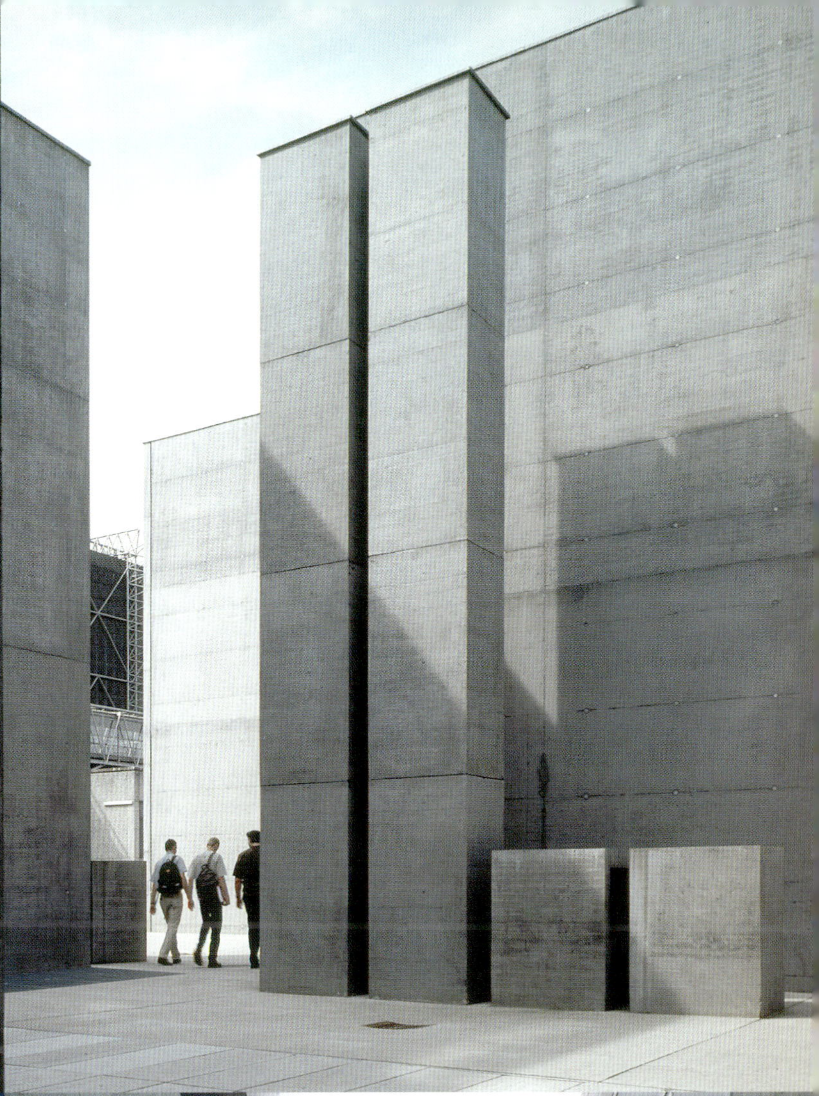
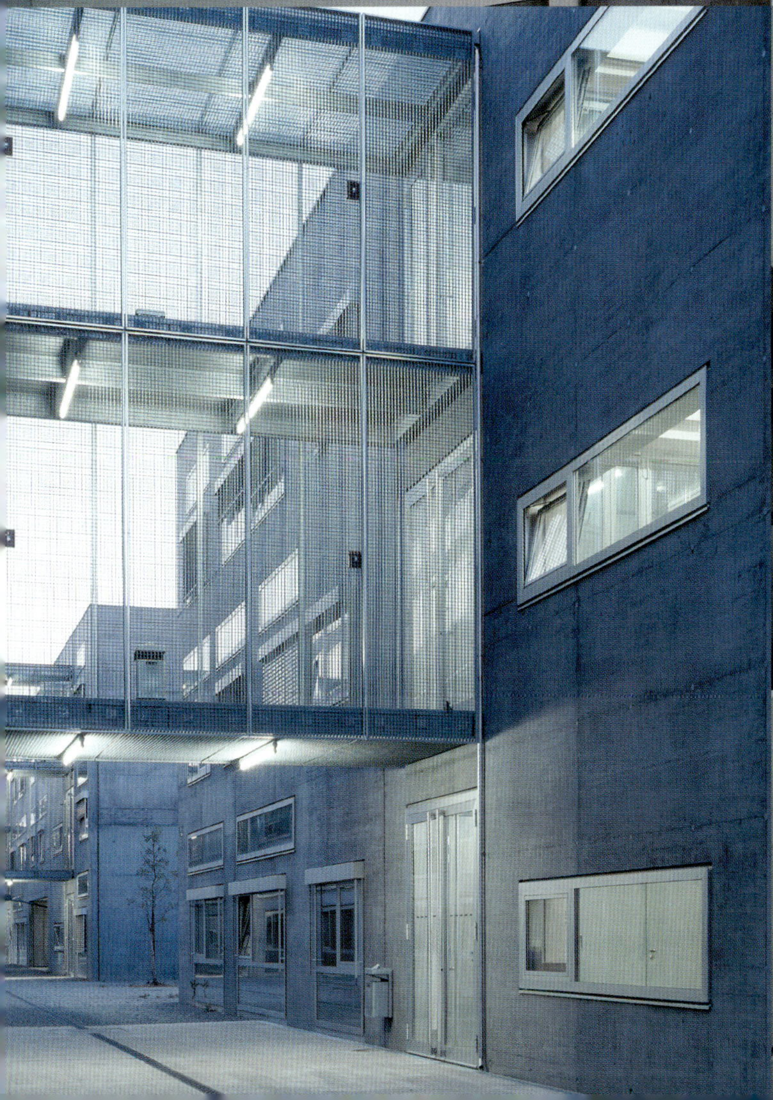
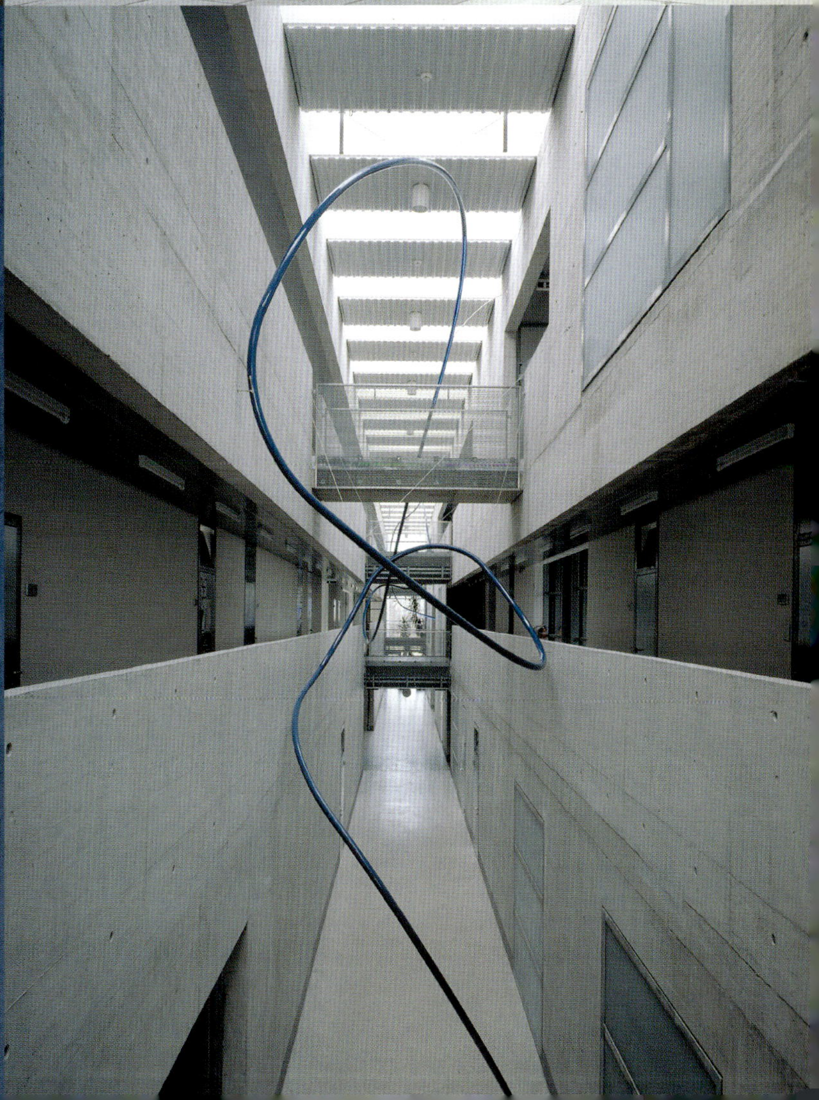

Japan
日本

Kazuyo Sejima + Ryue Nishizawa / SANAA
妹島和世＋西沢立衛/SANAA

Kazuyo Sejima + Ryue Nishizawa / SANAA was established in 1995 as a collaborating office. Aiming to investigate a diversity of design fields, the office designs various types of buildings as well as interiors, exhibitions, furniture, products and landscaping, recently on the international scene.

妹島和世 + 西沢立衛／SANAA／1995共同設計事務所設立。
様々な機能の建築の設計をはじめ、インテリア、展覧会、家具、プロダクト、ランドスケープ等幅広く設計を手がけている。

Kanazawa 21st-century Museum
Kanazawa, Ishikawa, Japan, 1999-2004

This building is located in Kanazawa's central city area, a location well connected to the various surrounding zones, which makes it very easy for citizens to access. The site belongs to the preparatory elementary school and junior high school of Kanazawa University, adjacent to the town hall.
A museum open to the public was requested, combining the two functions of a "museum zone" and an "art communication zone".
A circular building, without front or back, was placed in the center of the site to optimize the characteristics of a location which may be freely approached from any direction. Within this circular form, a space for creative activity encircles the perimeter of the building a communication zone with easy public access, which anyone may enter and leave without paying an entrance fee. The museum zone is located in the center of the circle, and requires an entrance fee. Independent exhibition spaces with distinctive proportions are arranged within a corridor space. Each of the museum exhibition spaces receives natural light via skylights to brighten the entire interior, and so courtyards were placed to prevent the center of the circular plan from becoming dark. In both the museum zone and the art communication zone, there are corridor spaces between each of the rooms, that allow one to catch glimpses of various activities while moving around within the building. In addition, this corridor space creates diverse connections between each of the rooms. Using the entire corridor space, visitors are free to choose their route, and there is sufficient flexibility to assemble exhibitions of various scales.

金沢21世紀美術館
石川県金沢市　1999-2004

この建物は金沢の中心市街地に位置し、敷地周辺にひろがる多様なゾーンをつなぐ場所として市民が気軽に立ち寄れる環境にある。市庁舎に隣接する金沢大学附属小中学校跡地を敷地として整備し、美術館ゾーンと芸術交流ゾーンという二つの機能を併せもつ、市民に開かれた美術館が求められた。
周囲から自由にアプローチできる敷地の特性を生かし、表と裏のない円形の建物を敷地中央に配置している。円形プランの中に入ると、まず無料で誰でも行き来できる交流ゾーンがあり、市民が気軽に利用し、創作活動を行なえるスペースが外周をぐるっと回っている。有料の美術館ゾーンは円形の中央部にあり、独立性が高く特徴的なプロポーションを持ったいろんなタイプの展示室が、廊下スペースを介して配置されている。美術館の各展示室はトップライトによる自然採光であるが、大きな円形プランの中央が暗くならないよう光庭を配置し、館内全体が明るくなるように計画している。
美術館ゾーンも交流ゾーンも部屋と部屋の間に廊下スペースがあり、そのスペースを介してお互いの活動を垣間見たりしながら館内を回遊することができる。また、展示室間では廊下スペースを介して各室のつながりが多様化され、この廊下スペースが全体に巡っていることにより、来館者が自由にルートを選べたり、展覧会に応じてサイズの異なる美術館ができあがるようなフレキシビリティを得ることができると考えている。

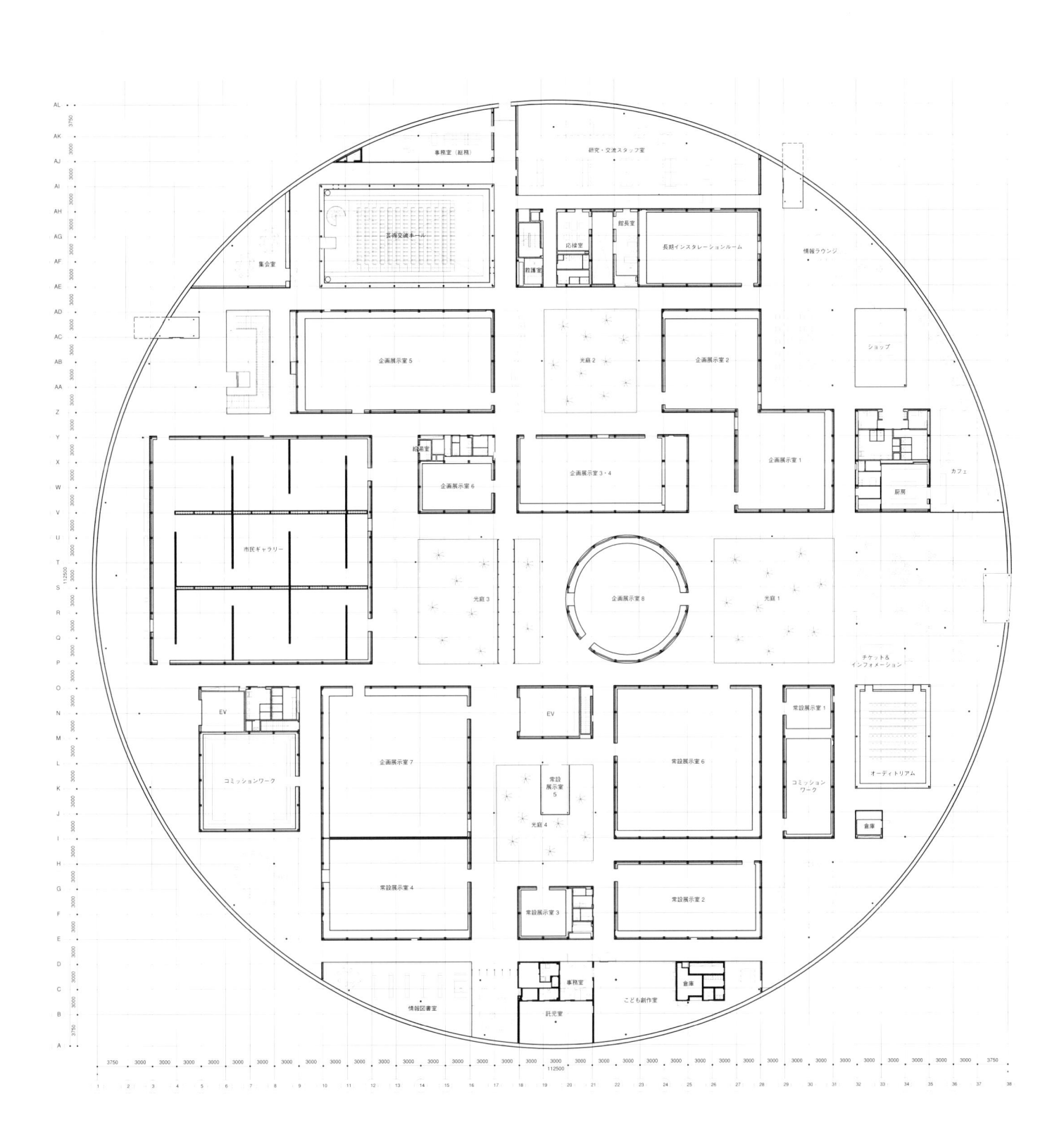

事務室（総務）
研究・交流スタッフ室
芸術交流ホール
集会室
館長室
記録室
救護室
長期インスタレーションルーム
情報ラウンジ
企画展示室5
光庭2
企画展示室2
ショップ
給湯室
企画展示室6
企画展示室3・4
企画展示室1
カフェ
厨房
市民ギャラリー
光庭3
企画展示室8
光庭1
チケット＆インフォメーション
EV
EV
常設展示室1
コミッションワーク
企画展示室7
常設展示室5
常設展示室6
コミッションワーク
オーディトリアム
光庭4
倉庫
常設展示室4
常設展示室3
常設展示室2
情報図書室
事務室
託児室
こども創作室
倉庫

Kanazawa 21st-century Museum
Kanazawa, Ishikawa, Japan, 1999–2004
© SANAA

Finland
フィンランド

Sanaksenaho Arkkitehdit Oy
サナクセンアホ・アーキテクツ

Student's House, Vaasa, Finland, 1996
© Jari Jetsonen

The Finland Pavilion in Sevilla expo '92, Spain, 1992
© Jari Jetsonen

The Sculptor's House, Sysmä, Finland, project 1999
© Raimo Träskelin

I was born in 1966 in Helsinki, Finland. As a young boy I wanted to become a painter. Later, becoming more interested in society and technology, I chose the studies of an architect.

I started my architect career designing the Finnish Pavilion in Sevilla world fair 1992, after winning the national competition with group Monark.

Nowadays I work with my wife Pirjo Sanaksenaho who is also an architect. Most of the buildings done by our office are a collaboration by her and me.

In ten years we have designed many kinds of buildings: a Chapel, a students' house, a studio for a sculptor, shop interiors, caves in Lapland, a summer cottage.
One value in this profession is that it has colors and variations, like life itself.

In this exhibition we present our latest project, House Tammimäki, which is our own home.

One afternoon, in the new house, while thinking about our approach to architecture, I was watching our five-year-old son play. He was studying little animals in the garden. Maybe in architecture we do the same thing: play and explore life.

私は1966年にフィンランドのヘルシンキに生まれた。子どもの頃は絵描きになりたいと思っていた。その後、社会と技術への関心が増すと共に、建築を学ぶことを選択した。

建築家としての最初の仕事は、1992年のセビリア万博のフィンランドパビリオンである。これは「モナルク」というグループで国内の設計競技により獲得したものである。

現在は、自身建築家である妻ピルヨ・サナクセンアホと仕事をしている。我々の事務所の手がける建物のほとんどは、私と妻の共同作業によるものである。

10年の間に、教会、学生宿舎、彫刻家のスタジオ、店舗の内装、ラップランドの洞窟、避暑地の別荘、というように様々な種類の建物を設計してきた。
この職業のひとつの意義は、人生と同様に、色彩と変容に満ちているということだと考えている。

今回の展覧会には、最も新しいプロジェクト「タンミマキの家」を出しているが、これは私たち自身の家である。

この新しい家である日、建築へのアプローチについて考えながら、5歳になる息子が遊んでいるのを見ていた。彼は庭にいる小動物を観察していた。多分、建築で私たちは同じ様なことをしているのだ。人生を楽しみつつ探求するということを。

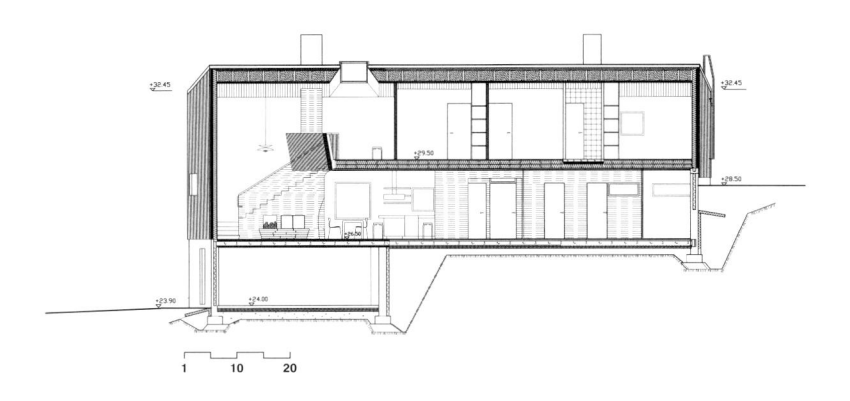

House Tammimäki
Lippajärvi, Finland 1998-2002

The house is situated on a lake-site out of Helsinki. The site is called "birdlake" because of the wide variety of birds. From the lake, a hill rises up and gives green shelter in a Northeast direction. There are a number of old oaks in the hill. That is how the area got its name, Tammimäki (Oakhill).

The project includes a one-family house built to the slope. For the future extension of the project there is room for a studio on the same plot.

The South -elevation turns with a gentle curve round the garden, leaving an old oak in the middle. The curved wall guides the sequence of exterior and interior spaces.

The building material for the basement is plastered stone. It is the stone foundation which carries the light timber structure of the rest of the building. The outside paneling is made of pine-wood which is heated with low temperature. That way the water disappears from the material and it has good resistance to the weather, like the wood in old cabins.

タンミマキの家
フィンランド、リッパジャーヴィ 1998-2002

建物はヘルシンキ郊外の湖畔にある。ここには多種にわたる鳥たちが棲むため、"鳥の湖"と呼ばれている。湖から北東には丘が上り、敷地のグリーンのシェルターとなっている。この丘にはオークの老木があり、それゆえこのあたりはタンミマキ（オークの丘）と呼ばれている。

斜面に一世帯の家が立つ。また将来の増築を想定してスタジオ用の空地を敷地内に残している。

南側の立面は庭を囲んで緩やかなカーブを描き、中央にオークの老木を残している。カーブした壁面が、屋外と室内の空間のシークエンスを誘起している。

地下階はプラスター塗をした石でできている。そしてこの石造部が建物の残りの軽い木造部分を支える基礎となっている。外装のパネルは低温で加熱処理した松でできている。この加熱処理によって木材の水分が失われ、古びた丸太小屋のように耐候性を増している。

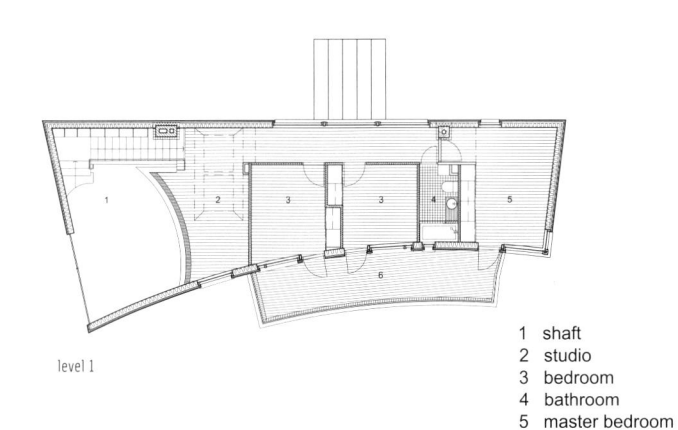

level 1

1 shaft
2 studio
3 bedroom
4 bathroom
5 master bedroom
6 balcony

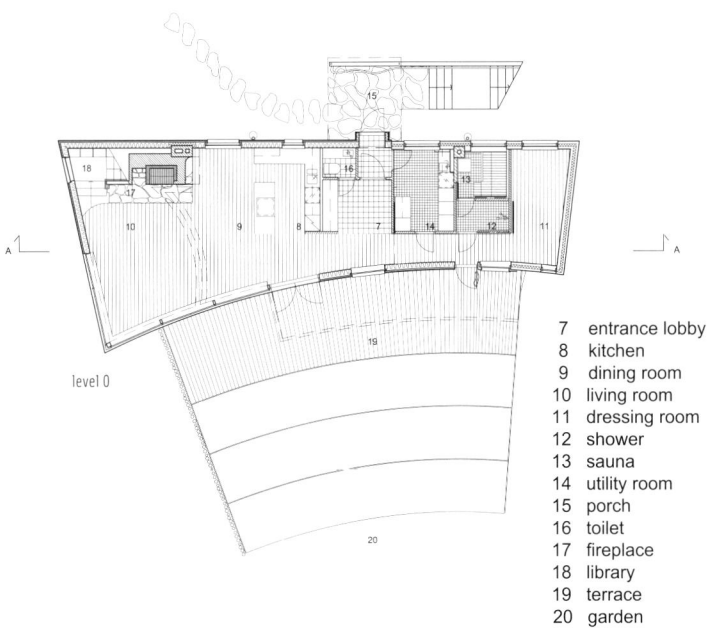

level 0

7 entrance lobby
8 kitchen
9 dining room
10 living room
11 dressing room
12 shower
13 sauna
14 utility room
15 porch
16 toilet
17 fireplace
18 library
19 terrace
20 garden

House Tammimäki
Lippajärvi, Finland 1998-2002
© Matti Sanaksenaho

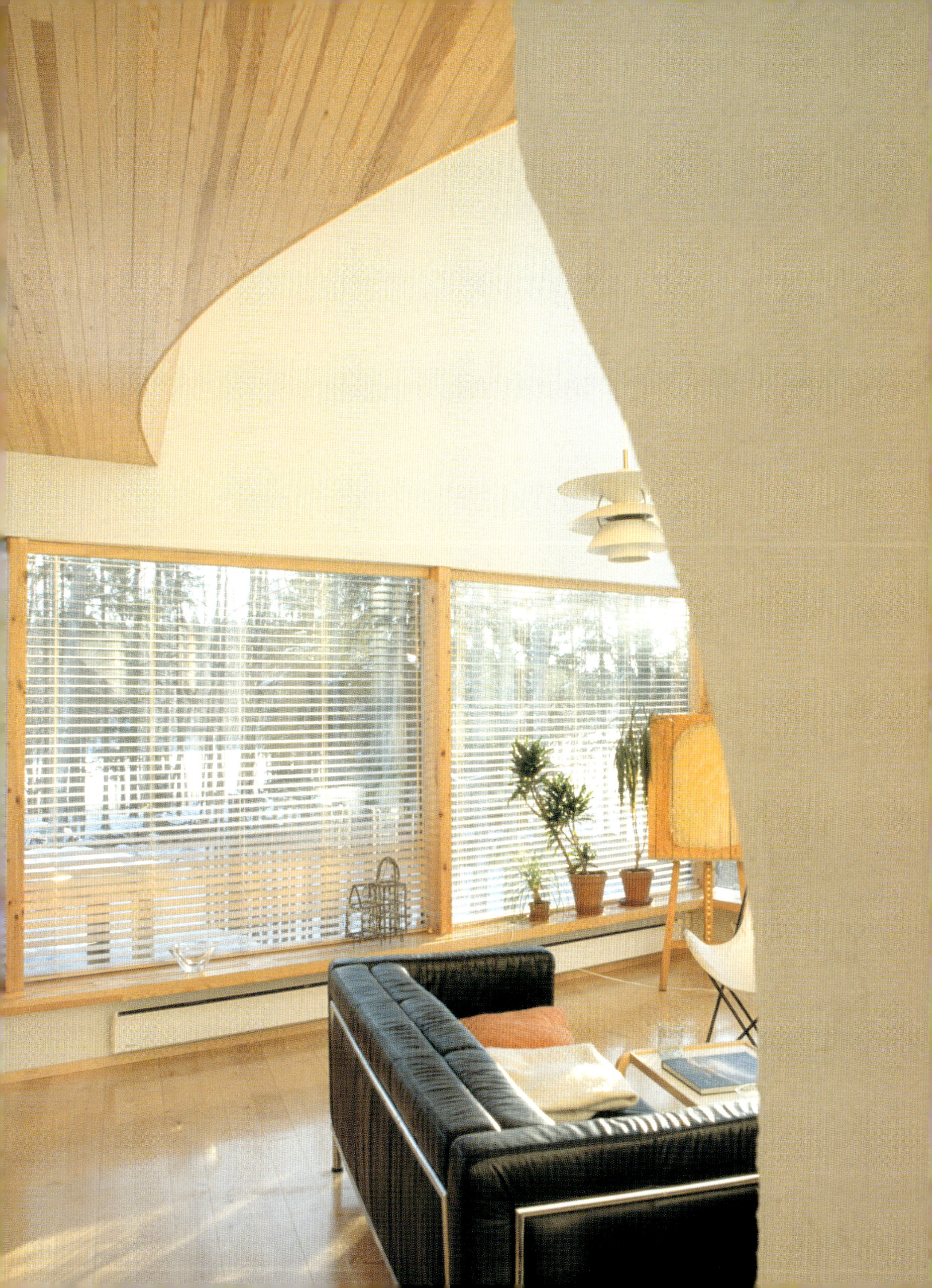

Italy
イタリア

UdA-Ufficio di Architettura
UdA

Lanzo-Ruggeri house, Torino, Italy, 1996
© Emilio Conti

D, L, V BBDO, advetising agency, Milano, Italy, 1998
© Mario Ermoli

City third millenium, international competition 2000
© UdA

Mole Antonelliana, Europan 5 international competition, mentioned project
© UdA

After obtaining their degrees, the UdA architects went abroad to continue their studies in Spain and in the United States.

What UdA pursues is an architecture made up of a few carefully selected signs, a sort of Platonic and even anorexic ideal. But their approach is not really minimalist; it can be described rather as eclectic.
What makes the group's work so interesting, and so Italian, is their love for complexity, for not being stuck in a precise category, for continual advancement and retreat.

UdA's sources are manifold. It borrows from Jean Nouvel and Herzog & de Meuron the poetics of disappearance, and from Steven Holl, Tadao Ando and Peter Zumthor, a taste for materials and the idea that matter matters, that architecture is not pure conceptual form, virtual reality, but concrete color, grain, and reality. UdA's stylistic approach also draws on trends in architecture in the fifties, and the modern way of conceiving form as pure form. But UdA regards architecture not just as form and tectonics, but most of all in terms of material, color, texture, and technology in its complex interaction with light, between natural and artificial.

Without being technological addicts, UdA likes playing with modern technologies.
It uses, for instance, electronic images, called finestre-paesaggio (which could be translated as changing windowscapes) for the furnishings. It has also put to use structural glass and a variety of new light materials.

国内で学位を取得した後、UdAのメンバーはスペインとアメリカに渡り勉学を続けた。

UdAが求めるのは、最小限の選ばれたサインからなる建築であり、ある種プラトン的な、あるいは拒食症と呼びたければそれも良いだろう。彼らのアプローチはミニマリストというより、折衷主義として説明可能かもしれない。
彼らの作品を興味深く、そして極めてイタリア的にしているもの。それは複雑なもの、細かなカテゴリーに縛り付けられないこと、継続して前進／撤退することへの愛情である。

UdAの作品の源泉は多様である。彼らはジャン・ヌーベルやヘルツォーク＆ド・ムーロンから消失の詩学を学んでいる。スティーブン・ホール、安藤忠雄、ピーター・ズントーといった建築家からは、素材の感覚、重要なことが重要であるという考え、建築は純粋にコンセプチュアルなフォルムやバーチャル・リアリティではなく、具体的な色であり粒子であり、リアリティだということを学んでいる。UdAにはまた、50年代の建築家のスタイリスティックなアプローチや、形を純粋なフォルムと捉える近代的な考え方へのあこがれも見受けられる。しかしUdAにとって建築とは単にかたちと構造体だけではなく、何よりも素材、色彩、テクスチャであり、テクノロジーとは、自然光と人工光の複雑な相互作用なのだ。

彼らはテクノロジーに熱狂しているわけではないが、近代のテクノロジーと戯れるのを楽しんでいる。例えばUdAは、finestre-paesaggio（変化する窓外の風景）と呼ぶ電子的なイメージを仕上げとして使っている。彼らはまた好んで構造的にガラスをもちいたり、透過性のある新しく軽い素材をあやつっている。

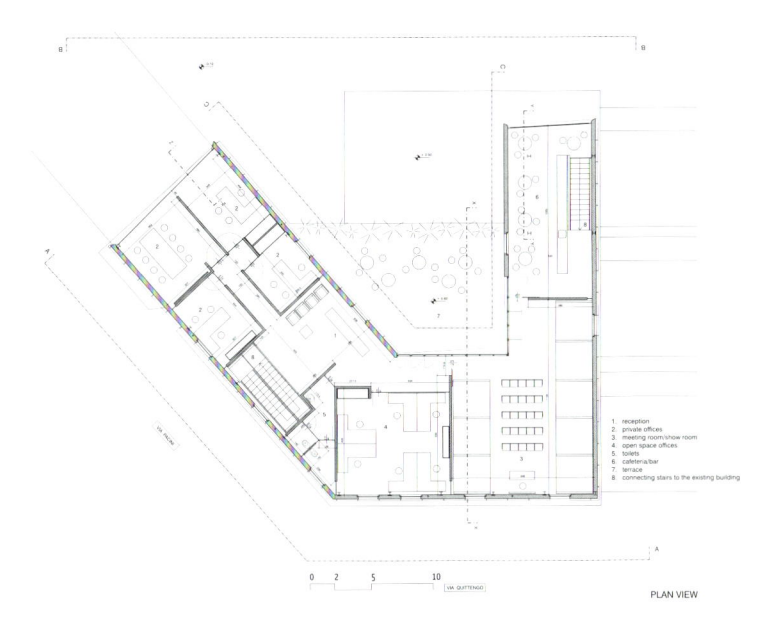

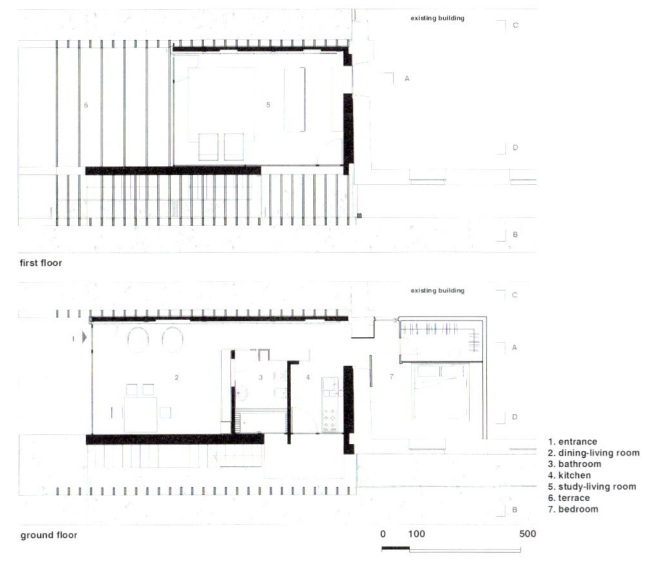

Ilti luce office building
Torino, Italy, 2001-2002

The building for Ilti Luce is located in an area near the suburbs of north Turin, in an industrial district with a nineteenth century shape, made of fragmentary urban structure and big holes as a result of the abandoning of the production activities. UdA work consists in a 400-square-meter elevation of an existing building, built in 1961.
The new building is structured as a stand alone entity: it goes on the flat roof of the building below, following the perimeter of it along the main public roads, and having a free progress along the other sides.
The building has been conceived as a tube with the extremes made of glass, a sort of screen or cathode-ray tube, one on the main road, the other on the courtyard. It is like an organism, an extraneous virus, lightweight and transparent with a virtual disquieting presence.

The main characteristic of the project is to represent a sort of emptiness, considered not as failure but as a chance, a possibility for a sum of energy not expressed before.
This is why the building has no elevations since it consists in a game of light and reflection which includes, a sequence of fading out the hill on the back and the existing landscape.
In substaining this, there are panels made of "pmma" (polymethil acrylate) which show the insulating panels underneath, and underline a gradual shade to the sky with different color divisions.
The photovoltaic cells underneath the pmma surface power the led strips in the horizontal joints of the panels in the front of the building.
During the night they light up giving a sense of dynamism to the building.
The surface, the skin gains deepness.
It beats, it flows.
And by flowing it introduces to a new disappearing.

イルティ・ル-チェ・オフィス・ビルディング
イタリア、トリノ 2001-2002

"イルティ・ルーチェ"の建物はトリノ北の郊外の近く、19世紀型の工場地帯にあり、そこは断片化された都市構造をもち、生産活動が放棄されて大きな穴があいたような場所である。UdAの仕事は、1961年に建てられた建物の400m²の立面である。

新しい構造物は自立して建っている。下部の平たい屋根の上を、主な公道に面しては下の建物の境界線に沿って、他の面に関しては自由に展開して建っている。この構造物は、ガラスでできたある種のスクリーンかブラウン管のような端部を、前面道路と中庭にもつチューブのように考えられる。それは有機体のようであり、軽さと透過性によってヴァーチャルで不穏な存在をあらわす異質のウィルスのようである。

それは周囲のほとんど放擲されたような工場地帯の環境と交信して、ほとんど何も意味しないサインのようである。
そしてこのことこそが、プロジェクトの大事な特徴なのである。ある種の空（から）の状態をあらわすこと。失敗ではなく、それまでは示されなかったエネルギーの蓄積の可能性、チャンスとしての状態。
建物が通常意図されるような、立面をもたないのはそのことによる。つまり、フェイドアウトする背景の丘と現存するランドスケープの序列の間の、ライトと反射のゲームからなっているのだ。
このために、建物は"PMMA"（ポリメチル・アクリレート）でできたパネルからなり、背面の断熱パネルが透けて見え、異なる色の区分により空へ向って次第に変化する陰影を強調している。
PMMAの表面の下の光電池が、建物正面のパネルの水平ジョイントに仕組まれたLEDに電力を与える。
夜間にそれは光を放ち、建物にある種のダイナミズムを与える。表層が深みを得る。
それは鼓動し、そして流れる。
流れが新たな消失をもたらす。

Levis house
Biella, Italy, 1998

Levis House is located in Biella on a gentle slope cultivated with fruit trees and endowed with views of the Alps. It is the enlargement of an existing rural building, on a plot of land occupied by a former barn. It is a little 85-squares-meter building on two levels Structure is in exposed concrete and iron. The exterior is punctuated by a laminated wood vertical structure. This is the most exciting characteristic of the house, a filter that has at least three reasons
First, it is the place that contains the beautiful concrete stair and the balconies. Secondly, it dematerializes the entire new building and makes it perceived more as an in-between space than a close box. Thirdly, it creates a complex interior/exterior relationship, a place in which you are neither inside nor outside. A veil that, gives the house an ultra-sensualist feeling.
The outside world is mediated, filtered. Landscape, considered as an intellectual man-made output, is inserted in architecture, treated as a series of pictures.

The new rooms are conceived as a sequence of filters which gradually lead from the enclosed interior spaces of the original building to the vastness of the landscape Architecture reveals itself not just as an organization of the external physical space but as a sensorial relationship with the external environment.
In Levis house the window is a complete wall substitute and it continues on the other side, by covering the concrete wall and by transforming the internal environment into a glass cover which, through a multiple reflections game comes out on the external landscape.
The building is a filter of perception and space, of memory and present; edges and limits are not defined. It's an exaltation of the intermediate space, a meditation on *shakkei*, a Japanese technique for being in contact with nature.

レヴィス・ハウス
イタリア、ビエッラ 1998

レヴィス・ハウスはビエッラの、果樹に覆われたゆるやかな斜面にあり、アルプスの眺めに恵まれている。これは既存の田舎の建物の増築であり、それまで納屋が立っていた場所に建築している。わずか85m²の2層というものである。構造は打放コンクリートと鉄骨である。

外部は断続する縦の積層板で覆われているが、ここが建物で一番重要な特徴であり、少なくとも3つの目的をもったフィルターをなしている。ひとつは、美しいコンクリートの階段室とバルコニーを内部に持つ場所であること。二つめには、新しい建物全体を非物質化し、閉じた容器よりも中間的な存在として知覚させるためであり、三つめは、複雑な内部と外部の関係、外でも室内でもない場所をつくりだすためである。家に超官能的な雰囲気を与えるヴェール。
外の世界は、調停され、フィルターにかけられる。ランドスケープは人間のつくりだした知的なものとみなされ、建築の中に挿入された、一連の絵画のようにあつかわれる。
ここでは建築は、何よりもまず素材であり、色彩、テクスチュアであり、テクノロジーとは自然と人工の間の、光の複雑な相互作用である。

新たな部屋は、既存の建物の閉じた領域から周囲のランドスケープの広がりに導く、フィルターのシークエンスだと考えられている。建築は外部の物理的な空間の構成としてだけではなく、周囲の環境との感覚的な関係の投影としてそこにある。
レヴィス・ハウスでは窓は完全に壁に代わってあり、他の面へと続き、コンクリート壁を覆い、室内の環境をガラスの覆いへと変容させ、さまざまな反射のゲームを通して外部のランドスケープへとあらわれる。建物は知覚と空間の、記憶と現在の、フィルターである。端部や限界は定められず、中間的な空間、日本的な自然との関係の技法、借景の瞑想が称えられている。

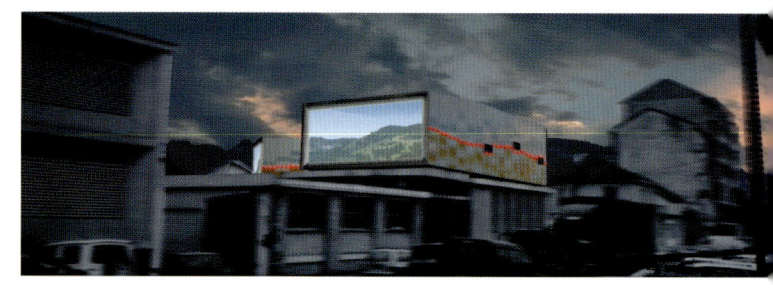

Ilti luce office building
Torino, Italy, 2001-2002
© UdA

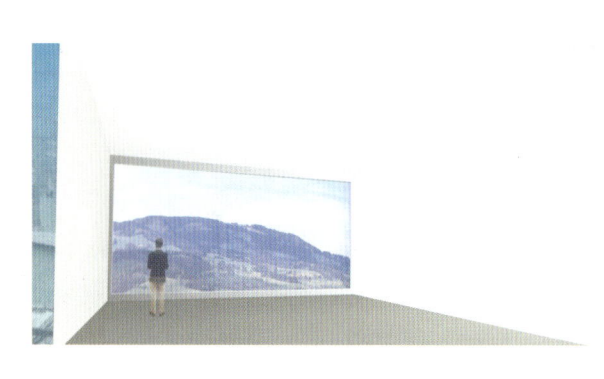

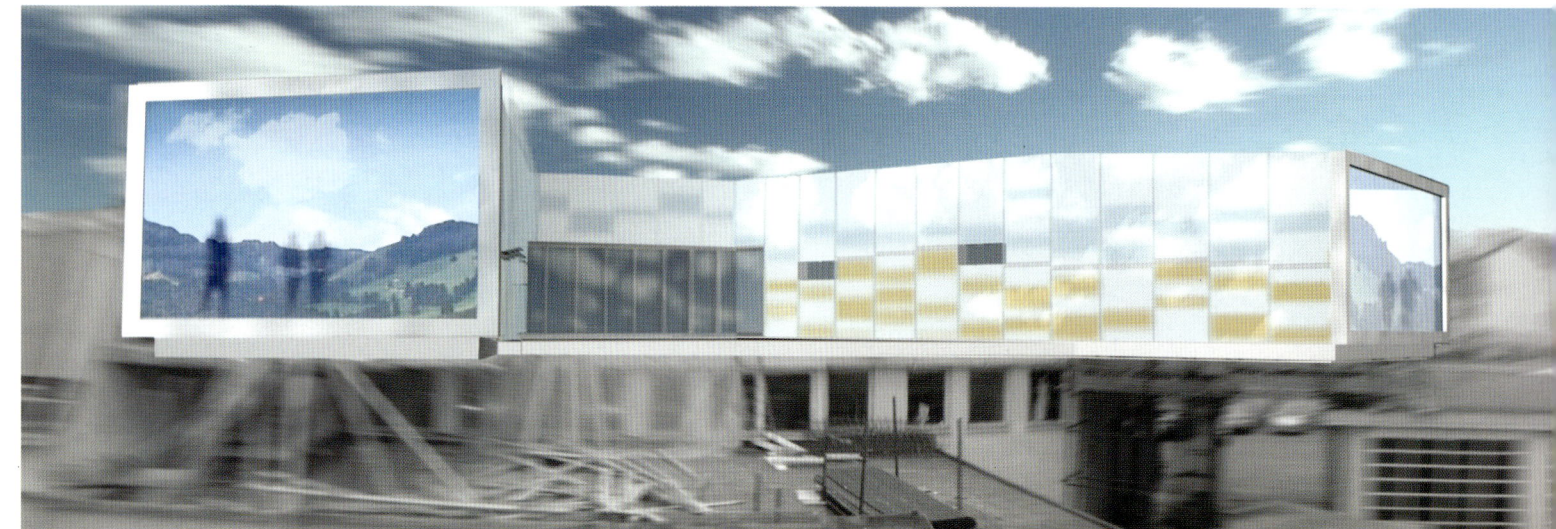

Levis house
Biella, Italy, 1998
© Emilio Conti

Japan 日本

Motomu Uno + Phase Associates
宇野求+フェーズアソシエイツ

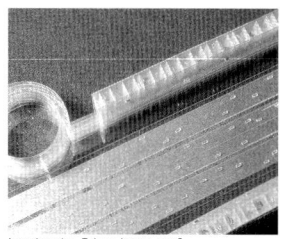

When I was in the graduate school, I started to practice architecture with my friends. At that time petroleum prices were soaring in the world, and Japanese economy was flagging. There were practically no job offerings and I thought unrealistic to get one. So we decided to open an office by ourselves. At that time I lived in a small apartment in Tokyo. One day, an Italian friend and a Japanese one came into my place, and strange days of three men in 6 tatamis' room started.

This Italian was an exchange student from University of Rome and had his title as a correspondent of an Italian sport journal. At night he used to make calls to Italy. When an Italian football team came to Japan, he almost made up funny stories, saying 'they will not know anyway, so funnier is better'.

The Japanese one was a graduate course student. But he went back and forth between Los Angels and Tokyo with an executive of a company for negotiations relating to the license agreement of portable electronic translator.

So my room became a place for International exchanges. Discussions with wine or sake went on and on every night over our future and the world. In those days I started to design architecture and have been doing so until today. But the world has so much changed.

Lately, I hear 60's music on the radio and TV. In my youth, I was a fan of Gigliola Ciquetti and Sylvie Vartan and had their records. Jean-luc Godard and Robert Enrico were my favorites in movies. People on the screen like Jean-Paul Belmondo or Joanna Shimkus attracted me very much. Although they were far away of Tokyo, I found the same urban atmosphere in them. I think that our digitalized cityscape has become unrefined, and people listen to analogue 60's songs as a reaction to this. I would like to make contemporary architecture with both digital and analogue feelings, which will explore and project lifestyles of today's over-modernize.

大学院の学生のときに、僕は友人と建築事務所をはじめた。当時、世界の原油価格が暴騰し日本経済は低迷していた。建築の求人はなかった。勤めることにリアリティがなく、いっそ自分たちでやろうということになった。

そのころ、僕は東京の小さなアパートに暮らしていた。そこに、ある日、イタリア人と日本人の友だちがふたりで転がり込んできた。6畳の狭い部屋で男3人の不思議な生活が始まった。ローマ大学から留学に来た彼はスポーツ新聞特派員の肩書きも持っていたので夜な夜なイタリアに電話をする。来日したイタリアのサッカーチームのレポートでは、あることないこと面白可笑しく伝えている。「どうせ日本のことは分からないから面白い方がいいだろう」と平気な顔でいう。大学院生だったもうひとりの友だちは、日本企業のトップとロスアンゼルスに通って当時世界最小のポータブル自動翻訳機技術のライセンス契約のビジネスをしていた。小さな部屋は国際交流の場となっていた。ワインや酒を飲みながらの毎夜の討論は自分たちの未来や世界のこれからについて果てしなく続いた。そうこうしているうちに、僕は建築をつくり始めていた。そのまま今日に至るのだけれど、当時とは随分世界も時代も変わった。

最近、テレビやラジオで60年代の音楽がよく流れている。少年時代、ジリオラ・チンクエッティやシルビー・バルタンの歌が好きでレコードを持っていた。映画ではゴダールやロベール・アンリコの作品を好んで見た。ジャン＝ポール・ベルモンドやジョアンナ・シムカスは、当時の東京とは別世界の人たちだったが、とてもひかれた。都市の雰囲気を漂わせていたからだろうと思う。60年代のアナログな音楽が好まれるのはデジタル化された今の街がだいぶ野暮ったくなってきた反動かなと思う。過剰に近代化した今日の日本における都市のライフスタイルやありようを探り投影するような、デジタルとアナログの感覚をあわせもつ現代建築をつくりたいと思っています。

Junction city, Tokyo, Japan, 1996

Muramatsu House, Tokyo, Japan, 1991

Yotsuya Temporary Office, Tokyo, Japan, 1990
© Shinhenchiku-Sha

Toyohashi Station Plaza, Toyohashi City, Japan, 1998

Villa Fujii
Kitasaku-gun, Nagano, Japan, 1999-2000

Technological villa on the threshold between nature and art

Our challenge of designing a contemporary villa on the site was to produce an architecture on the threshold between nature and art.

The design process was the following.
01. Set reinforced concrete slabs above the ground on each level.
02. Draw a zigzag walkway extending throughout the site, wooden decks in each dimension.
03. Roof over reinforced concrete walls with the hybrid structure of wood and steel.
04. Characterize spaces by adapting to each structural system, and open horizontal/vertical views of interior/exterior by cutting walls off freely.
05. Arrange furniture, fittings and structural components as the elements of interior landscape. Feature the combination of materials and lights to enhance the quality of space.

The figure and the form of the villa came out of editing its relation with the landscape. It features the local climatic conditions, the slight undulations forming different heights of ground, and the random pattern of trees such as oaks, cherry trees, and larches.

The design development with a landscape architect started from the beginning, and the tectonic image and the building methodology of the architecture were produced through the discussions with a structural engineer. The technological approach through the dialogues between architects and engineers brought forth the diversity of visual interrelations between architecture and landscape.

Villa Fujii
長野県北佐久郡　1999-2000

自然と人工の縁にたつテクノロジカルなヴィッラ

与えられたサイトに自然と人工の縁にたつ建築的環境を創りだすことをめざして、現代的ヴィッラとして設計しようと考えました。

設計プロセスは、次のようなものでした。

01　レベル差をもつ鉄筋コンクリートの床盤を地盤面から浮かせて設定する
02　内外を貫くジグザグのウォークウェイを描く
03　ハイブリッド構造（木×鉄）のルーフを架ける
04　複数の構造システムで場の特徴づけて縦長横長の開口部を自由に切り取り内外の景色を枠取る
05　インテリアを風景に見立て景観要素として家具や建具、構造のパーツを空間に配していく　空間の質を高めるために素材や光のコンビネーションを追求する

このヴィッラの姿形は、自然の気候の条件、敷地のなだらかな起伏、みずなら、さくら、からまつなどのランダムなパタンなど、周辺のランドスケープとの関係を編集、再構成してつくりだされました。

設計初期からランドスケープアーキテクトの三谷徹とともに打ち合わせをおこない、構造設計家の新谷眞人とのディスカッションをとおして、技術イメージと建築の構成方法をつくりあげていきました。アーキテクトとエンジニアの対話を重視したテクノロジカルなアプローチによって、建築とランドスケープのあいだに、多様で視覚的なインタラクション-相互関係をつくりだそうとしました。

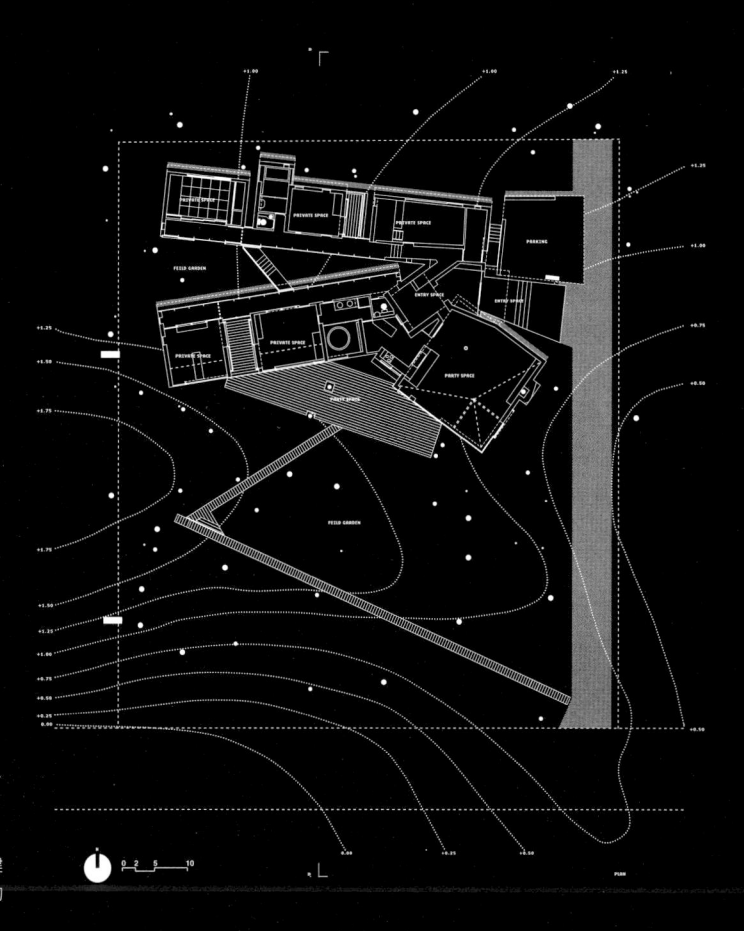

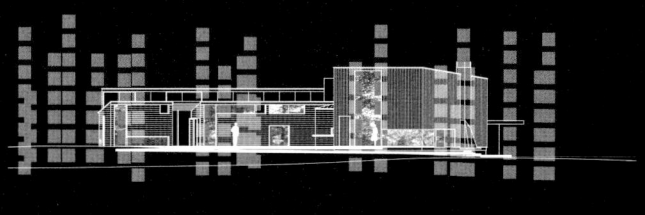

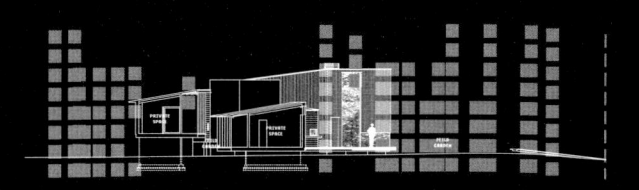

Villa Fujii
Kitasaku-gun, Nagano, Japan, 1999-2000
© Nobuaki Nakagawa

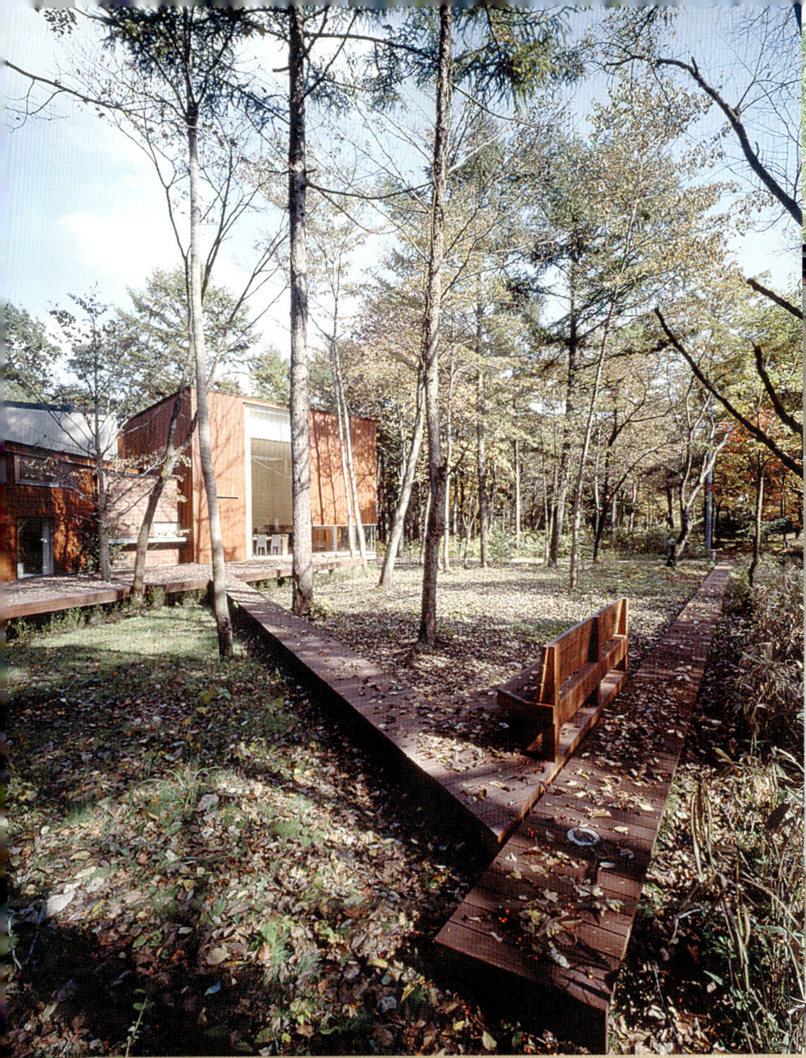
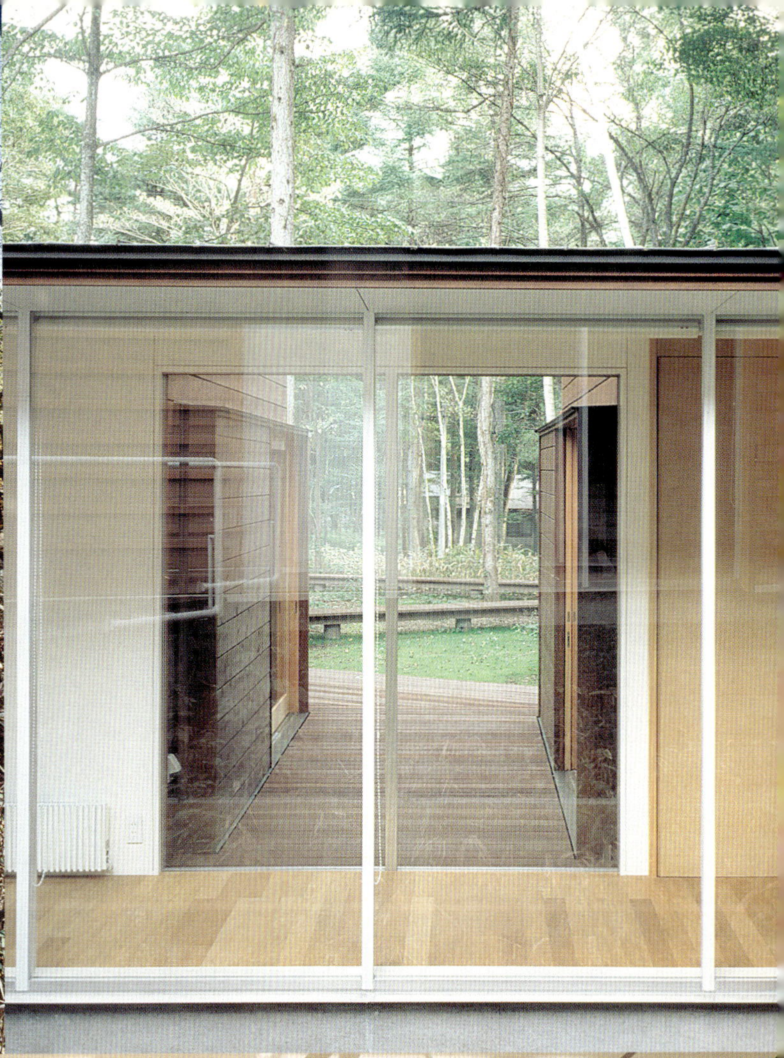
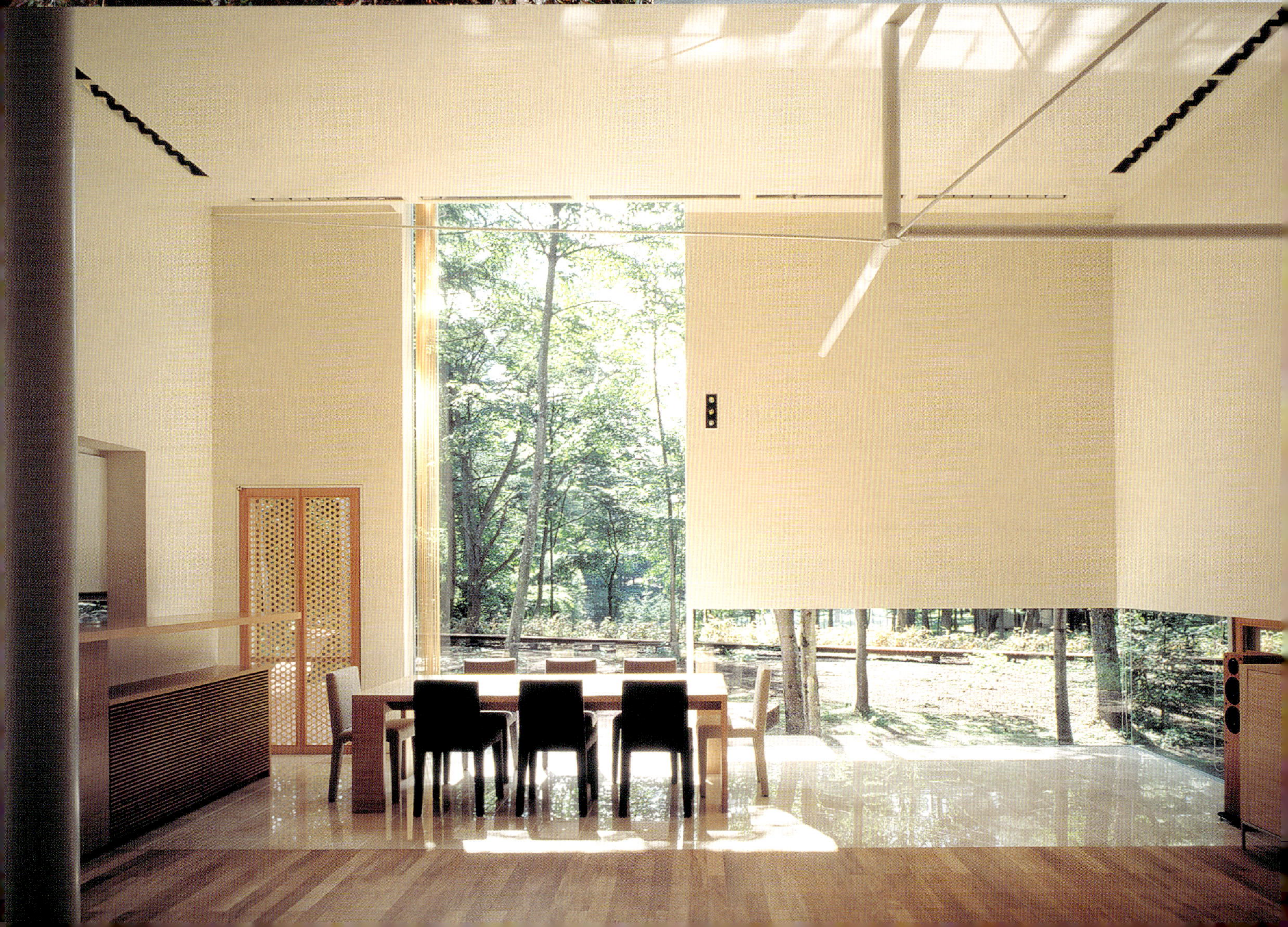

Profiles

Spain

Aabalos y Herreros

Principal Architects :

Iñaki Ábalos, Juan Herreros

Biography:

Iñaki Abalos and Juan Herreros have worked together since 1984. Since 1992 they have directed and coordinated the International Multimedia League, which is an organization dedicated to contributing to the simplification and intensification of artistic practice. Since 1994, they have edited ExitLMI, Documentos de Arquitectura. Since 1988 they are Senior Professors of Design at the Architectural School of Madrid.

Other Teaching Activities:

1984-88 Construction tutors, ETSA Madrid
1984-89 Buell Book Fellows and Visiting Teachers, Columbia University, New York
1997-99 Diploma Unit Masters, École Polytechnique Fédérale, Lausanne.
1998-01 Unit Masters and Master workshop teachers at the AA, London
Various courses, seminars and workshops in Spain, the United States and Latin America.

Awards (selection):

1995 First Prize: Public Library in Usera, Madrid (completed)
1996 Selected.III Bienal de Arquitectura Española.
MOPTMA. Office building for the Ministerio del interior (completed)
1997 First Prize: New Recycling Plant for Urban Waste. Madrid (completed)
First Prize: Río Cidade II Project, Área Ramos, Río de Janeiro (under construction)
First Prize: Headquarters for the Regional Government of Andalucía.Almería, Andalucía (under construction).
COAM Architectural Prize, Gordillo House(completed)
1998 Regional Government of Madrid Prize: Gordillo House (completed)
Regional Government of Madrid Prize, Social Housing Units on the M 30 (completed).
1999 First Prize: Central Headquarters for the Universidad de Mérida, Regional Government of Extremadura (completed).
Municipality of Barcelona Architectural Prize. Fabrications Installation (Ephemeral)
Second Prize: Urban Planning of the El Mirador Área, Algeciras
2000 Municipality of Madrid Architectural Prize. Recycling Plant for Urban Waste (completed)
First Price: Ekopark in Pinto, Madrid (under construction)
2001 COAM Architectural Prize: Recycling Plant for Urban Waste, Madrid
First Price: Woermann Tower in Las Palmas, Canary Islands (in construction)
First prize: Four Bioclimatic Housing Towers in Salburúa, Vitoria, (in construction)
2002 First Prize: Forum 2004, Barcelona

Publication / Writings:

1992 *Técnica y Arquitectura en la Ciudad Contemporánea*, Nerea, Madrid (translated into English as Tower & Office, MIT Press)
1993 *Abalos & Herreros*, Gustavo Gili, Barcelona. Monographs on Contemporary Architecture.
1997 *Areas of Impunity*, Actar, Barcelona
1999 *Natural -Artificial*, ExitLMI, Madrid.
2000 *Recycling, Madrid*, Actar, Barcelona

Japan

Atelier Hitoshi Abe

Principal Architect:

Hitoshi Abe

Biography:

1987 Master of Architecture, Tohoku University
1989 Master of Architecture, Southern California Institute of Architecture
1988-92 Coop Himmelblau
1992 Established Atelier Hitoshi Abe
1993 Ph.D., Tohoku University
1994-2002 Associate professor, Tohoku Institute of Technology
2002 Professor, Tohoku University

Principal Works:

1998 Miyagi Yomiuri Media Miyagi Guest House, Zao
1999 Miyagi Neige lune fleur, Sendai
2000 Miyagi Miyagi Stadium, Rifu
Miyagi Michinoku Folklore Museum, Kurikoma
Kanagawa n-house, Kamakura
2001 Miyagi i-house Hurukawa, Miyagi Sekii Ladies Clinic, Sendai
2002 Miyagi Ayashi Dental Clinic, Sendai

Awards:

1992 1st Place in Miyagi Stadium Competition (with Shoichi Haryuu)
1997 World Architecture Award, World Triennial of Architecture in Sophia
1998 The 14th Yoshioka Award (Yomiuri Media Miyagi Guest House)
2001 2001 Tohoku Architectural Award (Michinoku Folklore Museum)
The 42nd Building Contractors Society Award (Miyagi Stadium)

Publication/Writings:

1999 Kenchiku Junrei Series 43, *Los Angeles Locals, New Wind in California*, Maruzen
2001 *a-book, Atelier Hitoshi Abe, projet et realizations, 1993-2000*, IFA

Greece

Yannis Aesopos

Principal Architect:

Yannis Aesopos

Biography:

1966 Born in Athens, Greece
1989 Diploma of Architecture, National Technical University of Athens
1991 Master in Architecture, Graduate School of Design, Harvard University
1992-95 Member, Bernard Tschumi Architects, New York
1994 Guest Assistant Professor of Architecture, Graduate School of Architecture, Planning and Preservation, Columbia University, New York
1995 Established own office in Athens
1997 Co-Founder and Co-Editor, Metapolis Review of Architecture and Urban Culture, Athens
1998 Participated, 2nd Young Greek Architects Biennale, Athens
1999 Joint Curator, Landscapes of Modernisation: Greek Architecture 1960s and 1990s Exhibition, Netherlands Architecture Institute, Rotterdam. Presented also in Barcelona, Helsinki, Thessaloniki, Belgrade, Pescara.
1999 Assistant Professor of Architecture, University of Patras, Greece
2000 Participated, 7th International Architectural Exhibition, Venice Biennale

Principal Works:

1996 Zefyri Cultural Center, Athens (competition entry)
1996 Kansai-Kan of the National Diet Library, Japan (competition entry)
1997 Two Coffee-Bars, Athens (design and construction supervision)
1998 Omonoia Square, Athens (competition entry)
1998 Monastiraki Square, Athens (competition entry)
1999-02 Poly/mono-katoikia Apartment Building, Athens (design and construction supervision)
2002 Office Building, Athens (design, in progress)

Publication/Writings:

1996 Yannis Aesopos, Yorgos Simeoforidis (editors), *Landscapes of the Intimate*, Athens, Greek Ministry of Culture
1997 Yannis Aesopos, Yorgos Simeoforidis (editors), *Metapolis, nr. 1*, Athens
1999 Yannis Aesopos, Yorgos Simeoforidis (editors), *Landscapes of Modernisation: Greek Architecture 1960s and 1990s*, Athens, Metapolis Press
2000 Greek Entry, 7th International Architecture Exhibition, Venice Biennale 2000, Athens Greek Ministry of Culture
2000 Yannis Aesopos, Yorgos Simeoforidis, *Theorizing Athens*, Archis, nr. 7/2000, Rotterdam
2000 Yannis Aesopos, Yorgos Simeoforidis, "Athens: Paralogical Urbanization", in *Mutations*, Rem Koolhaas et al. (editors), Barcelona, Actar
2001 Yannis Aesopos, Yorgos Simeoforidis (editors), *The Contemporary (Greek) City/ Metapolis 2001*, Athens, Metapolis Press

Portugal

Aires Mateus & Associados LD.

Principal Architect(s):

Manuel Aires Mateus and Francisco Aires Mateus

Biography:

1963/64 Manuel Aires Mateus born in 1963 and Francisco Aires Mateus in 1964
1986 Diploma in Architecture in Lisbon-Manuel Mateus (87) Francisco Mateus (87)
1986 Assistant teacher in the University of Architecture in Lisbon – Manuel Mateus
Since 1997 Professor at Universidade Lusíada, Lisbon – Manuel Aires Mateus
Since 1998 Professor at universidade Autónoma – Manuel Aires Mateus and Francisco Mateus
2001-02 Professor at Accademia di Architectura, Mendrízio, Switzerland – Manuel Mateus and Francisco Mateus
Guest professors for seminars and lectures in Portugal, Spain, Italy, Switzerland, Argentina, England, Brazil, U.S.A., Mexico and Norway

Principal Works:

1990 Competition for the setting of 1st Triennial of Architecture in Sintra, 1st prize, Lisbon (constructed)
1991 International competition Samoná award, Italy, 1st prize
1993 Grândola Eders nursery, for Santa casa da Misericórdia of Grândola boco II (constructed)
1994 Invited to compete for the new headquarters of the engineers guild, 1st prize, Lisbon (constructed)
1995 invited to compete for the canteen at universidade de Coimbra, 1st prize (constructed)
1997 Competition for the Canteen at Universidade de Aveiro, 1st prize (constructed)
1997 Competition for pedagogical unit at Universidade de Coimbra, 1st prize (in construction)
1997 Rectory for Universidade Nova of Lisbon (in construction)

Awards:

2000 Architécti/ Arkial Award, 1st prize, Lisbon Portugal
2000 Luigi Cosenga Award, 1st prize, Nápoles Itália
2001 F.A.D. Architecture and Interior Award 2001, 1st prize, Barcelona
2001 II Biennial Ibero – American of Architecture 1st prize, Mexico City - Mexico
2001 European Union Prize for Contemporary Architecture; Mies van der Rohe Award (selected)

Publication/Writings:

1999 "Aires Mateus" in *Protótipo*, June 1999
2000 "Veterinary Clinic in Montemor - o - Novo and Library and Cultural Center in Sines", in *arq./a.* n°3 September/ October
2000 *Casa junto al agua*, Asensio Paco, Gili, México
2000 "Fraternal Order" in *A&V Monographs* n° 83
2000 Abstracció in *DPA*,"Presencia de la abstracción en la reciente Arquitectura Ibérica"
2001 *Student's Residence, Coimbra in Casabella*, June-August, Milano

United Kingdom

Allford Hall Monaghan Morris

Principal Architect(s):

Simon Allford, Jonathan Hall, Paul Monaghan, Peter Morris

Biography:

<u>Simon Allford</u>
1980-83 BA Architecture, Sheffield University
1984-86 Diploma, Bartlett University College of London
1986-89 BDP
1989 Founded AHMM
1989 Lecturing, Bartlett University College of London

<u>Jonathan Hall</u>
1980-83 BSc Architecture, Bristol University
1984-86 Diploma, Bartlett University College of London
1986-89 BDP
1989 Founded AHMM

<u>Paul Monaghan</u>
1980-83 BA Architecture, Sheffield University
1984-86 Diploma, Bartlett University College of London
1986-89 BDP
1989 Founded AHMM
1989 Lecturing, Bartlett University College of London

<u>Peter Morris</u>
1980-83 BA Architecture, Bristol University
1984-86 Diploma, Bartlett University College of London
1986-89 BDP
1989 Founded AHMM

Principal Works:

1996 Wilts, England, The Poolhouse
1998 London, England, The Broadgate Club
1998 London, England, Dalston Lane Housing
1999 London, England, North Croydon Medical Centre
2000 Essex, England,Notley Green Primary School
2000 London, England,Work & Learn Zone – Millennium Dome
2001 Walsall, England,Walsall Bus Station
2001 Birmingham, England, Caspar Housing
2001 London, England, Monsoon Headquarters
Current: London, England, Tulse Hill School
London, England, Union Square
London, England, Barbican Arts Centre
London, England, Clearwater Yard, Inverness Street
London, England, Raines Dairy
Leeds, England,Cloth Hall Street

Awards:

1996 Poolhouse, RIBA Award for Architecture
1998 The Broadgate Club, RIBA Award for Architecture
1999 North Croydon Medical Centre, RIBA Award for Architecture
2000 North Croydon Medical Centre, Civic Trust Award
Notley Green Primary School, RIBA Award for Architecture
Notley Green Primary School, Royal Fine Arts Commission Trust
School Building of the Year Award
Work & Learn Zone, RIBA Award for Architecture
CASPAR,British Construction Industry Award
Walsall Bus Station,RIBA Award for Architecture
2001 Walsall Bus Station, CivicTrust Award
Dalston Lane, Civic Trust Award
Raines Dairy,Housing Design Awards
Cloth Hall Street, Housing Design Awards

Publication/Writings:

1998 *New British Architecture*, The Architecture Foundation
1999 *The Power of Contemporary Architecture*, Academy
2000 *Young British Architects*, Birkhauser
2000 *New Work Future Visions British Architecture*, RIBA
2001 *L'Architecture Ecologique*, Le Moniteur

Germany

b&k+

Principal Architect(s):

Arno Brandlhuber
Bernd Kniess

Biography:

<u>Arno Hans Brandlhuber</u>
born in 1964
1984-92 Studies in architecture/urban planning and dissertation at the TH Darmstadt
1988 Guest studies at the Hochschule für Gestaltung, Darmstadt
1989-90 Erasmus scholarship, Universita degli Studi di Firenze
1994-96 Project partnership Neanderthal museum: Zamp Kelp and Julius Krauss, Arno Brandlhuber
1995-96 Office Brandlhuber, Cologne
1996 Foundation b&k+
1996-2000 Teaching post, Bergische Universität und GH Wuppertal
1999 Foundation +platform @b&k+, research platform
1999 Teaching post, Semaine Internationale, École d'Architecture de Nancy
2000 Professor replacement, Elementares Bauen, Bergische Universität GH Wuppertal
since 2001 b&k+ brandlhuber gmbh&co.kg

<u>Bernd Georg Kniess</u>
Born in 1961
1982-86 Gardener G+L
1986-95 Architecture/urban planning and dissertation at the TH Darmstadt
1991-92 Guest studies at the HdK Berlin
1996 Foundation b&k+
1997-99 Scientific assistance at the RWTH Aachen
1999 Foundation +platform@b&k+, research platform
since 2000 Teaching post Bergische Universität and GH Wuppertal
since 2001 b&k+ kniess gmbh&co.kg

Principal Works :

1996-97 Cologne, Dwelling and commercial house, Eigelstein
1997-00 Cologne,New Loft Building Kölner Brett
1997-00 Cologne, Dwelling and atelier house Geisselstrasse (b&k+ b,m)
1998-00 Aachen, Dwelling house Fabianek - Vaalser Quartier (b&k+ r)
1999-00 Cologne, Dwelling and commercial house Am Stavenhof
1999-01 Cologne, Dwelling, commercial and office building Neptunplatz
1998 Hannover Klimazone_n, Heating power station for the Expo 2000
1998 Hannover,Telematic landscape.org, EXPO 2000
1999 Frankfurt, Max, sky-scraper
1999 Cologne, Flora-n, office park Deutz (b&k+ ifau,le)
2001 Munich, BMW Event and Delivery Center
2002 Cologne, Loft complex Vulkan (b)
2002 Cologne, housing complex Ludwig-Jahn (k)

Awards:

1997 Architecture prize Beton BDA award
1998 Conveyor prize of the Land Nordrhein-Westfalen, architecture prize for exemplary commercial buildings (> 2.56 m), Architecture prize Nordrhein-Westfalen
2000 Cologne architecture prize (> 2.56 m)
Cologne architecture prize (Kölner Brett)
Cologne architecture prize (b&k+ b, m: Haus Romalgartz)
Wüstenrot prize (Kölner Brett)
Prix Rhénan (b&k+ b, m: Haus Romalgartz)
Architecture prize Zukunft Wohnen (Kölner Brett)
Architecture prize Zukunft Wohnen (b&k+b, m; Haus Romalgartz)
2001 Bauwelt prize (b&k+ b, m: Haus Romalgartz)
Bauwelt prize (b&k+ r: Vaalser Quartier)
German architecture prize (b&k+ b, m: Haus Romalgartz)
CoreDesign prize, 1st prize cat. Architecture (>2.56 m)
Architecture prize Nordrhein-Westfalen (b&k+ b, m: Haus Romalgartz)
2002 Building owners prize, high quality-low costs (Stavenhof)

Publication/Writings:

1996 Aedes, Neanderthal Museum, publication for the exhibition
1998/142, 1999/148, 2001/156 *Arch+*
Architektur natürlich, In vitro landscape
Von der Box zum Blob, Telematische Landschaft
Neuer Pragmatismus in der Architektur, Kölner Brett
2000/83 Av monografías, *edificio new loft*, colonia
1998/5, 2000/33, 2001/1-2, 2001/9 *Bauwelt*
Sonderbare Aufgaben, Zwischengehängt

zwölf Kölsch
Bauwelt Preis 2001
Schlauch und Staffel
1999/12 *b&k+ in vitro landscape*, exhibition catalogue, edition weißenhof, including audio CD
2000/4 Birkhäuser, *Junge Architekten in Deutschland*
2000 b&k+, Bergische Universität GH Wuppertal Akademie der Stadt Sindelfingen political landscape, book
2001 Archilab, Publication to the exhibition, Orleans 2001
2001/5 b&k+ Metazoon audio CD, Christopher Dell, 12 pieces to New Loft am Kölner Brett
2001/5 b&k+ to rococo rot.kölner brett audio CD, twelve tracks at three minutes verb, Architecture boogazine, telematic landscape, Kölner Brett
www.bk-plus.de
Exhibitions:
Aedes Galerie, Berlin, Neanderthal Museum
1998 Galerie Specta, Kopenhagen, Speculation
1999 Weißenhofgalerie, Stuttgart, in vitro landscape
1999 Museum Ludwig/ Josef-Haubrich-Kunsthalle, Cologne, At the end of the century
2000 Museum für Angewandte Kunst, Cologne, heilige-drei-Koenige. De
2001 archilab 3, Orléans
2002 Aedes Galerie Berlin, BMW Event and Delivery Center
2002 archilab4, Orléans

The Netherlands
Architect Agency Cepezed B.V.
Principal Architect(s):
Jan Pesman, Michiel Cohen
Biography:
Jan Pesman
1951 Born in Utrecht
1981 Technical University, Delft (department of Architecture)
1971-77 *Utopia magazine*, editor and layout
Start to 1992 *Items magazine*, editor
1974 Cofounder CEPEZED Architect Agency, Delft with M. Cohen
1994-95 Head lecturer, Academy of Architecture Rotterdam
Guest lecturer, Academy of Architecture Tilburg, Rotterdam, Amsterdam
President foundation Archit-act
Several lectures at Universities/High Schools in Delft, Eindhoven, Leuven
Several publications: personal, 1st prize ADCN Utopia nr. 8 (+ annex C)
Principal Works:
1999-00 NL Indoor Karting Track, Delft (winner Dutch Steel prize 2000)
1998-00 Austria Research Building for Austrian Academy of Sciences, Graz
1998-99 Germany Innovations Centre, Berlin
1999 Germany Porsche Showroom in Zuffenhausen, Stuttgart
1999 NL Own office building at Phoenixstraat, Delft
2000-01 Porsche Factory, Leipzig, Germany
1998-02 18 distribution centres for Dutch Post Telegraph Telephony
Started 2001 Studio building for VRT (Flemish Radio and Television Company), Hasselt + Kortrijk, Belgium
Awards:
1975 Tokyo International Lighting Design Competition, honorable mention, competition lamp
1997 European Steel prize, Centre for Human Drug Research, 1st prize Laboratory
2000 The Eleventh Colorcoat Building Award (CORUS) - best overall building - winner Cepezed for Cepezed offices, Delft.
2000 Belgium Steel prize 2000, Steel Construction Competition, winner cat. B. Villa Beckius, Luxembourg
Publication/Writings:
1995 *World Architecture*, "CEPEZED - Delft's prototypical practice"
1998 "Zwei vorbildliche projekte" by Michiel Cohen, *DeuBau*, Feb.
2001 "Une expérience aux Pays-Bas, sans chauffage apparent," *D'Architectures*, n°1
2001 "Total engineering by an architects' office" by Michiel Cohen, *Glass & Architecture*, Spring,
2001 "Intelligenz pro Kilo" by Jan Pesman*Intelligente Architektur*, 05/06

Belgium
evr.Architecten
Principal Architect(s):
Luc Eeckhout, Jan Van Den Broeke, Luc Reuse
Biography:
Luc Eeckhout
Born in 1960
1983 Architecture diploma
1984 Urban designer diploma
1994 Established office for sustainable building with J. Van Den Broeke
2001 established evr.Architecten
Jan Van Den Broeke
Born in 1960
1983 Architecture diploma
1994 Established office with L. Eeckhout
2001 Established evr.Architecten
Luc Reuse
Born in 1955
1979 Architecture diploma
1986-90 Collaborator OMA Rotterdam (NL)
1990 Office + teaching architecture Saint-Lucas Gent
1997 Partnership with Eeckhout - Van Den Broeke
2001 Established evr.Architecten
Principal Works:
2001 Vlaamse Landmaatschppij (VLM) low energy office building extension, Gent (construction 2002-04)
2000 Animal Centraal Besturingsgebouw Dijlevallei, low energy operating building, Leuven (construction 2002-03)
Campus VTI, Kortrijk (masterplan for technical school, in collaboration with H. Jult)
1999 Oxfam Wereldwinkels National Secretary, low energy office building and warehouse, Gent
1998 Zero-energy House, Aalst
1996 Arts Centre Vooruit, lobby and offices, Gent
1995 The Adobe Cube, bioclimatic dwelling construction, Tenerife (2002)
Awards:
1995 international tender: 3rd price / The Adobe Cube, Tenerife
1996 Electrabel Solar competition: 1st price / zero-energy dwelling Aalst
1998 City of Gent : 1st price / solar dwelling Gent
2001 VLM competition: 1st price / VLM - office building extension
2001 Gent / private contract / Port of Ghent Administration - office building
Publication/Writings:
1995-02 Several publications and lectures about sustainable building
1997-02 Publications about urban design and environment
1998-02 Publications about healthy buildings

Sweden
Studio Grön arkitekter ab
Principal Architect(s):
Fredrik Lund, Martin Forsby, Mika Määttä
Biography:
Fredrik Lund
1959 Born in Norway
1986 Diploma of architecture, NTH TRONDHEIM
1987-88 Employed lund- Hagem Oslo
1989-91 Employed Brunnberg Forshed Stockholm
1996-02 Owner Studio Grön
1991-96 PhD studies and teaching at Chalmers Gothenburg
1996-99 Lecturer at Chalmers
2000-02 Professor architectural design at Chalmers, Gothenburg
1996 Guest lecturer, Architectural association, Oslo, Norway
1996 Guest lecturer, School of Architecture, Trondheim, Norway
1996 Guest lecturer, School of Architecture (AAA), Aarhus, Denmark
1999 Guest lecturer, School of Architecture, Venice, Italy,
1999 Guest lecturer, Royal Academy of Art, Copenhagen, Denmark
1999 Guest lecturer, School of Architecture Bergen (BAS), Norway
2000 Guest lecturer, Architectural Association, Oslo, Norway
2000 Guest lecturer, Hochschule der Kunste, Berlin, Germany
2000 Guest lecturer, Isark Reykavik, Iceland
2000 Guest lecturer, School of Architecture, Oulo, Finland
2001 Guest lecturer, Architectural Association, Bergen, Norway
2001 Guest lecturer, Royal Academy of Art, Copenhagen, Denmark
2002 Guest lecturer and workshop leader, Graduate School of Architecture, Nanjing, China
Martin Forsby
1962 Born in Sweden
1993 Diploma of architecture, Chalmers, Gothenburg
1989-90 Employed Agora Arkitekter AB
1991 Employed Lars Forby AB, Stockholm
1991-94 Employed Blå Strek Tromsö, Norway
1994-96 Owner Bas X
1996-02 Owner Studio Grön
1995 Guest lecturer and workshop leader at Tau Tallin
2001 Guest lecturer, Architectural Association and School of Architecture, Warsava, Poland
Mika Määttä
1961 Born in Finland
1993 Diploma of architecture, Chalmers, Gothenburg
1989-90 Employed Wasa arkitekter, Gothenburg
1991-94 Employed Blå Strek Tromsö, Norway
1994-96 Owner Bas X
1996-02 Owner Studio Grön
1995-02 Lecturer at Chalmers, Göteborg
Principal Works:
1997 Restaurant Trädgårn, Göteborg
1998 Conversion of gymnasium to a college of media production, Göteborg
Awards:
1998 House of the year (National award)
1998 Gothemburg city prize (local award)
1998 SAR väst Prize (local award)
1999 Nominated for the 6th Mies van der Rohe award 1999
and the Kasper Sahlin Prize 1998
Publication/Writings:
2001
Byggekunst, Norway, n°6
Architectural Record, USA, July
Bauwelt, Germany, Bauwelt Preis 2001, n°1, Feb.
2000
"AV Monografias, 20 para el XXL", *Arqitectura Viva*, Spain, n°83
Area, Sweden, n°4
Byggekunst, Norway, n°7
Forum, Sweden, n°3
1999
Arhitectura Murator, Poland, n°9
Byggekunst, Norway, n°3
Scanorama, Scandinavian, Oct.
The Architectural Review, GB, April
Arkitektur, Denmark, n°2
Wallpaper, GB, March
1998
Byggekunst, Norway, n°8
Arkitektur, Sweden, n°7
Utblick/Landskap, Sweden, n°4
Spazio e socitá, Italy, n°83
Mama, Sweden, n°22
Glorian Koti, Finland, Nov.
Forum Nörmiljö, Sweden, n°3
Offentliga rum, Sweden, n°3-1998
Bibel, Sweden, n°2-1998
1997
Arkitektur, Sweden, n°3
Mama, Sweden, n°2

Japan
Kazuhiro Kojima
Principal Architect(s):
Kazuhiro Kojima
Biography:
1958 Born in Osaka, Japan
1982 B.Arch., Kyoto University
1986 Established COELACANTH Architects Inc.
1988-91 Research Associate, University of Tokyo
1994- Associate professor, Science Univ. of Tokyo
1998- Reorganized C+A (Coelacanth and Associates)
Principal Works:
1998 Kibikougen Elementary School, Okayama, Japan
2000 Space Blocks Kamishinjo, Osaka, Japan
2000 Big Heart Izumo, Shimane, Japan
2001 Hakuou Comprehensive High School, Miyagi, Japan
2002 EDUCATION CITY/ Bridge, Arts and Science, Doha, Qatar
2002 Hanoi Mode, Hanoi, Vietnam
Awards:
1985 Asakura Prize, SD Review 1985 (Himuro Apartment)
1990 Yoshioka Prize (Sakuradai Apartment)
1990 1st Prize, Osaka International Peace Center International Competition
1997 Prize, the Architectural Institute of Japan (Utase Elementary School)
2001 1st Prize, Isowand Isodach Design Contest
Publication:
1989 Special Issue "Coelacanth", *Kenchiku Bunka*, 1989, Dec.
1997 *Coelacanth Jam* (Gallery MA Books 06)
1998 Special Issue "Coelacanth"(*SD magazine* 1998,07)
2000 *Design Activities!*, Studies around educational space (Shoukokusha)
2002 *Plot 02, Kazuhiro Kojima: Process of Architecture* (GA, A.D.A.EDITA Tokyo)

France
Anne Lacaton
& Jean-Philippe Vassal
Principal Architect(s):
Anne Lacaton, Jean Philippe Vassal
Biography:
Anne Lacaton
1955 Born in St-Pardoux la Rivière, France
1980 Diploma at Bordeaux Architecture School, France
1984 Diploma of town planning, University of Bordeaux, France
Jean Philippe Vassal
1954 Born in Casablanca, Morocco
1980 Diploma at Bordeaux Architecture School, France
1980-85 Architect and Town planner in Niamey (Niger - Africa)
1987 Opening of the office
Principal Works:
1993 Floirac House Latapie, Bordeaux
1995 University of Arts & Human Sciences, Grenoble (completed 2001 / 2nd phase)
1998 House at Lège-Cap-Ferret
2000 House at Coutras
2001 Cafe of Architetur Zentrum, Vienna
2001 Palais de Tokyo, Site for contemporary arts, Paris
Awards:
1991 Lauréat des Albums de la Jeune Architecture, France
1997 Shortlist V° European Architecture Award, Foundation Mies Van der Rohe
1999 National Grand Prix of Architecture, Young Talent, France
2001 Shortlist World Architecture Award
Publication/Writings:
1994 *Une maison particulière*, Publisher Sens & Tonka, Paris
1995 *Il fera beau demain*, Publisher IFA, Paris (catalogue)
1998 *Premises: invested spaces in visual arts & architecture from France*, Guggenheim Museum, New York (catalogue)
2000 *10 x 10*, Phaidon Publisher, London
2001 *Archilab, Radical experiments in global architecture*, Orléans
2002 *Lacaton & Vassal*, 2G, Publisher G G, Barcelona, issue in April

Denmark
Dorte Mandrup Architekter
Principal Architect(s):
Dorte Mandrup-Poulsen
Biography:
1961 Born in Copenhagen, Denmark
1982-83 Georgia Southern University, Sculpture and Ceramics, USA
1987-88 Kolding School of Arts and Crafts, Graphics, Denmark
1991 Graduated from Aarhus School of Architecture, Denmark
1992-95 Employed at Henning Larsens Office, Denmark
1995-99 Established Fuglsang&Mandrup-Poulsen Architects with Niels Fuglsang
1992-98 Assistant professor at Royal Danish Academy of Art
1998-00 Part time professor at Royal Danish Academy of Art
1999 Established Dorte Mandrup Architects
Principal Works:
1997 Slagelse Antvorskov Church, competition winning entry
1998 Copenhagen, Home For The Future, exhibition 1:1
1999 Taarnby, Taarnby Courthouse
2001 Copenhagen Bookstore for Architecture Center Gl. Dok
2001 Copenhagen Seaplane Hangar H53, Headquarters for Cell Network, Denmark
2001 Copenhagen Neighborhood Center, Holmbladsgade
2002 Copenhagen Daycare Center Naestvedgade (in preparation)
Awards:
2001 National Wood Association Award for outstanding architectural work
2001 Copenhagen Cultural Foundation annual award
Publication/Writings:
2002 *Md moebel interior design*, Feb. 2002
DBZ Deutche Bauzeitschrifft, March 2002
2001 *Arkitektur DK*, July 2001
Rum, April 2001
2000 *Arkitektur DK*, August 2000
1999 *Young Danish Architecture and Design*

Japan
Mikan
Principal Architect(s):
Kiwako Kamo, Masashi Sogabe, Masayoshi Takeuchi, Manuel Tardits
Biography:
1962 Kiwako Kamo born in Kokura, Japan
1962 Masashi Sogabe born in Fukuoka, Japan
1962 Masayoshi Takeuchi born in Kamakura, Japan
1959 Manuel Tardits born in Paris, France
1995 Mikan established in Tokyo
1995-02 All partners have taught and lectured in many universities in Japan and abroad
Principal Works:
1998 NHK Nagano Broadcasting station, Nagano, Japan
1999 Community center, Yatsushiro, Japan
2001 Tokyo KH, Tokyo, Japan
2001 Tokyo Shibuya AX, Tokyo, Japan
2001 Kindergarten in Yatsushiro, Japan
2002 Saint-Julien Common Housing, Tokyo, Japan
Awards:
2000 Prize of encouragement from Kumamoto artpolis
2001 JCD Design award, honorable mention
2001 JCD Design award, honorable mention
Publication/Writings:
2000 *30 x 30 x 30*, Gap Publications
2001 *10 City Profiles from 10 Young architects*, Toto Shuppan
2002 *Quaderns*, n°231
2002 *50 Architects Under Age 40*, Ei Publishing
2002 *Danchi Saisei Keikaku*, Inax Publishing

Luxembourg
Ney and Partners sarl
Principal Architect(s):
Laurent Ney
Biography:
1964 Born in Thionville, France
1989 Graduated as civil engineer in Liège, Belgium
1989-96 Collaborated at the office of René Greisch in Liège

1996-02 Office T6, sàrl and Ney and Partners, SA
Principal Works:
1998-01 Brussels Tervuren bridge
1999-00 Antwerpen Canopies
2001-02 Alden Biesen Umbrellas
1998-00 Brussels Elena building
Awards:
2001 Prijze of the Sint-Lukasarchief

Ireland

O'Donnell + Tuomey Architects

Principal Architect(s):
Sheila O'Donnell, John Tuomey
Biography:
Sheila O'Donnell
1953 Born in Dublin Ireland
1976 B Arch, University College, Dublin
1980 MA Royal College of Art, London
1980-81 Worked in London with James Stirling
1981- Studio lecturer, University College, Dublin
1987 Visiting critic, Princeton University, USA
1988 O'Donnell + Tuomey established in Dublin
John Tuomey
1954 Born in Tralee, Ireland
1976 B Arch, University College, Dublin
1976-80 Worked in London with James Stirling
1980-87 Worked in Dublin with Office of Public Works
1987 Visiting critic, Princeton, USA
1988 Visiting critic, GSD Harvard, USA
1988 O'Donnell + Tuomey established in Dublin
Principal Works:
1990 Irish Pavilion "11 Cities 11 Nations" Leeuwarden, the Netherlands
1992 Irish Film Centre, Dublin
1992-96 Temple Bar Framework Plan, Dublin (Group 91)
1994 Blackwood Golf Centre, Dublin
1997 National Photography Centre, Dublin
1998 Hudson House, Navan
1999 Ranelagh School, Dublin
2001 Furniture College Letterfrack, Connemara
2002 Medical Research Laboratories, University College Dublin
Awards:
2002, 1999, 1997, 1992, 1990, 1988
Architectural Association of Ireland Downes Medals
1999, 1997
Architectural Association of Ireland Awards
2001, 2000, 1999, 1995, 1993
Royal Institute of Architects of Ireland Awards
2001, 1999, 1997
Royal Institute of British Architects Awards
1999
Stirling Prize, finalist,
Mies van de Rohe European Architecture Award, finalists
1997 Andrea Palladio International **1993** Award finalist
Publication/Writings:
1992 *The Irish Pavilion*, Gandon Editions
1996 *Domus* 781, Italy
1997 *Profile: O'Donnell + Tuomey*, Gandon Editions
1997 *20th Century Architecture Ireland*, Wilfried Wang, Prestel
1998 *Architecture and Urbanism* 332, Japan
1999 *Home The Twentieth Century House*, Deyan Sudjic
1999 *Architecture*, August, USA
2000 *Quaderns* 225, Spain
2001 *Europe The Contemporary Architecture Guide*, Vol. 3, Masayuki Fuchigami
2001 *Archi*, August, Kenneth Frampton, Switzerland

Austria

Riegler Riewe Architects Pty. Ltd.

Principal Architect(s):
Florian Riegler, Roger Riewe
Biography:
1987 Founding of Architekturbüro Riegler Riewe in Graz
1996 Founding of Riegler Riewe Architects Pty. Ltd in Graz, Austria
1997 Founding of branch office of Architekturbüro Riegler Riewe in Cologne, Germany
Florian Riegler
1954 Born in Mönichwald, Austria
Study of architecture at the Technical University in Graz, Austria
1991-97 Member of the board of the Austrian Society for Architecture, ÖGFA
1994-97 Member of the 5th Salzburg planning commission
1994 Berlage Institute Amsterdam, Netherlands
1995 RWTH Aachen, Germany
1996 Technical University in Prague, Czechia
1996 IAAS, Barcelona, Spain
1997 IAAS, Basel, Switzerland
1998 Lindauschool, Lindau, Germany
2001-02 ETH Zürich
Roger Riewe
1959 Bielefeld, Germany
Study of architecture at the RWTH Aachen, Germany
1989-99 Member of the board of the Central Union of Architects, (ZV) Styria, Austria
1996-99 Vice president of the ZV
1994 Berlage Institute Amsterdam, Netherlands
1995 RWTH Aachen, Germany
1996 Technical University in Prague, Czechia
1996 Caras-Workshop, Syros, Greece
1996 Institute for Advanced Architectural Studies - IAAS - Barcelona, Spain
1996 IAAS Malberg, Germany
1997 "Architekturwerkstatt" Augsburg, Germany
1997 IAAS Venice, Italy
1998 "Architekturwerkstatt" Biberach, Germany
1998 IAAS Venice, Italy
1999 William Sommerville Lectureship University of Calgary, Canada
since 1999 ESARQ (UIC), Barcelona
1994-00 External examiner of the diploma course at the Faculty for Architecture at the Technical University in Graz.
2000-01 TU Graz
since 2001 Professor TU Graz
Principal Works:
1989 Airport Graz, Austria
1993 Technical University Graz, Information Technology and Electronics Institutes, Austria
1995 Federal Institute for Social Pedagogy, Baden, Austria
1998 Railway station, Bruck/Mur, Austria
1999 Main Railway station, Innsbruck, Austria
2000 House of Literature, Graz, Austria
Awards:
1990, 1994, 1998 Styrian prize for Architecture
1993, 1999 Austrian clients' prize
1999 Finalist of the 6th Mies van der Rohe Prize
Publication/Writings:
1987 *Riegler Riewe*
Arbeiten seit, Hrsg.: Österreichische Gesellschaft für Architektur
1995 *Riegler - Riewe Graz*
Nicht determinierte Architektur
Hrsg. Aedes West, Berlin
2001 *Definite Indefinite*
Riegler Riewe, Springer Verlag Wien, New York

Japan

Kazuyo Sejima + Ryue Nishizawa / SANAA

Principal Architect(s):
Kazuyo Sejima, Ryue Nishizawa
Biography:
Kazuyo Sejima
1981 Graduated from Japan Women's University with M. Arch degree
1987 Established Kazuyo Sejima & Associates
1995 Established SANAA with Ryue Nishizawa
2000-01 Visiting Professor at ETH
Professor at Keio University, Visiting lecturer at Tokyo University
Ryue Nishizawa
1990 Graduated from Yokohama National University with M. Arch degree
1995 Established SANAA with Kazuyo Sejima
1997 Established Office of Ryue Nishizawa
Associate professor at Yokohama National University
Principal Works:
1997 Oogaki, Multi Media Workshop
Nakahechi, N-MUSEUM
Okayama S-HOUSE
Tokyo M-HOUSE
1998 Koga, Park Café
1999 Iida, O-MUSEUM
2000 Yokohama, Day-Care Center
Venezia, Italy Exhibition design "La Biennale di Venezia," Japanese Pavilion
2001 Italy PRADA Beauty Prototype
Tokyo, Hong Kong, PRADA Beauty ISETAN, Tokyo, LEEGARDEN Hong Kong
Project:
Kanazawa, Museum of Contemporary Art
Almere, Netherlands, Stadstheater
Toledo, Ohio, Center for Glass, The Toledo Museum of Art
Almere, Netherlands, Lumiere Park Café
Awards:
1996 1st Prize, Museum of Contemporary Art in Sydney Extension, Australia
1997 Selected for New Campus Center for Illinois Institute of Technology Design Competition, as last 5 architects
1998 The Prize of Architectural Institute of Japan for "Multi-media Workshop"
1st Prize, Edifici-mondo, a competition for the recuperation of the antiquities of Salerno, Italy
Selected for Center for the Contemporary Arts, Rome International Design Competition, as last 15 architects
1999 1st Prize, Museum of Contemporary Art Kanazawa Design Proposal, Japan
1st Prize, Theater and CKV in Almere, Netherlands
2000 Erich Schelling Architekturpreis 2000
2001 3rd Prize, Competition for the AMAG-BVK Commercial Buildings Zurich, Switzerland
Selected for the ASIA Society Hong Kong Center Design Competition as last 3 architects
2002 2nd Prize, New Mercedes-Benz Museum, International Competition, Stuttgart, Germany
Publication/Writings:
1999 "Kazuyo Sejima 1987-1999 / Kazuyo Sejima + Ryue Nishizawa 1995-1999," Special issue, *JA* vol. 35, SHINKENCHIKU-SHA Co. Ltd
2000 Monograph, *Kazuyo Sejima + Ryue Nishizawa 1995-2000*
El Croquis, n°99, Spain
2001 Monograph, "Kazuyo Sejima 1983-2000, Kazuyo Sejima + Ryue Nishizawa 1995-2000" *El Croquis*, n°77(I)+99, Spain

Finland

Sanaksenaho Arkkitehdit Oy

Principal Architect(s):
Matti Sanaksenaho,
Pirjo Sanaksenaho
Biography:
Matti
1966 Born in Helsinki
1993 Master of Architecture, Helsinki University of technology
1996 Guest professor at the Architecture School of Århus, Denmark
1997 Guest lecturer in several universities & seminars in architecture
Pirjo
1966 Born in Turku
1993 Master of Architecture, Helsinki University of technology
1988 Practice Raili & Reima Pietilä architects
1989-91 Practice Petri & Severi Blomstedt architects
1991-93 Practice Kari Järvinen & Timo Airas Architects
since 1993 Working together with Matti Sanaksenaho
since 2000 Teacher at the Helsinki University of Technology, department of architecture
Principal Works:
1992 The Finland Pavilion in Sevilla expo '92, Spain,
1993 The Empty Space in Saarijärvi, Finland
1996 Students House in Vaasa, Finland
1999-00 Designer Shops, Sweden/Finland
2001 House Tammimäki, Finland
1995- The Chapel in Turku (project), Finland
Awards:
1992 The state prize of architecture in Finland
1993 Participant of the European Architecture Award of Mies van der Rohe foundation 1993
2001 Reima Pietilä prize
Publication/Writings:
1992 Several books and publications in Finland, Europe, United States and Japan

Italy

UdA – Ufficio di Architettura

Principal Architect(s):
Walter Camagna, Massimiliano Camoletto, Andrea Marcante
Biography:
1992 Architect degree at Politecnico of Turin
1991-92 Working experiences and master in Spain and USA
1992 Opening of the office
Principal Work:
1994 Castiglione T.se (To), Playing area with recreational facilities
1994 Club Azimut, Turin
1995 Club La Barraca, Biella
1995 Borge house, Volpianto
1996 Bollarino house (apartment), Turin
1996 Torino, Lanzo-Ruggeri house (flat)
1997 A system of squares and pedestrian ways, Traversella
1997 Pininfarina – Historical museum with conference center, Cambiano
1998 D'Adda, Lorenzini, Vigorelli – Renovation and installation for the new head quarter, Milan
1998 Area della Mole Antonelliana – New service centre for entertainment and cultural tourism, Turin
1998 Biella, Levis house
1998 Hospital S. Giovanni Battista in Turin, requalification and new services for reception facilities
1999 Lobina house (apartment), Turin
1999 Boggetto house (apartment), Nizza
1999 Ciec Medica – Plastic surgery center, Rome
2000 Devecchi house, Foglizzo
2001 Interior design of the Prestige area for the Jewellery Show, Basel
2001 Argentovivo – Fitting of a new one-brand shop for Europe, Bologne
2001 Sahzà – Fitting of a new one-brand shop for Europe and Asia, Varese
Awards:
1997 Politeama Boglione theater City of Bra (CUNEO) (competition 2nd prize)
1999 San Giovanni Battista Hospital in Turin (competition 1st prize)
2000 City: Third Millennium - Venice Biennale, 2000 (competition selected project)
2000 Europan 5 (competition mentioned project)
2000 Borromini Prize 2000 (Young architects selection)
2000 GAC Prize (1st prize)
2000 GAC Prize (1st prize)
2000 Luigi Cosenza Prize (selected project)
Publication/Writings (1998-01):
1998 *Intorno alla fotografia 4*, France, Association JVBD catalogue
1998 *Wall paper*, n°9, England
1999 *Dieci anni di concorsi di architettura in Piemonte e Valle D'Aosta*, Italy, Clut catalogue
1999 *Siedimi*, Italy, Promosedia catalogue
1999 *Europan 5, Risultati in Italia*, Italy, Europan catalogue
1999 *Giornale dell'Architettura*, n°22, Italy
1999 *Europan 5 Resultats européens*, France, Europan catalogue
1999 *Abitare*, n°385, Italy
1999 *Ristrutturazione e progettazione degli interni*, vol. 3, Italy, edizioni Utet
2000 *City: Third Millennium*, Italy, Marsilio catalogue
2000 *Urban Interiors 3*, Italy, edizioni Archivolto
2000 *Caffè e ristoranti*, Italy, Federico Motta editore
2000 *Architécti*, n°49, Portugal
2000 *Diseño Interior*, n°95, Spain
2000 *Abitare*, n°398, Italy
2000 *Monument special 2000*, Australia
2000 *Giovani architetti europei*, clean catalogue, italy
2000 *Il futuro e la città*, image catalogue, italy
2000 *AV monografias - Young European Architects*, n°83, Spain
2001 *Pequeños espacios domésticos*, Spain
2001 *Architectures à Vivre n°3*, France
2001 *Blue Print*, n°181, England
2001 *Art Jonction*, Le Journal n°27, France
2001 *New Restaurants*, ed. Archivolto, Italy
2001 *New Bars Café & Pubs*, ed. Archivolto, Italy
2001 New Architectural Interiors, England
2001 *The Architectural Review*, n°1.251, England
2001 *Escaleras*, Spain
2001 *Le Moniteur*, n°5.078, France
2001 *Architektur Innenarchitektur Technisher Ausbau*, n°11, Germany
2001 *Minimalist spaces*, Links International, Spain
2002 *Stairs*, Edizione Archivolto, Italy
2002 *European Interior Style*, Checkout Publications, England
2002 *Abitare*, n°416, Italy

Japan

Motomu Uno + Phase Associates

Principal Architect(s): Motomu Uno
Biography:
1954 Born in Tokyo
1978 Graduated from the University of Tokyo, BA
1984 Graduated from Graduate School of Architecture, the University of Tokyo, PhD
1985 Founded Phase Associates present Professor of Chiba University
Principal Works:
1990 Yotsuya Temporary Office, Tokyo
1991 Muramatsu House, Tokyo
1995 Makuhari New City center Housing Block M2-2, Chiba City
1998 Toyohashi Station Plaza, Toyohashi City
2000 Villa Fujii, Nagano
Awards:
1982 Design Award, SD Review 1982
1992 The 9th Yoshioka Prize
1995 Architectural Culture Prize, Chiba Prefecture Government
1998 Special Prize for the Architects, Artist and Craftsmen Association of Japan
2002-02 Annual Architectural Design Commendation of Architectural Institute of Japan
2002 American Wood Design of the Year-Best of Residential
Publication/Writings:
1995 *Technoscape SD9504*, Kajima Publishing
1998 *New Wave of Waterfront PROCESS CITY*, (collaboration) Shinkenchiku-sha
2001 *New Concept of Architecture*, Syokokusha Publishing
2001 *Tokyo 2001*, (collaboration) Kajima Publishing

プロフィル

イタリア
アバロス&エレロス
イニャキ・アバロスとホァン・エレロスは1984年から共同している。1992年からはインターナショナル・マルティメディア・リーグを組織し、芸術活動の明確化、強化を目指している。1994年から建築誌ExitLMIを編集。1988年からマドリッド建築学校で教える。1984年から1988年までETSAマドリッドでチューター。1984年から1989年までコロンビア大学で客員講師。1997年から1999年までローザンヌ連邦工科大学でユニット・マスター。1998から2001年までAAスクールでユニットマスター。

日本
阿部仁史
1987年東北大学工学研究科建築学専攻博士課程前期修了。1989年南カリフォルニア建築研究所でM-ARK3課程修了、修士号取得。1988年から1992年までコープ・ヒンメルブラウ勤務。1992年阿部仁史アトリエ開設。1993年東北大学研究科建築学専攻博士課程後期修了、博士号取得。1994年から2002年まで東北工業大学建築学科で教える。2002から東北大学大学院工学研究科都市建築学専攻教授をつとめる。

ギリシャ
ヤニス・アエソポス
1966年アテネに生まれる。1989年国立アテネ工科大学で建築学位を取得。1991年ハーバード大学GSDで修士号取得。1992年から1995年までバーナード・チュミの事務所に勤務。1994年コロンビア大学大学院で客員助教授。1995年アテネに事務所設立。1997年建築と都市計画の批評誌Metapolisを共同編集。1997年第2回アテネ若手建築家ビエンナーレに参加。1999年ロッテルダム他で開催された近代化のランドスケープ・ギリシャ建築1960と1990展覧会を共同キュレート。1999年パトラス大学助教授。2000年第7回ベネチア建築ビエンナーレに参加。

ポルトガル
アイレス・マテウス&アソシアードス
1963年にマニュエル・アイレス・マテウス、1964年にフランシスコ・アイレス・マテウスが共にリスボンで生まれる。1986/87年にリスボンで建築学位を取得。1986年リスボン建築大学で助教師（マニュエル）。1997年からリスボンのルシアダ大学教授（マニュエル）。1998年からアウトノマ大学教授（マニュエルとフランシスコ）。2001年から2002年、スイス、メンドリツィオの建築アカデミーで教授をつとめる。

イギリス
アルフォード・ホール・モナハン・モリス
サイモン・アルフォード：
1980年から1983年シェフィールド大学で建築学位取得。1984年から1986年ロンドン、バートレット・ユニバーシティ・カレッジで学位取得。1986年から1989年BDP。1989年AHMM設立。1989年バートレット・ユニバーシティ・カレッジ講師。
ジョナサン・ホール：
1980年から1983年ブリストル大学で建築学位取得。1984年から1986年ロンドン、バートレット・ユニバーシティ・カレッジで学位取得。1986年から1989年BDP。1989年AHMM設立。
ポール・モナハン：
1980年から1983年シェフィールド大学で建築学位取得。1984年から1986年ロンドン、バートレット・ユニバーシティ・カレッジで学位取得。1986年から1989年BDP。1989年AHMM設立。1989年バートレット・ユニバーシティ・カレッジ講師。
ピーター・モリス：
1980年から1983年ブリストル大学で建築学位取得。1984年から1986年ロンドン、バートレット・ユニバーシティ・カレッジで学位取得。1986年から1989年BDP。1989年AHMM設立。

ドイツ
b&k+
アルノ・ブランドルフーバー：
1964年に生まれる。1984年から1992年までTHダルムシュタッドで建築／都市計画を学び、学位取得。1988年ダルムシュタッド造形大学で客員研究。1989年から1990年エラスムス奨学金によりフィレンツェで学ぶ。1994年から1996年ネアンデルタール博物館のプロジェクトに参加。1995年から1996年ブランドルフーバーオフィスをケルンに開設。1996年b&k+の基礎段階。1999年b&k+の第2準備段階。1999年ナンシーの建築学校国際セミナーで教える。2001年b&k+設立
ベルント・クニース：
1961年に生まれる。1986年から95年までTHダルムシュタッドで建築／都市計画を学び、学位取得。1991年から1992年Hdkベルリンで客員研究。1996年b&k+の基礎段階。1996年から1999年までアーヘンのRWTHで学科助手。1999年b&k+の第2準備段階。2001年b&k+設立

オランダ
アーキテクト・エージェンシー CEPEZED
ヤン・ペスマン：
1951年ユトレヒトに生まれる。1981年デルフト工科大学で学位取得。1971年から1977年まで雑誌Utopiaの編集をつとめる。1992年から雑誌Itemsの編集をつとめる。1974年CEPEZEDをミシェル・コーヘンと共同設立。1994年から1995年ロッテルダム建築アカデミーの主任講師。ティルブルフ、ロッテルダム、アムステルダムの建築アカデミー客員講師。Archit-actを設立。

ベルギー
evr.アーシテクテン
リュック・エークハウト：
1960年に生まれる。1983年建築学位取得。1984年都市計画学位取得。1994年オフィス・フォー・サステナブル・ビルディングをヤン・ヴァン・デン・ブルーケと設立。2001年evr.アーシテクテンを設立。
ヤン・ヴァンデンブルッケ：
1960年に生まれる。1983年建築学位取得。1994年リュック・イークホウトと事務所設立。2001年 evr.アーシテクテンを設立。
リュック・リューセ：
1955年に生まれる。1979年建築学位取得。1986年から1990年はOMAに勤務。1990年にオフィスを設立。同年、ゲントのシント・ルーカスで建築を教える。1997年エックハウトーヴァン・デン・ブルークと共同。2001年evr.アーシテクテンを設立。

スウェーデン
スタジオ・グレーン建築事務所
フレデリック・ルンド：
1959年ノルウェーに生まれる。1986年NTHトロンヘイムで建築学位を取得。1987年から1988年ルンドーハゲム事務所（オスロ）に勤務。1989年から1991年ブリュンベリ・フォーシェッド（ストックホルム）に勤務。1991年から1996年イェーテボリのシャルマーズ工科大学で博士課程。1996年から1999年まで同大学で講師。2000年から同大学で建築を教える。
マッティン・フォシュビュー：
1962年スウェーデンに生まれる。1993年シャルマーズ工科大学で建築学位取得。1989年から1990年アゴラ建築事務所に勤務。1991年ラース・フォシュビュー（ストックホルム）に勤務。1991年から1994年ブラ・ストレック・トゥロムソに勤務。1994年から1996年BasXを運営。1996年スタジオ・グレーン設立。
ミカ・マータ：
1961年フィンランドに生まれる。1993年シャルマーズ工科大学で建築学位取得。1989年から1990年ワサ建築事務所（イェーテボリ）に勤務。1991年から1994年ブラ・ストレック・トゥロムソに勤務。1994年から1996年BasXを運営。1996年スタジオ・グレーン設立。

日本
小嶋一浩／C+A
1958年大阪に生まれる。1982年京都大学建築学科卒業。1986年株式会社シーラカンス1級建築士事務所設立。1988年東京大学大学院博士課程修了。1988年から1991年まで東京大学工学部建築学科助手。1994年から東京理科大学工学部建築学科助教授。1998年C+A（株式会社シーラカンス アンド アソシエイツ）に改組。

フランス
アンヌ・ラカトン&ジャン・フィリップ・ヴァッサル
アンヌ・ラカトン：
1955年フランスに生まれる。1980年ボルドー建築学校で学位取得。1984年ボルドー大学でタウン・プランニングの学位取得。
ジャン・フィリップ・ヴァッサル
1954年カサブランカに生まれる。1980年ボルドー建築学校で学位取得。1980年から1985年までニアメイ（ニジェール）で建築・タウン・プランニング活動。1987年オフィス設立。

デンマーク
ドーテ・マンドルップ・アーキテクテー
1961年コペンハーゲンに生まれる。1982年から1983年アメリカ、ジョージア南大学で彫刻と陶芸を学ぶ。1987年から1988年デンマークのコールディング芸術学校に学ぶ。1991年オルフス建築大学院で学位取得。1992年から1995年ヘニング・ラーセン（デンマーク）に勤務。1995年から1999年までフールサン＆マンドルップーポールセン事務所で活動。1992年から1998年デンマーク王立芸術アカデミーで助教授。1998年から2000年までデンマーク王立芸術アカデミーで非常勤教授。1999年ドーテ・マンドルップ・アーキテクテーを設立。

日本
みかんぐみ
1962年生まれで共に東京工業大学に学んだ 加茂紀和子、曽我部昌史、竹内昌義と、1959年パリに生まれ、東京大学大学院に留学したマニュエル・タルディッツの4人により、1995年に設立された。

ルクセンブルグ
ネイ・アンド・パートナーズ
ローラン・ネイ：
1964年フランスに生まれる。1989年リエージュで土木工学の学位を取得。1996年までルネ・グレッシュの事務所に勤務。2001年にシント・リュカス・アーカイブ賞を受賞
ナタリー・リース：
1965年ルクセンブルグに生まれる。1991年から1992年までエラスムス交換学生としてミラノ工科大学に学ぶ。1992年にブリュッセルのラ・カンブル国立建築高等学院から建築学位を取得。1993年から1997年までベルギーのアルトー事務所で設計に協力。1996年に二人はT6 sàrlをルクセンブルグに、またネイ&パートナーズをベルギーに設立した。

アイルランド
オードネル+トゥミ・アーキテクツ
シェイラ・オードネル：
1953年ダブリンに生まれる。1976年ダブリン・ユニバーシティ・カレッジを卒業。1980年ロンドン王立大学で修士号取得。1980年から1981年までジェームス・スターリング事務所に勤務。1981年からダブリン・ユニバーシティ・カレッジのスタジオ講師。1987年プリンストン大学で客員批評。1988年オードネル+トゥミ・アーキテクツ設立。
ジョン・トゥミ：
1954年アイルランド・トラリーに生まれる。1976年ダブリン・ユニバーシティ・カレッジを卒業。1976年から1980年までジェームス・スターリング事務所に勤務。1980年から1987年までダブリンで公共事業事務所に勤務。1987年プリンストン大学で客員批評。1988年ハーバードGSDで客員批評。1988年オードネル+トゥミ・アーキテクツ設立。

オーストリア
リーグラー・リーヴェ・アーキテクツ
1987年リーグラー・リーヴェ・アーキテクツを設立。1997年ケルンに支所を設置。
フロリアン・リーグラー：
1954年オーストリアに生まれる。グラーツ工科大学で建築を学ぶ。
ロジャー・リーヴェ：
1959年ドイツに生まれる。ドイツ・アーヘンのRWTHで建築を学ぶ。

日本
妹島和世+西沢立衛／SANAA
妹島和世：
1981年日本女子大学大学院修了。1987年妹島和世建築設計事務所設立。1995年から西沢立衛と共同設計。2000年から2001年ETHにて客員教授。現在、慶応大学教授、東京大学非常勤講師。
西沢立衛：
1990年横浜国立大学大学院修了。1995年から妹島和世と共同設計。現在、横浜国立大学大学院助教授。

フィンランド
サナクセンアホ・アーキテクツ
マッティ・サナクセンアホ：
1966年ヘルシンキに生まれる。1993年ヘルシンキ工科大学で修士号取得。1996年デンマークのアーフス建築学校の客員教授。
ピルヨ・サナクセンアホ：
1966年トゥルクに生まれる。1993年ヘルシンキ工科大学で修士号取得。1993年からマッティ・サナクセナホと共同。2000年からヘルシンキ工科大学建築学科で教鞭をとる。

イタリア
UdA
ワルター・カマーニャ、マッシミリアノ・カモレット、アンドレア・マルカンテ
1992年トリノ工芸大学で建築学位取得。1991年から1992年までスペインとアメリカで職業経験と修士号取得。1992年オフィス設立。

日本
宇野求+フェイズアソシエイツ
1954年東京に生まれる。1978年東京大学工学部建築学科卒業。1984年東京大学大学院博士課程修了、博士号取得。1985年フェイズアソシエイツを設立。現在、千葉大学教授を勤める。

Data & credits

New Recycling Plant for Urban Waste
Architects: Abalos & Herreros
Location: Valdemingómez, Madrid, Spain
Project Type: New Building/ Industrial Installation
Use of the Building: Recycling Plant
Site Area: 50 ha
Building Area: 25,000 m^2
Total Floor Area: 25,000 m^2
Number of Floors: 1
Height of the Building: 4-18 m
Client: Vertresa-RWE Process
Structural Engineer: Obiol y Moya
Mechanical Engineer: Servicios Técnicos de Vertresa. Team Leader: Fernando Valledor
Constructor: IMES
Structure of the Building: Steel
Principal Exterior Material: Polycarbonate
Period: 1997 - 2000
Award: Ayuntamiento de Madrid Architecture Prize
Publication: *Recycling, Madrid*, Actar, 2000

Village Hall and Square
Architects: Abalos & Herreros
Location : Colmenarejo, Madrid, Spain
Project Type : New Public Building and Urban Space.
Use of the Building: Public Hall
Site Area: 1.5 ha
Building Area: 300 m^2
Total Floor Area: 400 m^2
Number of Floors: 2
Height of the Building: 6 m
Client: Comunidad de Madrid and Ayuntamiento de Colmenarejo
Structural Engineer: Juan Gómez
Mechanical Engineer: Juan José Nuñez
Structure of the Building: Steel
Principal Exterior Material: Polycarbonate
Principal Interior Material: Bamboo cane
Period: 1997 - 1999
Publication: *Recycling, Madrid*, Actar, 2000

Shiki Community Hall
Architects: Atelier Hitoshi Abe and Yasuaki Onoda
Location: Reihoku, Kumamoto, Japan
Use of the Building: Community hall
Site Area: 3,830.14 m^2
Building Area: 934.70 m^2
Total Floor Area: 993.36 m^2
Number of Floors: 2
Height of the Building: 9.95 m
Client: Town of Reihoku, Kumamoto, Japan
Structural Engineer: TIS & Partners
Mechanical Engineer: Sogo Consultants
Constructor: Nakamura Construction & Kanematsu Construction JV
Structure of the Building: Wood (Laminated lumber)
Principal Exterior Material: Wood
Principal Interior Material: Wood
Period: 12. 2000 - 03. 2002

Poly/mono-katoikia
Architect: Yannis Aesopos
Location: Athens, Greece
Project Type: Apartment building & single-family house
Use of the Building: Residential
Site Area: 623 m^2
Building Area: 249 m^2
Total Floor Area: 623 m^2
Number of Floors: 5
Height of the Building: 20 m
Client: ARIS SA
Structural Engineer: Georgios Christou (reinforced concrete structure), Mary Konstantakopoulou (steel structure)
Mechanical Engineer: Thomas Efthymiopoulos
Other Consultants: Alekos Aesopos (General supervision), Vassilis Douridas and Sotiris Yannoukaris (Construction coordination)
Contractor: ARIS SA
Structure of the Building: Reinforced concrete frame, steel frame
Principal Exterior Material: Plaster walls and chiseled plaster walls, grey sandblasted marble floors, aluminum windows, green-tinted glass railings
Principal Interior Material: Plaster walls, white and grey marble floors, wooden floors, wooden doors
Period: 1997 - 2002
Publications: Greek Entry, 7th International Architecture Exhibition, Venice Biennale 2000, Athens, Greek Ministry of Culture, 2000 / Yorgos Simeoforidis, "Architecture in Athens," *Archis*, n° 7/2000, Rotterdam

House in Alenquer
Architects: Aires Mateus & Associados LDA.
Location: Alenquer, Portugal
Use of the Building: Housing
Site Area: 677.60 m^2
Building Area: 48.60 m^2
Total Floor Area: 113.40 m^2
Number of Floors: 2
Height of the Building: 5.60 m
Client: Dr. Emílio Vilar
Structural Engineer: Eng. Augusto Marques Mendes
Mechanical Engineer: Ramalho Couto Lda.
Constructor: Ramalho Couto Lda.
Structure of the Building: Concrete and steel
Principal Exterior Material: Brick wall with painted stucco
Principal Interior Material: Brick wall with painted stucco
Period: 05. 1999 - 03. 2002
Publications: *Architécti* n° 46, April-June 1999, *Protótipo* n°4, June 1999-2000, "Casa en Alenquer," *Fenda*, 2001, *2G International Architecture Review* 2001, *Casabella*, Italia, 2002

Great Notley Primary School
Architects: Allford Hall Monaghan Morris
Location: Black Notley, Essex, United Kingdom
Project Type: New Building
Use of the Building: Primary School
Site Area: 1.8 ha
Building Area: Site footprint 1,044 m^2
Total Floor Area: 990 m^2
Number of Floors: 1
Height of the Building: 5.5 m maximum
Client: Essex County Council, Design Council
Structural Engineer: Atelier One
Mechanical Engineer: Atelier Ten
Other Consultants:
Quantity Surveyor: Cook & Butler Partnership
Landscape Architect: Watkins Dally
Planning Supervisor: Appleyard & Trew
Contractor: Jackson Building
Structure of the Building: Inner walls: loadbearing blockwork shear walls on strip footings / External walls: loadbearing timber stud walls / Roof: "Masonite" timber I beams
Principal Exterior Material: Walls: Western Red Cedar cladding with marine plywood "Plimsoll Line" / Roof: "Green" roof system
Principal Interior Material: Walls: Painted plaster finish / Ceiling: Birch-faced plywood / Floor: "Plyboo" bamboo flooring
Period: 03. 1997 - 09. 1999
Awards: Civic Trust Award 2001, RIBA Award for Architecture 2000, RIBA Sustainability Award, Royal Fine Arts Commission Trust Award-School Building of the Year 2000, CIBSE Award for Innovation, Millennium Product Status, Egan Demonstration Project, Construction Industry Award
Publications: *Architects' Journal* November 1999, *RIBA journal* July 2000

St Paul's Bus Station
Architects: Allford Hall Monaghan Morris
Location: Walsall, West Midlands, United Kingdom
Project Type: New Build
Use of the Building: Bus Station and public square
Site Area: 9,470m^2
Building Area: Main Canopy area: 3,171m^2
Number of Floors: Main bus station: 1, Concourse Building: 2
Height of the Building: 8.7 m maximum
Client: Centro
Structural Engineer: Atelier One
Mechanical Engineer: Atelier Ten
Other Consultants:
Quantity Surveyor: Appleyard & Trew
Civil Engineer: Clark Smith Partnership
Planning Supervisor: Appleyard & Trew
Landscape Architect: Watkins:Dally
Public Artists: Tanya Kovats, Alex Hartley
Contractor: Shepherd Construction
Structure of the Building: Main canopy: Reinforced concrete canopy supported on 12 steel "tree" columns and concrete shear walls / Satellite canopy: Ferro cement canopy supported on 4 steel "tree" columns
Principal Exterior Material: Main canopy: Reinforced concrete-combination of fair-faced and painted finish "Green" roof system to top surface / Concourse: Glazed curtain-wall system
Principal Interior Material: Concourse Walls: Fair-faced concrete / Floors: Resin-bound aggregate
Period: 07. 1996 - 07. 2000
Awards: RIBA Award for Architecture 2001, Design Council "Innovation Stories" accreditation, Civic Trust Awards 2001
Publications: *Architects Journal* May 2001, *Architectural Review* June 2000

Telematic Landscape
Architects: Arno Brandlhuber (b&k+) / Bernd Kniess (b&k+)
Location: Hanover Expo 2000, Germany
Project Type: Exhibition Pavilion
Site Area: 1,011.24 m^2
Building Area: 1,011.24 m^2
Number of Floors: Spatial structure without clear defined floors
Height of the Building: appr. 8 m
Client: Bosch
Structural Engineer: Werner Sobek, Stuttgart
Other Consultants: Meyer Voggenreiter (Casino Container), Cologne, Rudi Frings (Global Human AG), Cologne
Structure of the Building: Steel
Principal Exterior Material: Projection screens / glass
Principal Interior Material: All materials
Period: 1998 - unrealized
Publications: *Arch+* 1999 n°148, In vitro landscape, *Verb*, architecture boogazine

New Loft Building, Kölner Brett
Architects: Arno Brandlhuber (b&k+) / Bernd Kniess (b&k+)
Location: Cologne, Germany
Project Type: Loft Building
Use of the Building: Working and living
Total Floor Area: 1,660 m^2
Number of Floors: 4
Height of the Building: 12 m
Client: Ortner, Schultze, Mertens GbR
Structural Engineer: Führer Kosch Stein, Aachen
Constructor: Peters, Aachen
Structure of the Building: Concrete, prefab concrete slabs
Principal Exterior Material: Glass, fiberglass, steel (aluminum-gold anodized)
Principal Interior Material: Concrete, oak parquet, white tiles
Period: 1997 - 2000
Awards: Cologne architecture prize 2000, Wüstenrot prize 2000, Architecture prize Zukunft Wohnen 2000
Publications: *Av monografias* 2000 n°83, *Archilab catalogue* 2001, Arch+ 2001 n°156, *Verb*, architecture boogazine

BMW Delivery and Event Center
Architects: Arno Brandlhuber (b&k+) / Bernd Kniess (b&k+)
Location: Munich, Germany
Project Type: Delivery and event center
Number of Floors: Spatial structure without clear defined floors
Client: BMW
Structure of the Building: Hybrid
Period: 2001- unrealized
Publication: *Aedes Catalogue* 2002

Indoor Carting Track, Delft
Architects: Architect Agency Cepezed B.V.
Location: Kleveringweg 18, Delft (next to exit Delft Nord/A13), The Netherlands
Project Type: Business premises
Use of the Building: Carting track incl. restaurant/meeting room
Site Area: 5,280 m^2
Building Area: 2,942 m^2
Total Floor Area: 8,700 m^2
Number of Floors: 4
Height of the Building: 10 m
Client: Innoplan B.V./Sunergy, Rotterdam
Structural Engineer: Staalbouw Vianen B.V., Vianen
Mechanical Engineer: Croon B.V., Rotterdam
Builder: ECCS B.V., Hoofddorp
Structure of the Building: Steel
Principal Exterior Material: Steel and glass
Principal Interior Material: Steel and glass
Period: 1997 - 2000
Award: National Dutch Steel Prize 2000, winner 1st prize

Austrian Academy of Science, Graz
Architects: Architect Agency Cepezed B.V.
Location: Schmiedlstrasse 6, A 8042 Graz, Austria
Use of the Building: Research building, offices/laboratory
Site Area: 5,004 m^2
Building Area: 1,684 m^2
Total Floor Area: 6,018 m^2
Number of Floors: 4
Height of the Building: 14 m
Client: Austrian Academy of Science
Structural Engineer: Ingenieursbüro Wendl, Graz
Mechanical Engineer: TB Pickl, Graz
Other Consultants: Architekturbüro Herfried Peyker, Graz
Builder: Ingenieursbüro Wendl, Graz
Structure of the Building: Steel + prefab concrete floors
Principal Exterior Material: Steel, aluminum
Principal Interior Material: Steel, glass
Period: 08. 1997 - 06. 2000

National Secretariat & distribution centre for Oxfam Wereldwinkels
Architects: evr. Architecten
Location: Gent, Flanders, Belgium
Use of the Building: Office building and warehouse
Site Area: 5,200 m^2
Building Area: 1,970 m^2
Total Floor Area: 2,540 m^2
Number of Floors: 2 (partially 3)
Height of the Building: 8.9 m
Client: Oxfam Wereldwinkels
Structural Engineer: Herman Fraeye N.V.
Mechanical Engineer: De Klerck engineering
Other Consultants: Brink, The Netherlands
Constructor: De Coene Construct
Structure of the Building: Bearing masonry, concrete, wooden joints
Principal Exterior Material: Roof tiles, red ceramic
Principal Interior Material: Wood
Period: 05. 1997 - 04. 1999
Awards: Selection "Awards for Belgian architecture 2000"

Restaurant Trädgårn
Architects: Studio Grön arkitekter ab
Location: Göteborg, Sweden
Use of the Building: Restaurant
Site Area: Central public park
Building Area: 1,763 m^2
Total Floor Area: 2,600 m^2 net
Number of Floors: 3
Height of the Building: 10 m
Client: Higab gruppen AB / The city of Gothenburg
Structural Engineer: FB engineering AB
Mechanical Engineer: FB engineering AB
Other Consultants: Vent: ÅF_RNK AB Electr. KM AB
Builder: Selmer Göteborg AB
Structure of the Building: Cast in place concrete combined with steel framework and steel columns;
Exterior walls: lightweight concrete blocks stucco on both sides
Principal Exterior Material: Siberian Larch wood
Principal Interior Material: Birch plywood and birch ribs
Period: 06. 1996 - 06. 1998
Awards: House of the year 1998, Gothemburg city prize 1998, SAR väst Prize 1998, Nominated for the 6th Mies van der Rohe Award 1999, Kasper Sahlin Price 1998
Publications: *Arkitektur* 1998 (SV), *Bygge kunst* 1998 (N), *Wallpaper* 1999 (P), *Architectura* 1999 (P), *Architectural Review* 1999 (GB), *Arquitectura Viva* 2000 (SP), *Bauvelt* 2001 (G), *Architectural Record* 2001 (USA)

Hakuou Comprehensive High School
Architects: Kazuhiro Kojima C+A
Location: Kurihara-gun, Miyagi Prefecture, Japan
Use of the Building: Comprehensive high school
Site Area: 56,300.00 m^2
Building Area: 12,405.56 m^2
Total Floor Area: 18,119.56 m^2
Number of Floors: 2
Height of the Building: 14.61 m (maximum)
Client: Miyagi prefecture
Structural Engineer: Structural Design Office Oak Inc.
Mechanical Engineer: Scientific Air-Conditioning Institute
Other Consultants: Mambo (associate architects)
Constructor: JV of Hazama, Hashimoto, and Watanabe,
JV of Nihon, Ueda, and Onodera
Structure of the Building: Reinforced concrete structure, partly steel structure
Principal Exterior Material:
Wall: exposed concrete + translucent coloured water-repellent agent /
Roof: polyvinyl sheet waterproofing /
Openings: aluminum sash
Principal Interior Material: (classrooms, laboratories, offices)
Floor: natural linoleum, polyvinyl long sheet, carpet tiles /
Ceiling: baked painted steel perforated metal sheet, plaster board
Designing Period: 08. 1997 - 03. 2001
Publications: *Shinkenchiku* May 2001 (Shinkenchiku-sha), *PLOT02* Kazuhiro Kojima (A.D.A.EDITA Tokyo, 2002)

Arts & Science College / Qatar Education City
Architects: Kazuhiro Kojima C+A
Location: Doha, Qatar
Use of the Building: Liberal arts college
Site Area: 408,030 m^2
Building Area: 14,460.5 m^2
Total Floor Area: 36,363.1 m^2
Number of Floors: 2 + 1 basement
Client: Qatar Foundation for Science and Community Development
Structural Engineer: Schematic Design: Ove Arup
Design Development/Construction

INTERNATIONAL VIEWPOINT

France erupts

Italy: Rifondazione turns left
Palestine: Israel's destructive fury
Argentina: who decides?

NEWS AND ANALYSIS FROM SOCIALISTS WORLDWIDE   MAY 2002   No 340   US$4 £2.50   5

INTERNATIONAL VIEWPOINT

CONTENTS

FRANCE
- A political earthquake — 3
- The streets erupt — 4
- LCR candidate's statement — 5
- Breakthrough for the left — 5
- LCR statements — 5, 6

ITALY
- Refounding Refondazione — 7
- PRC Congress document — 8
- The general strike — 9
- Bertinotti's speech — 10

ISRAEL/PALESTINE
- A destructive fury — 12
- Behind Israel's offensive — 13

ARGENTINA
- Luis Zamora interview — 16

VENEZUELA
- Chavez' last chance? — 22
- Interview: Douglas Bravo — 23

SPAIN
- PCE Congress — 25
- Crisis in the CC.OO — 27

RUSSIA
- Signs of change — 28

EUROPE
- EU enlargement — 32

OBITUARY
- Ross Dowson — 35

INTERNATIONAL VIEWPOINT is a monthly review of news and analysis published under the auspices of the United Secretariat of the Fourth International, in conjunction with the French-language INPRECOR. Signed articles do not necessarily represent the views of the editors.
News closing date May 5th

Editorial office:
PO Box 112, Manchester M12 5DW, Britain.
Email: International_Viewpoint@compuserve.com
Printer: Ioannis Kotsatsos & Cia, Marinou Antipa 4, 163 46 Ilioupoli, Greece
Designer: Ed Fredenburgh

ISSN 1294 2925   ISSUE 340 MAY 2002

To our readers...

THIS ISSUE OF INTERNATIONAL VIEWPOINT is dominated by three themes - the dramatic political events in France, the congress of the Italian Party of Communist Refoundation (Rifondazione Comunista) and the Israeli war against the Palestinians.

The first round of French presidential elections threw all the political cards in the air. Coverage in the mainstream media world-wide has been dominated by the success of Le Pen, but much less so by the dramatic electoral success of the far left.

- The results of Olivier Besancenot of the Ligue Communiste Revolutionnaire and Arlette Laguiller of Lutte Ouvriere, who together won more than 10% of the vote, have shocked the French political establishment as much as the success of Le Pen.

The presence of Le Pen in the second round of the presidential elections provoked an extraordinary mobilisation of the workers' movement and young people, culminating with the huge demonstration on May Day in Paris. The forces of racism and reaction in France are very much a minority.

Both Le Pen's advance and the far left breakthrough are a result of the crisis of the traditional government left parties - the Socialist Party and the Communist Party (PCF). This in turn represents the complete disillusionment of large sectors of the population with the neoliberal policies which the Jospin government pursued. For the PCF the result is a catastrophe which puts the very survival of this party in question.

The crisis of the 'centre-left' is not just a French phenomenon. It led last year directly to the election of the 'savage neoliberal' Berlusconi government in Italy. Berlusconi's attempt to reform the labour law, making sackings much easier, has provoked a giant mobilisation of the Italian popular masses, including the two-million strong March demonstration in Rome, and the one-day general strike in April.

As the centre-left goes into crisis, the question posed for the militant left is how to construct a viable political alternative, which can have an impact at the level of mass politics - in elections as well as in the mass struggles. This is the question with which the leadership of Rifondazione around Fausto Bertinotti has been grappling. As our coverage shows, for the moment the party is steering left and staking a lot on the growing movement against neoliberal globalization.

Since the Genoa anti-capitalist demonstrations last year, Rifondazione has been at the centre of all the mass mobilisations in Italy. The future of this militant yet pluralist party is of vital interest to socialists internationally. We shall continue to cover its evolution in detail.

Israel's murderous assault on the Palestinians has provoked outrage world-wide. As Tikva Honig-Parnass explains, in Israel there is now open discussion about permanently expelling the Palestinians from the West Bank. This would represent the fulfilment of the most extreme Zionist position, for the creation of a 'Greater Israel'. Tikva's article explains the relationship of Israeli actions to the regional plans of the United States, the situation of the Palestinian national movement and the role of the Palestinians within Israel.

Finally, this issue is the first using our new design. This is part of our push to professionalize the magazine and make it more accessible. IV is the only English-language magazine which regularly presents the voices of revolutionary Marxists from across the continents. We ask all our readers to help us get the magazine more widely distributed and read. □

A political earthquake

Francois Duval

PHOTO: Olivier Besancenot and LCR demonstrating against Le Pen

The first round of the French presidential election provoked a real trauma, particularly among the masses and traditional left supporters. The constitutional rules for this election mean that only the two candidates who top the poll go through to the second round. Thus the final election will be a run off between outgoing president Jacques Chirac, a particularly corrupt rightwing figure, and Jean-Marie Le Pen, representative of the racist and fascist far right. Lionel Jospin, the outgoing Prime Minister and Socialist Party candidate, got a few hundred thousand votes less than Le Pen. He was thus eliminated from the second round.

Bankruptcy of the traditional left

This unexpected situation should not hide some other lessons of the 21st April election. First of all, there was a high rate of abstention (27.8%), the highest since the introduction of direct elections for the president. Second, we saw the collapse of the Communist Party, which has been in the government led by Jospin for the last 5 years: it got just 3.7% of the vote. Third, a historic phenomenon: the CP was overtaken by two revolutionary far left candidates. Arlette Laguiller for Lutte Ouvriere got 5.7% of the vote and Olivier Besancenot, candidate of the Ligue Communiste Revolutionnaire (LCR-French section of the Fourth International) got 4.3%, that is 1.2 million votes.

Widespread abstentionism, like the collapse of the parties that had been in government (with the notable exception of the Greens who succeeded in bringing out their differences with social democracy), bear witness to a widespread phenomenon. There is a clear rejection of the policies of austerity and social injustice implemented over the last few years, and discredit of the parties that implemented this. Opinion polls published during the campaign showed that three quarters of the electorate had difficulty in telling the difference between the political programmes of Chirac and Jospin.

The EU summit in Barcelona a few weeks before the election deepened this inability to tell the difference. Chirac and Jospin, in partnership, accepted the privatisation of the Electricite de France (a state company which still has the monopoly on the supply of electricity), the raising of the retirement age by five years, and a commitment to reduce the public deficit, which means budgetary austerity in the years to come.

This confusion, already very strong on social and economic questions, worsened with the eruption into the election campaign of the "law and order" or "insecurity" question. Chirac made it his central theme in order to highlight his difference with the left, supposedly more "lax", at least so he thought. But most of the candidates, right and left, rushed onto this slippery slope.

Jean-Pierre Chevenement was not slow to up the stakes But very rapidly Jospin followed him. During the campaign only Noel Mamere, the Greens' candidate, and in particular Olivier Besancenot, refused to give in to this pressure and abandon the defence of democratic freedoms or criminalise young people.

What was the result? There was a huge wave of law and order demagogy under the slogan "zero tolerance", young people from the underprivileged suburbs, in particular of immigrant descent, being implicitly or explicitly held responsible. Le Pen, whose linking of law and order to immigration has been his stock in trade for thirty years, only had to pick up the winnings.

Both the elimination of the parliamentary left from the second round of the presidential election and the strengthening of the racist far right, are obviously defeats for the workers' movement in France. They will obviously encourage wide-spread soul-searching and a discussion on future perspectives for the entire left: the parliamentary left parties, trade unions, associations and the radical left: how did we get here; how can we prepare the fightback, on a political and social level; how can we regain ground?

LCR chooses its candidate

These elections also showed that, despite the failure of the free-market left, another left exists, not only in the social movements and in the electoral arena. That is the starting point for rebuilding. This presidential election also showed that the radical left, the non-free-market left, the left that defends the interests of workers and different layers of oppressed in society, exists mainly through two organisations: Lutte Ouvriere and the LCR. The LCR was always conscious of this situation and the responsibilities of activists who identify with a revolutionary perspective. This is why the LCR proposed to Lutte Ouvriere to make a political agreement on joint candidates in the presidential and parliamentary elections, to offer the strongest possible alternative for people who did not want to vote for the traditional left. Of course, this was not to deny the major differences that exist between the LCR and LO but to make it possible for them to exist in a common framework that would not harm the political struggle on major questions that clearly differentiate revolutionary left organisations from the free-market left. This was achieved in the European elections of 1999 where a joint LO-LCR list led to the election of five revolutionary MEPs.

Conscious of the popularity of Arlette Laguiller, the traditional candidate of Lutte Ouvriere, the LCR proposed that Arlette be the joint candidate. Lutte Ouvriere did not accept this proposal and made their own sectarian choice without even agreeing to a discussion. A national conference of the LCR, in June 2001, then decided to present one of its own leaders, Olivier Besancenot a 27-year old postal worker, and trade-union and global justice activist.

The goal was to have a candidate who would put forward an action programme of urgent demands against the bosses' offensive, which is also relayed by the "pluralist left" government and the European Union. The LCR also wanted a candidate who, like the members of the LCR, is a real activist of the global justice movement, unlike Lutte Ouvriere. For LO this movement is simply a diversion from the "real" anti-capitalist struggle. The LCR put forward a candidate brought the struggle against all forms of exploitation of oppression and of discrimination created and strengthened by capitalism, particularly of young people, women and immigrants to the centre stage.

Another goal was to propose the building of a new anti-capitalist party, to bring together not only revolutionaries but all those who reject the barbarism of capitalism, members of the SP, CP and Greens who no longer who identify with the governmental left and above all the tens of thousands of activists from the trade-unions and associations who today no longer have any party political reference point, after the collapse of the Communist Party and the betrayals of the Socialist Party.

FRANCE

Our goal in choosing Olivier Besancenot was also to bring a new element into political life, by offering millions of people the possibility to vote for someone who is not a professional politician but, like themselves, a wage worker, who has the same pay slip as they do, and who, once the elections were over, would find himself like them...back at work. It was also a question of speaking to young people, presenting somebody unknown but in step with their struggles, whether the mobilisations against capitalist globalisation or against casualised labour which are growing in France today in big retail firms such as the FNAC book and record shop chain or MacDonald's. This wager was in large part successful. It was among the youngest electors that Olivier got his best scores (13.9% of 18-24 year olds, and 6.3% of 25-34 year olds according to certain breakdowns).

This campaign, waged under the slogan "Our lives are worth more than their profits" enabled the LCR to speak to a far wider audience than usual. In a few months of campaigning, the European members of parliament, Alain Krivine and Roseline Vacchetta, and above all Olivier Besancenot, spoke at a hundred public meetings attended by more than 25,000 people, mostly workers and young people. We had not seen this for more than thirty years!

In the last three weeks, after the 500 sponsorships were deposited and Olivier was at last invited by the major television channels, this unknown candidate made a breakthrough. The numbers attending meetings reached record levels, hundreds of messages of support and encouragement and asking to join the LCR were received every day. This increased after the results of the first round were announced.

The electoral success has obviously changed the LCR's relationship with the workers' movement, the social movements and with the other organisations on the left and far left. First effect: LO has agreed to meet the LCR to discuss the possibility of an electoral agreement for the parliamentary elections in June. It is too early to know if the outcome will be positive. But the mere fact that there will be such a meeting shows that something has changed on the far left.

Building a leftwing of the left

The current situation, shaped by the crisis of the traditional left, the threat of the far right and the rise of the far left, confers new responsibilities on revolutionaries. First of all we must be the spearhead of the mobilisation against the far right, which has been growing notably among young people since the 21st April. The LCR has been at the forefront of these demonstrations. Then we have to prepare the conditions for a massive response to the offensive that is in preparation, whoever is going to constitute the next parliamentary majority, against social security, public services and democratic rights, particularly for immigrants.

Then we must develop a perspective for emerging from this unprecedented crisis, a perspective that gives a new hope to a traumatised workers' movement. Moving towards a new party capable of responding, refounding a fighting left, rehabilitating the project of revolutionary transformation of society, will not be easy. The results of the far left in general, and of the LCR candidate in particular, do not in themselves resolve this problem. But they make the conditions a lot more favourable than in the past. This is the task the LCR sets itself in the period to come. Paris 25th April 2002. □

WHO VOTED FOR OLIVIER BESANCENOT?

Young people. In the 18-24 age group Besancenot was the second most popular candidate with 13.9% of their votes to Chirac's 15.7%, and unlike Arlette Laguiller who got only 1.8% of the youth vote and scored best with 35-49 year olds, of whom 9.1% voted for her. He did best with white-collar workers, teachers and other public service employees (around 6% in all these categories) and his electorate was fairly evenly divided between women (4%) and men (4.7%).

The streets erupt

Dominique Mezzi

Since Sunday April 21, 2002 a massive movement, essentially made up of young people, has erupted onto the streets of France. Organizations like the anti-fascist network Ras l'Front, the LCR, sometimes the MJS and the JC (youth organizations of the Socialist Party and the Communist Party) as well as networks organizing through the Internet sounded the alarm that evening, and college and high school students in particular have responded in their thousands.

According to AFP, 100,000 people demonstrated on the Monday following the first round election. The demonstrations continued in the days that followed. Typically, actions were initiated from a high school, technical college or university faculty and spread from there: that was the scenario in Lille, Lyon, Rennes and elsewhere. In the evening, the two components merged, the youth and the networks of activists, trades unionists, Besancenot voters, or those who had voted for Mamère, Laguiller, Hue or even Jospin.

In Paris, Ras l'Front called the first action, on Sunday at 10 p.m. Supported by the LCR, the young socialists, the Greens, the gathering had swelled to 20,000 by the time it reached the place de la Bastille. The CP and Lutte Ouvriere were absent on this occasion although they supported the Monday evening demonstration (15,000). Demonstrations have taken place in cities,

FRANCE

towns and even villages up and down the country, often on the initiative of the LCR, with varying support locally from political organizations (the far left, the Greens, the PCF, sometimes the Socialist Party), trade unions, anti-racist organisations and feminist groups. The culminating point was on May Day where a massive demonstration in Paris and other in cities all over the country mobilized almost two million people in a clear rejection of Le Pen from a clearly left and trade-union standpoint.

In some towns, a slogan is raised which expresses a widespread sentiment: 'Votez escroc, pas facho!' ['vote for the crook, not the fascist'] The media have tried to focus attention to those who say: 'I voted Besancenot for fun but now I regret it.' But the overwhelming sentiment is to stop Le Pen, including by a vote, but to maintain the mobilizations. And all parties on the left, including even the Socialist Party, but notably the LCR, are receiving a flood of requests from people who want to join, rejoin, or in some other way be linked to organized political activity.

This massive reaction is the first step in a new wave of radicalization that will have an important impact in France. □

LCR STATEMENT 5TH MAY 2002

A huge popular mobilisation, in the streets and in the polling stations, has blocked Le Pen at the level of the far right votes of the first round.

This is not a plebiscite for Chirac's anti-social, law and order policies.. Starting this evening we must preapre a massive mobilisation against the proposals of the right and the bosses' organisation, the MEDEF.

We cannot rely for this on the forces of the "pluralist left" whose governmental policies led us to this calamitous situation. Only a radical left with a social action programme can offer a perspective of social transformation in opposition to the plans of the right and making a balance sheet of the 5 years of the "pluralist left" in government. This is also the only alternative which could put a definitive stop to the rise of the far right.

Candidates defending these positions will be standing everywhere during the parliamentary elections in June.

Political Bureau LCR, 5th May 2002 at 8 pm

(Unofficial figures at 8pm:
81% Chirac, 19% Le Pen 19 % abstentions 4% spolit and blank votes)

Statement by Olivier Besancenot, LCR presidential candidate, April 21, 2002

Tonight there has been a political earthquake in this country. It is a victory for the worst enemies of the wage earners and of youth. The Front National is a current that represents a direct continuity with Vichy, fascism and the Nazi crimes of World War II. Tonight I share the sadness of millions of people in the face of this advance of the far right, in particular the millions of immigrants who live in our country.

This is the result of the campaign waged by Chirac and the right – and accepted by Jospin – on the question of 'insecurity'. It is also the result of the policies of the governing 'plural left' which has dramatically cut itself off from the popular classes.

At the same time, these elections indicate a change in the relationship of forces on the left, with more than 10% for the far left: Lutte Ouvriere and the LCR.

I would like to thank the 4.3% of electors who voted for my candidacy, the candidacy of somebody who shares their concerns and their hopes.

The multiplicity of candidates on the left is not responsible for the rise of the far right; it is rather the policies followed by successive governments for some years that are responsible.

Now we have to re-establish hope on the left. First by relying on the forces of renewal which have expressed themselves, in the candidatures of LO and the LCR – organisations which have special responsibilities in this new situation.

Hope lies also in the youth who are massively resisting capitalist globalization and fascism. I ask all the electors of the left, Socialists, Communists, ecologists, but also the community and trade union activists, to organise a popular resistance to the rise of the far right, all together against fascism and the employers.

Historic breakthrough for the far left

Léonce Aguirre

The score of the far left in the first round of the French presidential election is a major political event even if it has been relativized by the electoral success of the Front National.

The mobilisations against the far right and the preparation of a response to the coming attacks on pensions and public services, as well as the upcoming parliamentary elections, present the opportunity to consolidate and build on this result.

Two political earthquakes took place at the first round of this presidential election. The first is the presence of the Front National in the second round. It has relegated to the second level the other earthquake; the fact that the results of the far left exceeded 10%. And if the presence of Le Pen in the second round is effectively the major political element of this election which upsets the traditional political chessboard, and demands a unitary and immediate mobilisation to bar his road – we should not minimise the achievement of the far left and its political impact.

With 10.4%, its results were more than triple those of the PCF and almost equivalent to the sum of the PCF, Green Party and Movement of Left Radicals vote. This electoral influence was not limited to certain departments or regions but was nationwide in scope. With the exception of the DOM-TOM [France's overseas territories] the scores in every department were higher than the 5.3% obtained by Arlette Laguiller in the 1995 presidential election. In 16 departments, the far left exceeded 12% with the best results in Haute-Vienne (13.42%), Seine-Maritime (13.55%), Pas-de-Calais (13.56%) and Puy-de-Dôme (14.10%). In a general manner, these scores are in line with the deep phenomena of recomposition of the workers' movement that has been going on for some years.

FRANCE

Plurality of the far left

If some polls indicated that the far left could reach or even exceed 10%, the division of the electorate between the LCR and LO, up until three weeks before the ballot, indicated a relationship of between 1:5 and 1:10.

The two last weeks of the campaign substantially modified this relationship, to the extent that Olivier Besancenot received 4.23% of the vote and Arlette Laguiller 5.72%. And even if the respective electorates of the two far left organisations do not coincide exactly, it is obvious that a substantial part of the 10% of voting intentions that the polls had called for Arlette Laguiller went to the LCR candidate.

The breadth of this phenomenon is all the more important in that the latter was totally unknown – the LCR had not contested the presidential election in its own right since 1974 – whereas Arlette Laguiller was candidate for the fifth time, benefiting from the start from popular recognition, electoral capital and substantial goodwill.

This result shows, if it was necessary, that the far left is plural. Any attempt at hegemonism is not only vain but constitutes an obstacle to the unity of the diverse components of the far left. Lutte Ouvrière's decision to reject a common candidacy was certainly in part determined by the appreciation that this campaign could allow it to exert a political hegemony on the far left, either because the LCR would not succeed in gaining the 500 sponsorships or because there would be a substantial electoral gap between the two organisations.

Neither happened, and in the immediate it would be better to return to the spirit of the European electoral campaign of 1999 rather than seek false justifications concerning the allegedly petty bourgeois nature of those who voted for Besancenot (as implied in Arlette Laguiller's statement following the first round). For our part, we rejoice at the score of our candidate but also that of the whole of the far left, because it clearly expresses a rejection of the policies followed by the government of the plural left and the search for an anti-capitalist alternative.

That goes also for at least some of those who voted for Daniel Gluckstein, [candidate of the (Lambertiste) Parti des Travailleurs], although in the case of this organisation, its total absence from the social movement or any framework of unitary mobilisation, together with its manipulative and sectarian political practices, render any unitary approach more problematic.

A major political responsibility

The success of the far left should not lead us to fall into triumphalism or smug and sterile self-satisfaction. Some hundreds of thousands of workers and youth look to us today. The LCR and Lutte Ouvrière have immediate particular responsibilities that will be discussed in the framework of a joint meeting scheduled for the coming days. Our tasks: to be the spearhead of the necessary mobilisation against the Front National and the far right without falling into the trap of the republican front; to prepare the conditions of a massive unitary mobilisation to counteract the anti-worker offensive that is being prepared by the Medef [the employers' federation] and the next government on social security, pensions, the dismantling and privatisation of public services; and the challenge to democratic rights.

Finally, the unprecedented crisis of the traditional workers' movement and the Communist Party in particular, poses objectively the question of the construction of a new anti-capitalist workers' party. There is no royal road to advance in this direction, but politics abhors a vacuum and if we do not seize all our opportunities, the reformist leaderships will take the initiative and occupy the terrain.

These are the stakes, and they are sizeable. ☐

Statement adopted by LCR Central Committee

Bar the road to Le Pen in the streets and in the elections! On May 5, vote against Le Pen!

For a week now demonstrations against Le Pen and the Front National have continued. Hundreds of thousands of young people are expressing their anger against the far right.

● Le Pen is a fascist. He claims to be the defender of the 'small people' but he is a millionaire demagogue who defends the rich and powerful. He wants to increase the givebacks to the bosses, liquidate social and democratic rights, send women back to the home and expel immigrants.

● Le Pen's score is the result of the campaign around 'insecurity' unleashed by Chirac and the right and accepted by Jospin, but it is also the consequence of the policies followed for 20 years by successive governments. The plural left, by adapting to neoliberalism and capitulating to the Medef, has turned its back on popular aspirations.

The right prepares its attack

● Le Pen's road must be barred by any means possible, through mobilisations and in the elections; but a radical political change is also needed in the country. Among wage earners, among the unemployed, in the popular neighbourhoods, among all those who feel themselves despised, laid off, without a decent income, without rights, too many setbacks have been suffered, and too many promises have not been fulfilled.

● Chirac is not a rampart against the far right. Already, he is preparing the recuperation of Le Pen's voters by combinations with the ultra right, the likes of Millon, Soisson and company... He is preparing, from his election, attacks against wage earners, youth and immigrants.

For a new anti-capitalist force in the service of workers and youth!

The parties of the governmental left have been punished by the popular electorate. The leaders of the plural left cannot be relied upon to genuinely oppose neoliberalism. It is necessary to rebuild a new hope for millions of young people and wage earners.

● A new anti-capitalist political force is needed. A force of combat, intransigent against the far right, the right and the bosses. A force which draws the lessons of the bankruptcy of the traditional left.

● Millions of electors have voted for the far left, notably for Olivier Besancenot, the LCR candidate, and Arlette Laguiller.

● We are ready to open a new road, with all those who occupy the street, with the new generation which is often getting involved in politics for the first time, with the activists in the social, trade union and community movements, with the Communists, Socialists and ecologists who seek an alternative to the governmental left. We want a new political force, 100% on the left.

● Yes, we must bar the road to Le Pen, through demonstrations against the Front National in the street, the neighbourhoods, and the workplaces. On May 1, hundreds of thousands of wage earners and youth will demonstrate against Le Pen and for their demands.

On May 5, vote against Le Pen!

Through this mobilisation, we prepare a huge social movement, as in the strikes of May 1968 or winter 1995, all together against unemployment, poverty, inequality, for the defence of social and democratic rights, for another division of wealth, an anti-capitalist policy which is radically opposed to the bosses, a politics which is 100% on the left.

Time for a general mobilisation! ☐

The Fifth Congress of the Italian Partito della Rifondazione Comunista (PRC) which took place in Rimini from April 4th-7th 2002 was an extraordinary event, which cemented the transformation of the party that has been taking place over the last year. Through its key involvement in the massive demonstrations in Genoa and the consolidation of Social Forums across Italy, the PRC has not only championed the anti-globalization cause but at the same time questioned key aspects of the political tradition from which the majority of its members come. At a moment when the old European Communist Parties are reeling from the rout of the PCF in the first round of the French Presidential Elections, a discussion on the way the PRC under the leadership of Fausto Bertinotti has made this shift could not be more timely. In the pages that follow, Livio Maitan assesses the key dynamics of the Congress and we carry major extracts from Bertinotti's speech together with shorter extracts from the main Congress resolution. We also carry an article on the extraordinary general strike on April 16, in which once again the PRC played an important role

ITALY: Refounding Rifondazione
Livio Maitan*

At its fifth congress since its foundation in 1991, Italy's Party of Communist Refoundation confirmed its specific, indeed unique, character in the history of the Italian workers' movement. It would today be difficult to find its equivalent not only among the parties of the European left, but also among those parties which identify with the working class and socialism in Europe and other continents.

The choice of slogan for this congress – Refoundation – could at first blush appear as a tiresome cliché. In fact, it amounted to an admission and indicated a goal: refoundation had not yet taken place and it was necessary to undertake it now.

In 1991, when the party was born, it was necessary to reaffirm a primordial demand: to continue the struggle of the workers' movement under the banner of Communism. However, in spite of the good intentions expressed in the new party's adoption of its name, and in spite of the analyses and concepts introduced in the texts of the four congresses from 1991 to 1999, a refoundation in the widest sense of the word did not take place at the level of theoretical and strategic definitions. Still less did it take place at the level of the political practice and consciousness of a good part of its membership. The PRC's subsequent political choices and divisions have been a striking confirmation of this.

The party's first major crisis came in early 1995 when, after the fall of the first centre-right government, the problem was posed of an eventual participation in the heterogeneous coalition led by Lamberto Dini, a former Berlusconi minister. On this occasion the party lost a majority of its parliamentarians and its national secretary Sergio Garavini, who had been elected at the founding congress. After the 1996 elections, the party descended into sterilising support for the Prodi government – something it paid for heavily in electoral setbacks in the following years. Then, in autumn 1998, Bertinotti, observing the drift of the centre-left coalition, proposed that the PRC abandon the parliamentary majority. Armando Cossutta, the president of the party, then took the initiative of a second split, even more important than the first. It was a further confirmation that an overall reflection on the strategy of the workers' movement in an anti-capitalist dynamic had not yet taken place. Neither had a reflection taken place on the nature of Stalinism and the problem of the transition to socialism.

Fausto Bertinotti should be given credit for understanding that the party risked finding itself in a dead end, foundering, indeed suffering an irreversible erosion. He decided to open a campaign against Stalinism and at the same time stimulate a strategic reflection on the basis of an up-to-date analysis of the fundamental traits and the dynamic of capitalism in an epoch of globalization. In principle, it could legitimately be said: the very fact that a campaign against Stalinism is launched more than 70 years after the struggle of the first Communist oppositionists to the bureaucratization of the Soviet Union, is revealing of the prolonged drift of the workers' movement, in Italy and elsewhere. Nevertheless, as they say, better late than never. Bertinotti's initiative is all the more praiseworthy in that it happened in a context where, at the international level, the reaffirmation of an anti-capitalist, socialist perspective remains difficult despite the growing contradictions of the system and the rise of new oppositional movements.

We will not go back over the themes raised in the texts submitted for debate at the congress[1]. We should recall that last November the National Political Committee (NPC) had adopted by a large majority, draft theses to which a historic minority had opposed an alternative overall text[2]. But the new reality had been the emergence inside the outgoing majority of a significant differentiation leading to the presentation of four amendments by a notable minority of the NPC, the national leadership and two members of the Secretariat. These amendments concerned the question of imperialism (the minorities reject the argument of the theses that the classical notion of imperialism should be transcended); the characterisation of the movement against neoliberal globalization and the relationship between the party and the movements (the minority argue that the majority blurred the centrality of the capital-labour conflict and slid towards a dilution of the party in the movement); the assessment of the history of the Communist movement (according to the minority, the majority's verdict was over-negative); the self-reform of the party (the minority held, in the view of the majority, an over-traditionalist approach)[3].

It would be abusive to characterise the partisans of these amendments as 'Stalinist' or 'neo-Stalinist'; Stalinists in the strict sense only represent a completely marginal fringe of the party. We could more pertinently qualify them as 'continuists', for they identify above all with the traditions and conceptions of the old PCI. It is on this subject that the majority text has often been the target of criticisms. More generally, those who defended of the amendments adopted different attitudes in the debate, with oscillations in the course of a single meeting; they have sometimes tried to minimise their divergences with the majority; at other times they have vehemently denounced the supposedly liquidationist tendencies of the latter[4].

Stalinism and communism incompatible

At the national congress the different alignments did not change. It should nonetheless be stressed that Bertinotti has sharpened his critique of Stalinism, and advocated innovation still more vigorously. Replying to Claudio Grassi, a member of the outgoing Secretariat and a supporter of the amendments, he affirmed that Stalinism was incompatible with Communism. He also rejected the theory of socialism in one country and, in relation to the criticisms of Stalin made at the 20th congress of the CPSU, he recalled that other currents had opposed Stalinism much earlier[5].

The election of the new NPC was marked by two

difficulties: its size had to be reduced from more than 350 to 135 members – a completely rational reduction, but problematic – while respecting the statutory quota of at least 40% women. There was another complication: while the proportional distribution of seats between supporters of the majority text and partisans of the alternative was obvious enough, things were much more complicated concerning the representation of those who had put forward amendments. Finally, the list was adopted thanks to some draconian measures – like the exclusion of parliamentarians (although the presidents of the two groups will be permanently seated at all levels) – with 350 votes for, 120 against, and 12 abstentions (out of 549 who were able to vote). Bertinotti was re-elected secretary by the NPC, with 105 votes against 13 for Ferrando, candidate of the alternative text, and two abstentions[6].

The majority who supported Bertinotti enjoyed an undoubted political success, which should also have international repercussions. Nevertheless, it would be a great error to underestimate the gap between the adoption of a line by a congress and its translation into practice. Bertinotti himself stressed once again the persistent and grave weaknesses of the party. In addition, it is a negative note that, for such an important event, only a little over 30% of members attended their local congresses to vote. Moreover, our own direct experience allows us to note the extent to which the majority which supports Bertinotti is heterogeneous, leaving aside differences which have long been out in the open. So the majority is far from relaxed: all the more so in that this majority current only enjoys a relative majority in two of the four most important cities (Milan and Turin).

The renewal of the PRC embarked upon at the congress can only be realised on two conditions. The first only depends partially on us: this is, that the so-called movement against neoliberal globalization maintains itself, indeed develops, under its current forms or under other forms, which today seems very possible. The second condition is that the composition of the party changes substantially through the influx of the new generations. Recently the PRC has recruited many youth: in the near future, these new recruits must acquire a determinant specific weight, and mature in and gain experience from the mass movements. What is more, it is crucial that the youth are immunised against the insidious poisons produced by the perverse mechanisms of functioning which have subsisted, despite everything during the preparatory congresses and in the national congress itself. This is the key political-organisational question, which is in the last analysis decisive.

NOTES

* Livio Maitan, a leader of the Fourth International, was re-elected to the National Political Committee of the PRC at this Congress.

1 See IV 336, December 2001, which contains extracts from Fausto Bertinotti's report opening the debate for this congress (the general line of this report was adopted by the majority of delegates) and extracts from the resolution adopted at this congress.

2 This minority was also present at the 4th congress. At the 3rd congress it was part of a bigger minority, which also involved, supporters of the magazine Bandiera Rossa (Fourth International), based on rejection of support for the Prodi government.
Liberazione summed up thus the intervention of its main spokesperson: "Marco Ferrando put forward a clear rejection of any opening of the PRC to the centre-left. In his view the Olive Tree is only a different form of political organisation of the bourgeoisie. Only the emancipation of the movement from the Olive Tree could defeat Berlusconi: concrete results would only be obtained through radical struggle. The experience of Argentina refutes the categories of the anti-globalization movement, which should not be presented as a myth. It is not about demanding the Tobin tax or advocating non-violence, but of starting from the counter power of the masses. An Olive Tree government would only be a new neoliberal government: the only government in which the Communists could participate is a government based on the workers and their power."
This current, which has chosen to marginalize itself in relation to the process of historic transformation in the PRC, allies a sectarian vision of the anti-globalization movement with accusations against the PRC majority based on an assessment of the Olive Tree that this majority in fact shares. Its draft resolution obtained 13.7% of votes.

3 A much more restrained minority, concentrated mainly in Lombardy, presented amendments advocating a more flexible attitude to the Left Democrats (DS). In some cases, these amendments were also voted for by the partisans of the four amendments mentioned.

4 A ruling according to which votes on the alternative texts could only be expressed at the level of local branches whereas the amendments could be presented also at the provincial level and at the national congress led to some rather disreputable operations: some did not present the amendments in the branches and were elected as majority supporters and then voted for the amendments at the provincial level, in some cases overturning the majority.

5 The report which appeared in the PRC daily Liberazione left out these passages. This was not deliberate, but it remains the case that those who were not present do not know what was said.

6 The calculation of votes for the amendments was complicated in that if as a rule the delegates supported them in their entirety, in other cases there were delegates who voted one, two or three amendments and not all four. In the vote for the NPC it should be said that the partisans of the alternative text voted for, their candidates having been included on the list on a basis of strict proportionality. The alternative text won 13.7% against a little more than 15% in 1999 (4,330 votes against 5,300) and the majority text 87.28% (of which around 25% were in favour of the 'continuist' amendments).

DOCUMENT: MOTION ADOPTED BY PRC CONGRESS (EXTRACTS)

With this conference our party completes a determined and innovative step forward in the process of refounding modern thought and communist action to meet the great challenge that faces us with the deep transformations taking place in the capitalist system world-wide in the current phase of globalization.

This task is today possible precisely because the challenge of being communist in the present age has already been won.

The whole of humanity finds itself at a crossroads between the return to barbarism and the construction of an alternative society, that we continue to call Socialist.

This development and innovation in analysis and political theory are only possible if at the same time we put into effect a serious, brave and also a harsh balance sheet of the history of the communist movement of the last century and the experiences of constructing socialist societies.

Those ideas, those conflicts, those struggles, those revolutions have indelibly marked the history of humanity as for the first time the masses have been protagonists of their own destiny in this way. But in this history, that therefore we do not want to put to one side or to fossilise, mistakes took place and also horrors – those of the Stalinist age – that we must look at in order to avoid them happening again – in the present or the future.

This is an indispensable and also a possible task today, because we are facing a world-wide movement against globalization that is fighting for 'another possible world', and that therefore raises questions about the nature and the characteristics of a new society – one without exploitation, alienation and wars. This search, on the basis of a return to the basic elements and foundation of Marxist thought, must continue and be expanded and our conference is a definite contribution in this direction.

With this conference, our party proposes and effects a turn to the left. This has been made necessary by the present crisis in the process of globalization, which it is an economic, cultural and political crisis and a crisis of legitimacy, to which the capitalist system responds with a permanent state of war.

It is necessary in order to be in tune with

13 million strike against Berlusconi

Flavia D'Angeli

On April 16 2002 around 13 million Italians took part in a general strike in opposition to the social policies of the Berlusconi government.

The strike was called by the three main Italian trade-union confederations (CGIL, CISL, UIL) and by all the alternative trade unions, in particular the network of Cobas (alternative trade unions). Hundreds of thousands of people, moreover, took part the same day in multiple regional and local demonstrations, organised by the CGIL, CISL and UIL and by the social forums and the movements against neoliberal globalization. The general strike, the first for twenty years, attracted record levels of support – around 90% of workers, according to the unions.

The initiative, which had become increasingly urgent in a climate of social mobilization, was inevitable (despite the moderate leaderships of the big union confederations) after the decision of the Berlusconi government to continue its ultra-neoliberal reform of the labour code and in particular to pursue the abolition of article 18 which lays down the right to be re-employed for any worker wrongfully laid off.

Once again, and in an even more significant manner, Italian society has shown its vitality and its capacity for mobilization, with this strike coming after an impressive series of demonstrations and movements throughout the past year: Genoa, opposition to the war, the mobilization of students against the educational reforms and anti-racist demonstrations.

All this has been accompanied by a resumption of strikes and labour struggles almost everywhere in the country. Thus the general strike and the more 'traditional' mobilization of the workers to defend their own rights can link up, almost spontaneously, with the 'movement of movements', organised in the Social Forum which had also participated in the big CGIL demonstration of March 23.

On April 16, alongside the workers and the trade unions, the global justice movement participated, with the idea of a 'generalization of the general strike', and a multiplicity of local initiatives, like the occupations of temporary job agencies, colleges or universities, and a very youthful and lively presence in the trade-union demonstrations. Now a new phase is opening, where the movement must take the initiative in social mobilization, given the uncertainties of the trade-union leaderships, which are once again disposed to reopen negotiations with the government rather than to pursue the social struggle.

In this context, the idea of a referendum for the extension of article 18, to companies of less than fifteen employees, has been floated by the metalworkers' federation of the CGIL, and taken up by the PRC at the institutional level.

At the political level, the need to build a common front of opposition to the right wing government remains obvious, according to the proposal advanced by the PRC, but without losing sight of the idea that any alternative must involve a break with neoliberal policies and war. In this context of huge social effervescence, the perspective advanced by PRC leader Fausto Bertinotti on the eve of the general strike, of the construction of a European anti-capitalist left based in the social movements, becomes more credible – with the European Social Forum in Florence in November being central to this. ☐

---

the growth of the movements when, in our country in particular, we see more and more a meshing together of the movement against globalization, war and neo-liberalism, and the extraordinary upturn in the combativity of the working class movement itself.

It is necessary because of the defeat of the political project of the Centre left and the so-called third way put forward by the moderate left, which not just in Italy but on a European level, has demonstrated its total inability to face and defeat the right wing, its neo-liberal policies and its wars. We commit ourselves to these fundamental aims on all necessary and possible fronts, whether social, political, cultural or institutional, working inside the movements for their growth and participating politically at an international level. (....)

This congress reaffirms that the strategic objective of our party in the current stage is the construction of the alternative left. This objective is today possible precisely because of the growth of the social movements; the alternative left then can only be built by an interaction with and in liaison with the movements. It is not about putting together the fragments of an old political layer, but of bringing together, at the level of thought, an alternative politics and practice, from experiences of parties, associations and movements, that is of various forms of aggregation.

That is why we launch the invitation to open a constituent phase of the alternative left, by the construction of a network of stable relationships between multiple and autonomous subjects. It is a task that is all the more urgent in that the constituent phase of the movements is under way for some time. It is necessary to project different and contemporary levels of initiative, going from that of intervention in society to that of political action and theoretical reflection which will contribute to the transformation of our current scientific committee. The construction of the alternative left is a task which imposes itself already, including at a European level, where it is realistic, not just necessary, to fix concretely, on the basis of the experience of the European United Left, the objective of the construction of a new European political subject bringing together, in their political and organisational diversity, the communist and alternative forces. It is in this framework that the strengthening and innovation of the party should progress. This congress confides to us an important task: to innovate our way of thought, to act, to ensure a broader opening to society and the movements within it. (...)

We must change our modes of functioning, overcome hierarchical conceptions and practices of separation, we must privilege political initiative in relation to a simple action of propaganda or reaffirmation of identity, we must privilege in our ranks the culture of knowing how to do things rather than how to say things. ☐

ITALY

THE LEFT TURN

From the speech given by Fausto Bertinotti at the opening of the PRC Congress

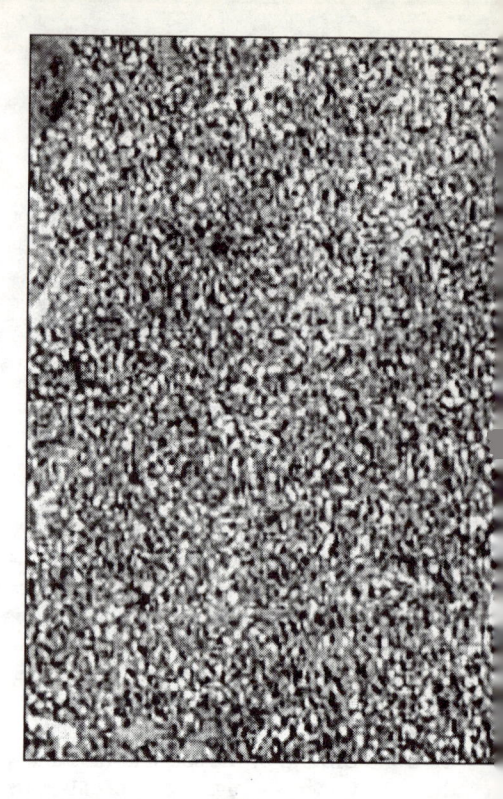

RIGHT
The 'movement of movements'
– mass demonstration
called by CGIL on 23 March

BELOW
Fausto Bertinotti at PRC Congress

In today's world there are two great antagonistic currents, two long-waves that are destined to mark the future of the humanity, of work and life. They go in opposite directions. The first is a cold current speaking the language of competition, the supremacy of the market and commodities, of the economy, of domination and war. The other, a warm current, speaks the languages of the people, of another possible world, of peace; and is critical of this economy. Our individual and collective destiny depends on which of the two prevail. Global capitalism has changed its pace and is ever more riven by the crises which it itself generates and feeds.

War is accompanied by neo-liberalism, so that capitalism marches forward unstably on these two legs. But at the same time an unknown and extraordinary movement has been born and is growing, fighting against just this neo-liberalism and war.

The spirit of Seattle gave birth to the "movement of the movements", from which have grown fights, resistance, opposition and new social experiences, and alongside this movement a diffuse and diverse criticism of globalization has taken shape.

These two contrasting currents are in conflict, with the first continuing to dominate while the second one, which contests and criticises, still has not succeeded in blocking the first or putting it into crisis or producing societal alternatives on a wide scale which could reverse the general tendency.

This is the political problem that we are facing. I am putting it sharply because we see a real possibility of transforming society, but also a serious risk that capitalist globalization will concretize the destructive tendencies latent within it.

The problem in terms of the development of the movement is to be able to construct a new political project within the necessary timescale and that can win the space, in Europe and the world that is needed to meet the challenge.

The problem is how to reconstruct the critical strength and mass to restore effectiveness to alternative politics, a politics of transformation. The political project is born from our class-based criticism of capitalist globalization and the experience of the movement. It proposes to construct an alternative social model and idea of democracy, which can also become governmental alternative, founded on the two distinctive principles of "no to war" and "no to neo-liberalism", in Italy and in Europe....

Recent attempts of reformism, so intimately connected as they are, and not coincidentally, with the dictates of capitalist globalization, show that it is completely wrong and misleading to search for a left perspective tied to the problems of a political way out in the short term and to the search for a particular rigid pattern of alliances as the basis of an alternative politics. We have made a completely different choice, to restore the primacy of politics, and to rescue politics from a subordinate role.

These two bench marks are a radical repositioning of the PRC on the left and making the social and political fight for the transformation of capitalist society a reality.

'No global' and the new workers' movement

Our relationship with the movement is the main foundation. We want to help open a new chapter in the history of the class struggle, of the fight for the liberation of women and men from exploitation and alienation....

It is important for the movement that the party made this choice – which was an innovation given our historic tradition – of discussing with others in the movement as equal partners, contributing along with others to its growth. We put forward our political ideas, but at the same time operate in a unitary manner, putting aside every propensity to vanguardism.

We are not interested in the hegemony of the party over the movement, but in contributing to the hegemony of the movement in society....

The March 23 demonstration was a great, extraordinary and new event. Without lessening the importance of the decisions of the different trade unions and the direct engagement of all the workers who took strike action, I would argue that this would not have happened in this way, on this scale and at this level of intensity, without the movement. The general strike was born out of the movement, and could not have taken place without the movement's growth....

This is not an explicitly anti-capitalist movement – at least, not at the moment. We will work for this, and we know there is a huge potential for this. This is shown in the movement's approach to the great problems of the world: war, hunger, disease, the environment. It opposes the philosophy of the globalization which it defines as neo-liberalism, and, if it does not unanimously see the roots of the problem in the capitalist mode of production, it certainly understands that they are imbedded in the social model and the system of power constructed by globalization....

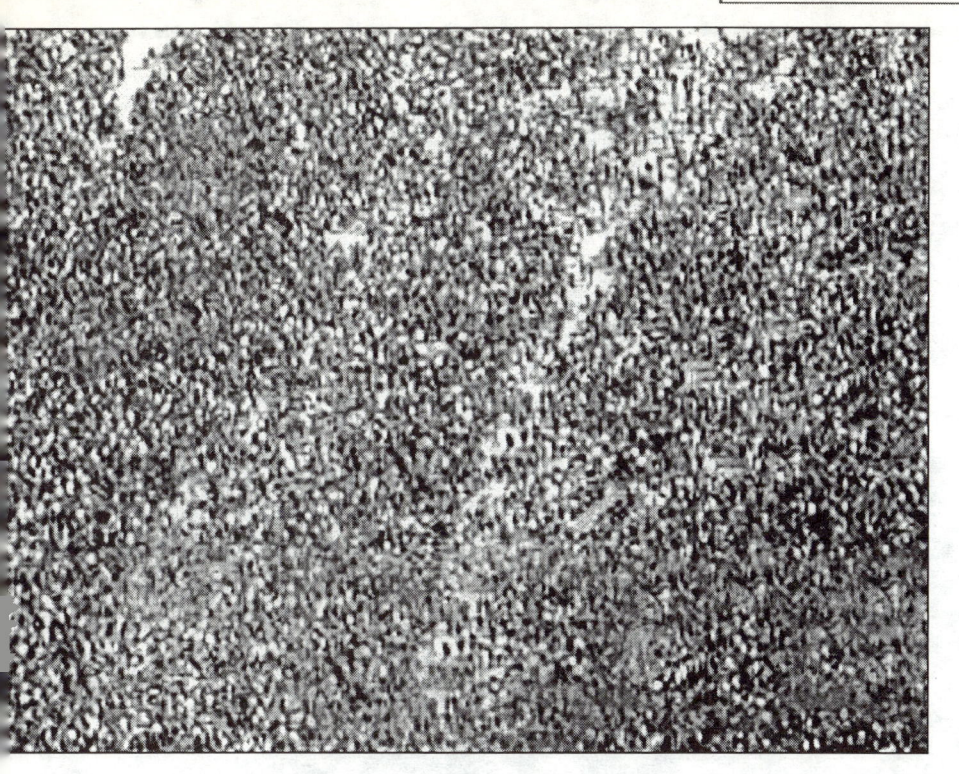

Our strategic objective is ambitious but clear: the birth of a new workers' movement. The PRC can help immediately by travelling the difficult but necessary road of finding the connections between immediate questions and longer-term perspectives, between the present and the future. The construction of an alternative platform is a defining moment in this process. An ambitious task lies ahead for the alternative forces of the left, for the movement.

A constituent process for the alternative left

The proposal that we have advanced, and which we are launching from this conference with a great sense of urgency, is to open a preparatory phase in building the alternative left in Italy.

We are not going to pretend we are the movement, whose autonomy, pluralism, ways of organising, diversity and political originality we understand as decisive for its history and its future. On the contrary the alternative left must come into being through its relationship with the movement, starting by opposing war and neo-liberalism in order to create itself as a political subject, and in an open and plural process, giving itself a visible identity and an organised shape.

We communists want to work with others who are not communist. We, as a party, want to work with those who are not in a party and do not want to become part of one, or who want one, but do not yet have it,-mutually acknowledging our differences and sharing in a joint political project. The alternative left, and ourselves as part of it, can stop being a minority and become a real actor in the public life of the country. So far, this perspective has come up against difficulties. But today it is posed anew from a twofold requirement: to exit from the crisis of politics, which will not happen spontaneously; and also from the growth of the movement and the accentuation of the social and political crisis....

The refounding of the party

The party is being subjected to formidable strains. What was not possible yesterday is today becoming possible. Resistance has ended, a new cycle of politics has begun. An opportunity is unfolding ahead of us, but also, perhaps, an extreme challenge.

The debate at this conference is another step on the road of *rifondazione*. The debate serves to clarify the positions....

For my part I have noticed that on the ideological basis of *"L'Ernesto"*[1], this magazine legitimately supported a package of amendments as the expression of a determined political position. I also noticed that most of those speakers who supported that position, expressed ever more openly a global critique of the document that I strongly support. This led to a political choice which I do not support, because it seemed to me to be a total brake on innovation – in the name of a history which is behind us, and which we are supposed to share without criticism. But that is not the case.

I see that position as a weakening of the radical character of the left turn that we are proposing. Such a weakening, a reduction, a brake, I believe, would condemn this turn to impotence.

The political choice that we propose consists, on the other hand, of radicalism and openness, exactly what is needed to seize the opportunity present in the historical moment we are witnessing today.

To put the question another way: if not now, when? I am convinced that this turn of ours, from what I can make out, has already been shown to be correct in more than one way. Without it we would not have gone through Genoa in the way that we did. With it we can now try to tackle the building of our future.

To construct it we need all the comrades, the whole of the party, its sympathizers, and also those who observe it with interest. Above all we need all the different cultures, tendencies and histories that live in the party, and we also need so many others who stand outside the party and who do not accept the existing order of things.... In this conference we have discussed everything including our joint history. We have done it not in an ideological conference, which in fact would be a good thing to do, not in a closed debate between the full timers, but in the circles, amongst the party membership, without claiming titles and science, which would not have corresponded to people's familiar cultural and political, individual or collective environment.

Stalinism is incompatible with communism

"Why," someone asks "from Livorno[2] onwards have you continued this profound and persistent settlement with Stalinism?" Because when the opponent resists, it is he who chooses the battleground and sets the hierarchy of problems, hence some negligence in the debate is always possible.

But when the chance comes again, when the possibility and the necessity to refound your politics is confronting you, then you cannot drag your feet. This time you must start from the movement itself, and seize this new opportunity with both hands as the movement has reached its highest level, posing the transformation of the society. Then you have to show that you can do both these things, showing which side you're on, how you react, the culture that you carry with you, and the idea of society that you put forward. The movement of the movements, the idea that another world is possible which for us is socialism, rise up against this capitalist modernization in name of a process of liberation of women and men. Our communism can speak the same free language if it can free itself from a big defeat that is part of our history, if it can free itself from the burden that it carries along behind it. The comrades who witnessed it, far from the epicentre, but inside a story as unique as the Italian story itself, carry the marks of it in different ways, but all with the honour of people who fought for a great cause, the democratic Republic.

But this story cannot dazzle us. Stalinism is incompatible with communism. This critique of a part of our heritage, the eradication from our rules of every form of authoritarianism and the substitution of the power of the representatives for the liberation of women and the men. This together with the fight against the idea that politics is autonomous from life, from work and from society, is part not of one struggle in the 1930s in the East, but of the 20th century in the world. ☐

1 *A political magazine published in Bologna, which organizes nationally the "orthodox"-"communist" current, led by Grassi-Burgio*

2 *The place where Bertinotti launched the real debate for the PRC congress*

Translated by Sarah Parker

ISRAEL / PALESTINE

A DESTRUCTIVE FURY

MICHEL WARSCHAWSKI

Israel today resembles a bus driven by a crazed drunk at 100 miles an hour. This bus crushes everything in its path, does not stop at any red lights and plunges straight into the abyss. We are witnessing a destructive and murderous fury that knows no limits. Ambulances and medical teams are fired on, as are churches and mosques, diplomatic convoys and journalists. US or European citizens who come to see at first hand the situation in the occupied territories are deported as if they were hooligans – and the same treatment is meted out to a European Union ministerial delegation. Men are killed by being shot through the head (at least six in Ramallah), entire streets are destroyed by shelling and missiles, with the inhabitants in their houses. Torture is practiced in the detention camps where thousands of civilians have been rounded up. How many deaths? 2,000? More?

In the refugee camp at Jenin, in any case, there has been a veritable massacre, like that in Kibyeh in 1953, like in Sabra and Chatilla in 1982. All carried out by Sharon.

What lies behind this destructive madness? As far as the government is concerned, it is the result of an ideology that mixes ultra-nationalism, hatred of Arabs and messianic fundamentalism (the presence of Shimon Peres only confirms the confusion of those elements in international social democracy who believed the Israeli Labour Party were anything other than national socialists). Their war is a holy war for *Eretz Israel*, cleansed of Arabs. As far as the Israeli people are concerned, and in particular those hundreds of thousands of men and women who, for a time, supported the peace process, it has – very easily, it should be said – been mystified by the discourse of Ehud Barak, who stated that at Camp David he had succeeded in proving the Palestinians never wanted peace with Israel, and in fact was only engaged in a subtle manoeuvre to destroy Israel. Sharon's victory was the corollary of such an argument.

It should be said and repeated: this is not a war between Israel and the Palestinians, for a war supposes two armies confronting each other, even if their forces are sometimes very unequal. Nor is it an anti-terrorist operation, because you don't dismantle networks with 30,000 soldiers, more than a thousand tanks, combat helicopters and fighter jets. What is it all about then? A punitive operation combined with a vast operation of pacification, two concepts which will be immediately familiar to all those who have experienced or studied colonialism.

The punitive operation is not a reaction to suicide bombings (it began at the end of September, well before the first such bombings), but rather to the refusal by the Palestinians and their national leadership to accept the diktats of Ehud Barak at Camp David in July 2000. To the generous offer of the Palestinians to content themselves with 22% of their historic homeland, Ehud Barak had responded with the demand to annex some 20% of Palestinian territory, to maintain a significant number of settlements and above all to impose Jewish sovereignty on the Haram al-sharif[1]. A proposal as absurd as it was unacceptable, it was seen by the Palestinians as an Israeli rejection of their historic compromise and more generally of their will for coexistence based on the realisation of UN resolutions and the principles of law.

However, the essence of the Israeli aggression is not the punitive aspect, but pacification: it is about bringing a whole people to its knees, to make it capitulate and accept the Sharon plan. For, contrary to what is often thought, Sharon has a plan: to enclose the Palestinians in the zones they inhabit, transform them into veritable Bantustans, put the finishing touches to the process of settlement in the remainder of the occupied territories (50-60%) and annex them to Israel. These Bantustans (or 'cantons' as Sharon calls them) would be governed by collaborators, put in position after the neutralisation of Yasser Arafat and the destruction of the Palestinian authority.

A crazy objective, doomed to failure because of the obstinacy of the Palestinian people who, despite thousands of deaths and the destruction of the infrastructures of their society, show absolutely no sign of capitulation. On the contrary, with the determination of those who have nothing more to lose the women and men of the West Bank and Gaza Strip continue to heroically resist Israeli violence.

That is why the murderous violence of Sharon and the Israeli army will not stop until the Palestinians surrender or another force which is still more determined than that of the far right government which leads Israel obliges it to cease its aggression, begin a withdrawal from the occupied territories and dismantle the settlements built in those territories.

ISRAEL / PALESTINE

Behind Israel's offensive

Interview with Tikva Honig-Parnass, co-editor of *Between the Lines* Jerusalem. Questions asked by Daniel Berger for German *Inprekorr*, and for *Avanti* (monthly paper of the German Socialist Organisation, the RSB)

More than 10 years ago the former Israeli chief of staff, general Dan Shomron, said that the Israeli army, before deciding on what methods to employ to break the Palestinian popular movement, should take into consideration two factors: possible international pressure and the existence of a strong internal opposition. These two factors, said the general, fixed the limits of the means of repression available to the army of occupation. These two factors have been cruelly lacking in the course of the last 18 months.

International pressure does not go beyond verbal reproaches and vague threats in the case of Europe; while since September 11 the US has given a green light to what is presented as the front line defence in the world crusade against terrorism. As for Israeli society, apart from a peace movement which is slowly waking up from a more or less active collaboration with the terrorist policies of Barak and then Sharon, it is for the moment united behind its government of national unity and its army, and genuinely believes that it is 'them or us', and that it is imperative to return to the behaviour and reflexes of the 1950s when Israel was entirely mobilised in its war against the Arab world. As if nothing had happened since the war of 1973, neither the coming of Sadat, nor the peace with Egypt, nor the Madrid Conference, nor the Oslo process, nor peace with Jordan nor the Saudi plan. A schizophrenic and murderous, but also suicidal, psychosis.

The Geneva conventions are trampled underfoot, the laws of war are violated, the norms of international civility swept aside. With complete impunity: no serious sanction has been taken by the European states. As for the US, they support Sharon, who gives an example of how to lead the crusade of the civilised world against barbarism.

Certainly, civil societies have woken up, from Rabat where 2 million people demonstrated their solidarity with the Palestinians to Berkeley, California, from Brussels where more than 15,000 demonstrated against war crimes to Noumea in New Caledonia. The European Parliament reflected this awakening in calling for economic sanctions against Israel, as did President Mubarak in recalling his ambassador from Tel Aviv. However, it is all too little and tragically late.

The murderous madness of the Sharon government and its army and the warlike schizophrenia of the majority of Israeli people demand a strong and immediate international intervention, If this latter is delayed Palestine will cease to exist, Israel will experience the fate of the combatants of Massada, and the whole Middle East will become a field of radioactive ruins. Apocalyptic exaggeration? No, it is enough to remember what happens to those who don't stop at red lights. ☐

1 *Jerusalem's Al-Aqsa mosque and environs*

Q What is the aim of the current military attack on the Palestinians?

A The current brutal military offensive of the Israeli army against the Palestinians, entitled 'Defensive Wall Operation', typical to Israel's Orwellian double talk, indicates the opening of a new stage in the long process that aims at destroying the Palestinian national movement embodied in the Intifada strugglers and 'liquidating the existence of the Palestinian people on the land of Palestine' (Haidar Abdel Shafi in an interview to Yossi Algazi, Ha'aretz, April 2). This strategic aim of the Jewish-Zionist state is in accord with the US imperialist interest in eliminating any independent nationalist regime or political movement in the Middle East (as well as in the third word in general) which by definition constitute a barrier to the capitalist globalization project in the area. The Oslo Agreement, initiated and executed by a government led by the Labour party, which represents the Israeli capitalist class, was an attempt to implement these US-Israeli aims. However, the Israeli military operation which has begun two weeks ago, signals the end of the former stage of the Oslo process.. The central assumption upon which the Bantustan plan of Oslo was founded was that the Palestinian Authority headed by Arafat, would fulfil the function of repressing any opposition to this plan, thus abolishing the Palestinian national movement and bringing about the 'Kurdization of the Palestinian question', as Azmi Bishara formerly coined the term. That assumption has proved to be wrong. The Intifada has erupted precisely because the Palestinians refused to play the role assigned to them in Oslo and to accept the humiliating proposals of Clinton and Barak at Camp David and Taba. It indicates the awakening of the national popular forces that seemed dormant during the 7 years since Oslo. During this time, the entire '67 Occupied Territories were covered with settlements and split by roads, that have been the central elements for their fragmentation into a Bantustan state.

Palestinian resistance fighters

The Intifada however, which is led by all Palestinian political organisations including Fatah and supported by almost the entire populace, marks the breaking away from the Oslo framework and the efforts to establish an alternative agenda to its 'peace negotiations', which proved to be but a cover for the continuity of the Israeli occupation. The entire people with their popular leadership which developed here and fought against the occupation, have now returned to the path of resistance, which at the same time includes critical positions towards the Tunis bourgeois, bureaucratic leadership and the authoritarian regime that has emerged under their rule.

It is this struggle for liberation that Sharon's government is determined to destroy in the current offensive. The professed aim of 'dismantling the terrorist infrastructure' has nothing to do with the premeditated, systematic demolition of the minimal infrastructural means of carrying on daily life such as PA ministries and institutions, roads, hospitals, schools and electricity and water networks and demolishing of houses of the civil population. Indeed, Israel has declared total war on the Palestinians as a civic and national entity along with a decision to finish with Arafat who has come to symbolize the national movement which is now under attack, and with the PA which is the creation of the Oslo framework.

Sharon has refused to obey the demand of US president Bush to immediately stop the operation and retreat to the areas in which Israeli troops have been situated prior to the 'Defensive Wall' operation. It seems that even the ceasefire mission of US secretary of State, Colin Powell is doomed to fail, and that he is going to let Sharon complete the operation until 'the infrastructure of terror is dismantled.' This indicates that within the parameters set by the US for Israel's polices, Israel has a relative free hand in selecting the time and methods of implementing the joint strategic goals of both states.

In the post-Oslo era, Israel is returning to a version of direct colonial rule. This time however Israel cunningly attempts to 'only take over security responsibility in Area A' (since Areas B and C - representing 82% of the West Bank - are already beneath Israeli security control) thus leaving the Palestinians to take care of their daily needs (senior political commentator Akiva Eldar, Haaretz, April 11), apparently beneath the strangling conditions Israel imposes on them. As emphasized by Sharon, this situation will continue until 'an alternative responsible Palestinian leadership will be found', which apparently can arise only after the Palestinian national movement is abolished. The opening of Sharon's government to the extreme-Right National Religious Party (now headed by the fanatic messianic Brigadier (res.) Efi Eitam who is preaching for 'Transfer' of the Palestinians), and to David Levi ('Gesher') together with the forthcoming re-entrance of the right-wing extremist Avigdor Liberman, aims at ensuring a majority in the government for the implementation of the re-conquest plan, with or without the Labour party.

Q Will the Israeli government succeed in catching or killing all the Palestinian activists/militants?

A We have to be careful not to play into Israeli hands and present the brutal onslaught on the civilian population and infrastructure, as if it is aimed only at catching the alleged 'terrorists' whom the army can identify according to a list of names at their disposal. As the Israelis themselves emphasize it is the 'terror infrastructure' they are after, which is a very blurred concept and one that includes political leaders as well as military commanders, like Maruan Barghouti (Fatah) [who was arrested after this interview] and Ahmed Sa'adat the general secretary of the Popular Front for the Liberation of Palestine (PFLP) who is currently hiding in the besieged Arafat compound. Thus the Israeli media, when announcing a number of Palestinians killed (not often), takes care to emphasize that they had been 'armed', as if the participation of civilians in defending their camp or neighbourhood justifies depicting them as 'terrorists'.

Of course, catching the 'heavy' wanted persons has been one of the aims of this military attack. Indeed according to Israeli officials, the hundreds who have been killed and the four thousand who have been arrested during the first two weeks of the invasion (one thousand of them have been released to date) include 300 wanted activists. However, the success in catching these activists and the demolition of some 'laboratories' in which weapons have been produced cannot stop the resistance, including its military operations and suicide bombers, as has been already proved by the bombing operations near Haifa and in Jerusalem, and the military attacks on settlers and soldiers which took place while the Israeli military operation continues.

A senior military command estimated that the infrastructure of 'terror' can be rebuilt in four months time and thus, as Israeli commentators emphasize, in a very short time the army is bound to reenter the Palestinian cities (which at the time these words are written, it has not yet withdrawn from) and the entire area A and commit an harsher military offensive than the present. Moreover, this may be the opportunity for Sharon to finally commit 'the big blow' which will light the fire in the North as well, and under whose pretext Israel would try to finish once and for all with the Palestinian 'problem'.

Q I suppose the long term aim of the Israeli government is to mount the pressure on the majority of the Palestinian population in order to make them 'leave the country'. Is this what the government is trying to do: Putting into practice the politics of transfer without describing it in this way?

A The policies which are aimed at making the life of the Palestinian population unbearable in order either to make them surrender or leave the country, has been adopted by all Israeli governments, both Likud and Labour. However, Sharon's plan of mass expulsion of Palestinians under the cover of 'the stormy circumstances' of the coming premeditated 'big blow', has never been pronounced publicly. Until around two years ago, the explicit call for 'transfer' has been looked upon as a 'barbaric' idea to which only the marginal messianic circles held. This is not any more the case. The unified government of Sharon-Peres has included within it the 'Transfer Party-Moledet' whose leader (Gandi) was killed by members of the military wing of the Popular Front for the Liberation of Palestine (PFLP). Also the recent entrance into the government and the 'security' cabinet of the above mentioned General (Res.) Efi

Etam who calls for transfer of Palestinians has not been considered by Labour a sufficient reason for leaving this extremist Right government.

Moreover, transfer of Palestinians has become a legitimate topic of discussion in the Israeli media and among different circle of academics and research centres. These plans include the expulsion of the Palestinian citizens of Israel as well, whose national identity and solidarity with the struggle for liberation of their brothers in the 1967 occupied territories has been strengthening rapidly. Moreover, a total change has been taking place in their political demands regarding the relations between the Palestinian minority and the Jewish-Zionist state. Inspired by the National Democratic Alliance movement (Tajamu), they no longer suffice in calling for equality in civil rights, but also demand the recognition of their collective rights as a Palestinian national minority.

This demand constitutes a genuine challenge to the definition of Israel as a 'Jewish state' which almost the entire Jewish population of Israel perceives as the essence of Zionism and which even amongst those termed 'Left' find wholehearted adherence and identification. Moreover, the prevailing interpretation of the 'Jewish state' definition is the notion of a numerical majority of Jews which is claimed to be a necessary condition for sustaining the 'Jewish identity' of Israel, and whose violation puts in danger that of the entire Jewish people. This interpretation is doomed to bring its followers, including those amongst the Zionist 'Left' who genuinely believe in the two states solution, to support policies aiming at fighting the 'demographic danger' of a Palestinian majority, through different policies of oppression aiming at encouraging Palestinians to leave, including that of 'inevitable' ethnic cleansing. (as recent articles by Israeli 'peace-seekers' Amos Oz (novelist) and Benny Morris (historian) attest).

Q Who are the potential allies for a long term policy for a real alternative? Are there political movements/organisations that can be won for such a perspective?

A At present, there are no political forces among the Jewish population in Israel which can lead the struggle against the US-Israeli colonialist project. All Jewish political parties actually represent the interests of the Ashkenazi[1] capitalist class and the Ashkenazi bourgeoisie whose hegemony has not been seriously challenged yet. Not only is there no difference between the neoliberal ideologies of Right and 'Left' but also it is precisely the Labour Party which has led the Oslo policy, that serves as their political home. The Zionist ideology with the notion of the Jewish state at its centre which constitutes the hegemonic ideology of Israel, has proved a successful tool in uniting the Jewish population, including the working class, behind the ongoing Zionist colonialist project.

The Israeli working class is split along national and ethnic lines. The Mizrahim Jews[2], who (together with the Palestinian citizens of Israel) comprise the majority of the lower layers of the proletariat lack any independent organisations that express their economic, social and cultural oppression. Their past cooptation by the Labour has been replaced by the political Right, now with the help of the false leadership of the apparent 'Mizrahi' party of Shas. The entire working class, both Jews and Palestinian Arabs lack even trade unions which fight for their minimal basic rights as workers. The past powerful Histadrut, which traditionally has served the needs of Zionism in cooperation with Jewish capital is now serving the sheer interests of 'The big Committees', which comprise largely the Ashkenazi elite of the organised working class.

What is mistakenly named the 'Left' in Israel refers only to those within the Jewish population who support a political solution to the 'Palestinian-Israeli conflict' which includes the 'concessions' of 'withdrawal to the 1967 borders' and the creation of 'a Palestinian state' - with different opinions regarding the fate of the settlements and the extent of the indirect control that Israel will have on the Palestinian entity. Most of them have wholeheartedly accepted the Oslo agreements, while ignoring the Bantustan nature of the solution which was offered by them. No real soul searching regarding the essence of Oslo has been committed by even the more 'radical' sector which constitutes a minority of the peace camp. This minority adheres to the belief that the failure of Oslo has been a result of Israel's violation of both its written articles and the 'understandings' on which Oslo was founded.

The peace camp mainly consists of Zionist Ashkenazi middle class whose fight for the 'end of occupation' and the establishment of a Palestinian state (with different meanings attributed to these slogans) are generally not contextualized or couched within any comprehensive anti-imperialist perspective, any understanding and challenge of Israel as a US client state in the region and the US as the prime supporter of the Israeli occupation. Nor are these 'Leftists' in opposition to capitalist globalization and the neo-liberal policies of Israel's economy.

For too long the anti-Zionist socialist analysis has concentrated largely on the prevailing slogans and confessed values and self images within the Israeli peace camp, as the main basis for explaining their political positions and has drawn from them alone conclusions regarding their main potential allies. Thus we too often have forgotten to insert into our analysis the basic Marxist assumptions regarding the inter-relationships between their membership in the hegemonic bourgeoisie Ashkenazi class, and their interests in keeping this hegemony through the 'Jewish state' and the Bantustan regime it would govern in the whole of historic Palestine. Their class origin as well as their Zionist ideology makes them incapable of leading the democratic struggle here, which is a condition for the implementation of Palestinian national rights. Moreover, if we stop seeing in their consciousness and declared motives, the only explanation for their political behaviour we shall find out that their European origin and class belonging which makes them benefactors of the different versions of the Bantustan solutions offered till now, is a significant factor in determining the allies they search for among the Palestinians.

Thus, even the more radical sector of the Israeli Peace camp has, till the current military offensive (which will reshuffle the relations of forces within the Palestinian leadership), been committed to the bureaucratic leadership of the PA, most of whom Arafat brought when he returned from Tunis and remain alienated from the popular strata in the refugee camps and villages, student and labourers who are the backbone of the resistance. The Israeli peace camp has preferred to disregard the rise of local leaders who represent the revived spirit of the Palestinian national movement, which embodies the seeds of social and political transformation of the corrupted autocratic regime which has emerged under the PA as well.

Q What role do the Palestinian citizens in Israel play? Are they of any importance concerning the fight for an alternative?

A The Palestinian citizens of Israel are oppressed both in national and class terms and are assigned no share in 'peace dividends' of the era of capitalist globalization of the 'New Middle East'. They have emerged as the only genuine democratic force in the Israeli political scene who seriously challenge the Jewish Zionist state. Inspired by the National Democratic Assembly party, headed by MK (member of Knesset) Azmi Bishara, they have increasingly taken a step forward from the traditional demand for 'equality of citizen rights' to that of 'collective rights as a national minority'.

This demand negates the very foundations of the Jewish state, as emphasized by ex Prime Minister Ehud Barak in the midst of the hot public debate which took place after the October 2000 militant demonstrations in which 13 Palestinian

Continued on bottom of page 16

ARGENTINA

"Permanent, uninterrupted revolution in the heads of millions"

Interview with Luis Zamora

Luis Zamora was elected as a deputy to the National Congress of Argentina in October 2001. He is a leader of the Autonomia y Libertad (AL) group.
Aldo Andres Romero interviewed him for the Argentine review *Revista Herramienta*

How would you describe the situation in the country, or more precisely the confrontations that are taking place?

A First, a completely new experience opened up and came to the surface in December, 2001. A new experience, because the popular assembly process, of debates and collective action that has taken place for two months, out of necessity, continues to rethink and reassert itself.

The weakness of the political regime has deepened. And not only in relation to the government, as expressed in the pots and pan banging demonstrations against the Court -- but in the series of incidents in the street with politicians being repudiated, insulted and harassed.

Another element is the sharpening of the internal ruptures or confrontations within the dominant class, although they have been going on for a long time, they can be seen very clearly in the last two months. But the fact or phenomenon that's most important – at the level of consciousness – or the collective subjectivity, as it's termed – is in 'people's heads'. I don't wish to counter-pose this to the actions, the stream of mobilizations leading to two new governments, but indeed to emphasize that there is a revolution, permanent and uninterrupted, going on in the heads of millions of people.

One of the slogans seen on the demonstrations states: "They should all go, none should remain". It's understandable that the politicians would be angered with this slogan and they say that it's subversive, but one can also hears supporters of the 'progressive moderates' complaining about it, saying that the slogan could possibly be exploited by the authoritarians. "They should all go" isn't only a mere expression of current circumstances, it's the cry of the streets which is yelled out with the most fervour and about which there is no discussion by those who bang their pots and pans. It's a cry and a watch-word which brings unity to the movement.

And so, as a consequence, the workers, the youth, the people who are mobilizing, will be faced with this reality. What will we do then? Will we return to a delegate system? Will we look for others, better, more honest, or whoever? Or will we go towards a structure of more direct democracy? Will we make the decisions? Will we decide?
The so-called 'progressives' are really afraid of self-determination and talk about keeping our eyes open, in case some authoritarian comes along. There is also an effort by the government and other institutions, and some of the communications media, to prevent the population from making decisions.

"Let's be careful...we will not push Duhalde out until we have an alternative", the 'progressives' say. "They shouldn't all go, we have to have someone, it's only a phrase", they say in regard to the slogans. These are the arguments of those who defend the governmental institutions. I believe it's beautiful to debate them, and in the popular neighbourhood assemblies they're being debated. I believe the question of 'uncertainty' is an argument which benefits the government and it spreads this idea, because it's their only

citizens of Israel were killed by the police:" "We, as a Jewish state, can agree to equality of individual rights of Arabs which does not harm the democratic Jewish-Zionist state. But the Jewish state cannot accept the aspiration to define another national collective identity within it, with the long run vision of 'a state of all its citizens' held by extremists".

The strengthening of the national identity of the 1948 Palestinians and their growing solidarity with their brothers' and sisters' resistance in the 1967 occupied territories, indeed may grow to be a threat to the Jewish state which is the embodiment of the Zionist movement. The question of Palestine has been for decades defined only in terms of the 1967 occupied territories (including by the majority of the Israeli 'Left'), which it is said, can be solved by the two state solution. The atomization and marginalization of the Palestinian citizens of Israel has been mistakenly taken for granted, as has been proved when they boycotted the last general elections and during the 18 months that have passed since the outbreak of the Intifada. Moreover, the assumption that underlined the very 1947 UN decision to partition Palestine that the destruction of the entire Palestinian National movement could be easily achieved, has proved false as well. Thus after more than 50 years since the establishment of the state of Israel, we have witnessed the return of the old concerns of Imperialism and Zionism that an uncontrolled uprising of a united Palestinian people in Israel and in the 1967 occupied territories will stir the oppressed masses in the Arab countries and in the entire Middle East.

This growing awareness of the false assumptions regarding the Palestinians in Israel, is the reason for the war that has been opened recently by the Israeli establishment against the Palestinian leadership and citizens within Israel, who have been defined as a 'time bomb'. No doubt, a second front has been opened by the Palestinians inside Israel against the Zionist implementation of the apartheid regime throughout historic Palestine, which may prove to be no less important than the struggle of the Palestinians in the 1967 occupied territories. That is why I have concluded that anti-Zionist internationalists and socialists among the Jewish population should support this growing genuine nationalist stream among the Palestinian citizens of Israel. Indeed, their members are not committed to class politics, or to socialist programs regarding the future of Palestine. But their nationalism should be estimated according to the only criterion that true internationalists should adopt in deciding whether any national movement is progressive, namely its challenging imperialism (which in Israel/Palestine equals the struggle against the Zionist project), as Aijaz Ahmed emphasizes in his book *Lineages of the Present* (p.300): "I have long been very suspicious of nationalism, because a great many nationalists strike me as at least very chauvinistic if not altogether fascist. But the blanket contempt for all nationalisms tends to slide over the question of imperialism. I think that they who are fighting against imperialism cannot just forego their nationalism"...

The daily struggles led by the Palestinians in Israel against the Jewish-Zionist nature of the state as well as the struggle of the 1967 Palestinians for liberation is at the same time a struggle against US imperialism in the region. Therefore joining them as well as accepting their leading role in determining the agenda of the Jewish radical circles in Israel is the most progressive democratic assignment confronting internationalists. ☐

NOTES
1 Jews of European origin
2 Jews of Niddle Eastern origin

point to justify supporting them. The 'uncertainty' argument has support in other sectors like the so-called centre-left too, but the idea is also favourable terrain for constructing something new.

Q Systematically people resist the constitutional formula: "people only deliberate and govern through their representatives". The same ones who used to close their eyes when the military violated the constitution now cannot accept that there are neighbourhood assemblies, piqueteros and the unemployed who challenge the classical criteria of parliamentary representation. But I have the impression that, for part of the left, these expressions are also uncomfortable, because these movements are not able to fill the space with the 'demand for power', even though at some point these demands may be useful. What's your opinion?

A For part of the left, there is something to this because according to my criteria, they form part of the 'system of representation'. They decry the idea of the bourgeois representative system, even though some of them will be standing in elections as 'the best representatives'. They have a conviction that electoral representation must continue. They don't really value the fundamental role of a mobilized population and of fighting, working people but they do value the role of an elected representative.

Others on the left are afraid of the possibility of the people's self-determination because it would signify that they, themselves, could be questioned about their programme and they are not prepared to give an opportunity to the people to be self-acting, unless it coincides with such a programme.

What can happen in face of a power vacuum in the country? Who will fill this vacuum? All right, as we are exploring ways to institute an alternative, we can think of a kind of parliament even though we might have a week without a government while the popular assemblies are voting for delegates (who could be replaced on a rotation basis). It's not important today what the precise slogan will be – the government falls and then we fill the vacuum according to such and such predetermined formula –what is important is to continue the practice of the popular assemblies and to put forward these ideas in the discussion. This is exciting because one could contribute right to the end in the search for something different, new and revolutionary. Why accept the minimum at this time? I don't share the characterization that some organizations have, that, "the people are ready to take the power, they wish to do it, they only lack leadership". I don't believe this matches reality.

It also seems evident to me that there is a process underway which is very rich and revolutionary. 'Revolutionary' is the way a government can immediately be pulled down, and more; but 'revolutionary' is what's happening in people's heads and in the actions during these past weeks.

We must push forward the possibilities opening up to us, possibilities that, if they develop, could permit us to attempt to go much further than has happened in many other similar situations in the twentieth century. We can advance measures that build power from below, a culture constructed from below and with a practice constructed from below, different from that of the capitalists, instead of attempting the transformation of society from above. But this implies confronting, within the left, the same problems of dogmatism, sectarianism and substitutionism.

The other day I listened to a very important leader of a traditional left organisation who said that the popular assemblies are going to end up being watered down, and that what is important is that they be channelled into the political parties; for him what is important is the party, and not the organization and construction of people's power... It's significant here that a leader of the left doesn't realize it would be a serious retreat if the popular assemblies were dissolved... The mobilization and the creativity displayed during these two months has been impressive, but we must observe that these forces from below are now competing with calls for meetings by the CTA[2] and FreNaPo[3]. At the same time the movement from below has to confront the street gangs of Duhalde, and the union bureaucracy which is looking for ways to reposition itself and is also blundering into the same sectarian methods and formalism of the organized left.

Q The measures adopted by this government since it took over don't seem to be improving the situation. Does the 'New Productivity Alliance', proclaimed by Duhalde, really exist?

A I don't believe it exists, in reality... It's true that unlike the Menem decade, when there was a plan which pleased the big bourgeoisie and imperialism, today such a plan doesn't exist. The IMF used to say: "Here's the plan, apply it, and afterwards we'll give you support." Now they say: "You present us with a plan and after that we'll talk". Apparently, the IMF doesn't seem to have plans for countries such as Argentina either. Before, they could say: "Privatize, deregulate and open up the economy!" Today they can't say this because it's ridiculous. There is nothing to privatize and nothing to deregulate...they can only demand adjustments to pay the debt...

Duhalde is working with the financial sectors and with the privatized businesses, attempting to base himself on the so-called, 'productive' sectors, saying that they'll be the engines for development. Firstly, these 'productive' sectors don't exist like that: they don't have Argentina's development as an objective. Secondly, the foreign or trans-national sectors are dominant and they're not tied to Argentina's development, but to its plunder, or, through speculation and parasitic intermediation, obtaining super profits which go outside the country. And in any case, Duhalde has not been given support by such groups to confront the financial sector, but to negotiate with it; and it's difficult to base oneself on the trans-nationals in order to blackmail other multi-nationals. And obviously Duhalde doesn't question what the imperialists tell him through the IMF or other international financial insitutions.

He negotiates with the banks, large businesses, multi-nationals and with imperialism... conceding a little to each one but not reconciling himself to any single one. But I reject the notion that there may be a project that can be based on some 'productive' sector to confront the financial sectors, and least of all, imperialism. The failure of this idea has been demonstrated over the last two months. The popular sectors not only don't support Duhalde, they mobilize against him, weakening his power even more. He doesn't have authority, and this again was clearly revealed in his discussions with the petroleum companies. I was on a television programme when Duhalde stated: "I'm not going to tolerate an increase in energy prices", when the representative of Esso who was there immediately answered back: "It's impossible not to increase prices." And then the other day Duhalde declares: "Alright, the increase wasn't much, it's reasonable." And this is what happens with everything.

Q What is the extent of the "harmonizing" that

was put forward by the Church and the United Nations?

A The 'harmonizing' has gone totally unnoticed by the population. The lack of prestige of the governmental institutions is so great that to save the political regime they have to look to the Church and the United Nations to show some kind of agreements, somewhere. However, the people are moving in an opposite direction. There is a sector of the population that is participating in actions against the government and its institutions. It is perhaps, not the majority, but the rest of the people, who do not participate actively, support it, regard it with sympathy and are in solidarity with it. This sector is questioning the banks, denounces the privatizations as doing serious harm to Argentina, and there are no important sectors of the population who dispute the speeches of those who are mobilizing. On Friday, in the Plaza de Mayo, there was some 'few thousand' there and it looked as though it would have been very easy to repress them, if the government had wished. But these 'few thousand' are accompanied by the sympathy of millions.

I remark on this to contrast it with what is happening with the 'harmonization': it has gone unnoticed, no one follows these conversations, in the popular assemblies it isn't discussed. On the other hand, it's an arena where again the divisions and the discussions in the dominant classes have become more apparent; who put their demands forward, looking to increase their share of the pie.

The Church says the same thing about them: "They behave selfishly". I believe that the Church, and I refer here to the hierarchy, and the UN, are institutions with little prestige. As the population shouts: "They should all go", the Church attempts to protect them (the politicians) from the pots and pan bangers with a rescue operation. We are reminded that, earlier, the Church had tried to save De la Rua[4] in Caritas, with a 'harmonization" that came late. Possibly, now, the "harmonization' is discredited in the collective imagination of the country. Obviously, when they invite us, we don't go.

Q Days before the social explosion of December 19th and 20th, the CTA had called a 'popular consultation' which has had many reper-cussions, and in the excitement of this process, FreNaPo was formed, which has joined the 'harmonization' project. What do you think?

A I went to vote in the 'popular consultation', but it seems to me that this activity came late in the process: it had been planned a year and a half before, so already, by this chronological fact it was evident that it would finish up being something very bureaucratic, that would not correspond with the active reality that was developing in the country. But anyway, it had an impact. It invited the people to participate, it talked about unemployment and many people, for different reasons, went to vote. I voted, at any rate, with criticism, because after the 'consultation', what was necessary, in my opinion, was that the three million who voted, be summoned to encircle the Congress.
And in reality, this is what, in a few days, the mobilization began to do, spontaneously. I believe that FreNaPo – and the CTA, of course – suffered a decline because of their behaviour in the immediate events around the actions of December 19th and 20th. They lost prestige and there was much questioning among people. In the middle of the police's tear gas in the Plaza Congreso we met delegates from the CTA who were indignant at the CTA's order to retreat. This generated discussion inside the CTA.

Because of some feeling of rebuff throughout the CTA institution and apparatus, faced with such an important mass action, some CTA members stayed away and others became directly involved in the confrontations with the authorities...there is now, at any rate, an attempt to achieve re-accommodation with the CTA and we should not underestimate the strength that this would have. This week was the first in the last two months where there were activities - within the arena the of the pots and pan bangers and picketers – called by organisations that were not members of the neighbourhood assemblies: the "Seize the Congress" convoked by the CTA and the CCC[5,] who placed themselves in front of the media talking about things which until then, they had not been able to do...

But it is certain that the CTA is reappearing. D'Elia[6] has made some very damaging statements raising the possibility that the BNP[7] might begin to pose itself as an alternative reference...

The CTA has a capacity for organization and organizational machinery and can try to show that they are part of the popular assembly process, without confronting it directly. On the other hand, I believe they chose the confrontation with the BNP, because of the very strong presence of a structured left within the Bloc, which runs the organization of the popular assemblies and the direct democracy process, the mobilizations and the mass participation

Q The daily world of Argentineans has crumbled. The lives of millions have changed abruptly owing to the impact of the government's measures, the pauperization, etc. An expression of this new situation is the phenomenon of the pots and pan bangers, and all kinds of mobilizations, demanding concrete measures in face of the disaster produced by capitalism. But this brutal change opens up the possibility, for the first time in Argentina, that millions of people will catch a glimpse of the possibility of constructing and thinking of a different world, precisely because the old world has tumbled down. As socialists, what can we put forward in the face of these new possibilities?

A Regarding an 'emergency programme', I consider it interesting what the various left economists see as being effective. They take shelter in ideas that are a somewhat traditional, even though today they are part of the urgent[8] search for answers to the most elementary things the population demands. There is lot to be learned about this.

The other day in a neighbourhood assembly, "Nationalisation of the banks" was posed, and no one said anything. Then one of the neighbourhood participants mentioned the case of the Santander Bank, which is threatening to leave the country, saying they can't pay the cost of the peso-change. Then someone else interrupted, saying, "the Santander Bank should go if it wishes to go. But the bank, its buildings, its documents and our money stays here."
What he was proposing was expropriation rather than nationalization... and the rest of the audience who before then had been quiet, because they didn't understand what was meant by 'nationalization', gave this neighbour an ovation. What's important to understand is to not try to put forward demands without proposing methods that can be understood...The measures that are being proposed, such as "the re-taking over of the privatized businesses", "solving the matter of the pensions terminated by the AFJP[8], "retaining the earnings of REPSOL-YPF[9], "no increase of rates", and other measures

open the road to an 'emergency programme'.

When I 'm appearing in the media, I talk a lot about the barbarism of capitalism, even though, obviously, in the popular assemblies I don't raise as a demand "a march against capitalism" – because it's important that those who are mobilizing, do it within a programmatic framework – but this is a contribution I'm making in the media, even though it may not be a so-called 'emergency' measure... in this I see that the left organizations are very weak, almost electoralist, only pointing to what they more or less like. But it is important to talk about world globalization, about the war, about what the IMF is doing and about the massacre of the poor, to show that capitalism is cruel and barbaric.

Today it appears possible that an 'emergency programme' may emerge from integrating the theoretical and technical suggestions of professionals and intellectual Marxists with the initiatives and models coming from those who are mobilized. To construct an 'emergency programme', which is not only strong, because of its logical coherence or abstract theory, but also because of its harmony with the new logic imposed by the demands and needs of the people. Certainly, for example, the question of 'control' by service-users and workers, connects with what the rest of the population is demanding.

"They should all go", is shouted by the masses, but alongside this, new methods of direct democracy are being built. I recently talked on television about the idea of re-nationalization of the enterprises under workers and the service-users control, and the other day organizations of service-users telephoned me to ask me about this. Members of the Caballito neighbourhood popular assembly approached me to talk about this also. They too wanted to see how this could be expanded.

These slogans must be linked with the discussion that is going on now in the popular assemblies, but it's no big deal. If we want to make a contribution to this discussion however, before we do so we should realise we can learn a lot from it.

Q How do you think the development of the various forms of autonomy and self-organization of the people should be articulated? On the political and cultural terrain, what specific contribution can socialists make?

A I remind you of what we are thinking of doing: calling a meeting around 'the five points' which the Autonomia y Libertad movement is promoting. It will be a meeting to link ourselves to other activists, to push forward the popular assembly process, to develop more powerfully our anti-capitalist, anti-imperialist and socialist 'points' to develop our ideas about self-determination and the levelling out of society.

After a period of exploration, better to say going and coming, with respect to organizational functioning, with time we will find it easier to get together to exchange ideas, for example, about what's happening in the popular assemblies in which we are all participating or in the other areas where the activists are functioning.

Some militants are not participating in the popular assemblies because they live in places where they have yet to develop. Some are not involved in them because they are active in their work places, or active with the unemployed workers in the 'roadblocks movement', the piqueteros, or in places in the country where the popular mobilization movement is much further behind... It seems to us this would be a modest achievement: to join with the fighters who are participating in the social process and who have written and phoned, who raise the need to know what's happening here or there in the country, and to answer more collectively questions such as: "Will this process last?"
"How do you defend the popular assemblies?"
"How do you stimulate the political debate that is going on in the popular assemblies?"
"How do we link up with the other sectors?"
"How do we help strengthen the process of struggle that is going on and extend it?"

Q Is this meeting strictly an Autonomia y Libertad project or does it have a more open character, to be defined in the course of the activity?

A We are calling a meeting around the 'five points', to give a report... not for the purpose of raising the profile or the building of the Autonomia y Libertad movement. The idea is to link ourselves broadly – even though there are organizational limits: we are addressing those who are not constructing another political organization – and establish bonds... We want to listen and bring forward our ideas, in a two way exchange with those who participate in the social organizations, or groups, or collectives, or trade union locals or neighbourhood organizations...some will come with documents, others with their experiences...

But the idea, from the political point of view, is enriching to the maximum, without having to approve political characterizations, policies, or orientations that might go beyond promoting the "five points"...

And from an organizational point of view, we are thinking of establishing an ongoing connection, but which would not signify assimilation into Autonomia y Libertad or reproduce Autonomia y Libertad everywhere, but to establish some kind of networking organization that would maintain the autonomy of its member organizations and which will serve to exchange information and perhaps get out some kind of periodical which could be sold throughout the network, ...perhaps to link struggles and to learn from them... Wherever we have been posing this idea these days, people are telling us: "Good, the truth is it's about time this happened!"

Q Autonomia y Libertad's "five starting points" raises, and explicitly leaves open, some policy questions, strategies and theories, which have greater importance and urgency now, it seems obvious to me, after what has happened in the country... our journal, Herramienta, has come up against similar problems. Do you believe that it would be possible and useful to propitiate an exchange in our journal, more or less systematically, of opinions about the "five points" in the pages of the magazine, to begin thinking about them, with contributions from yourselves and others?

A Yes, it seems to me that it would be useful to discuss them...as was expected, we have found questioning in the more orthodox and traditional left. But we ourselves didn't realize that there are unresolved matters regarding them. Now we see these "five points" as very valuable and exciting, among other things, because they synchronize very much with the process that is presently going on, but there is no doubt it would be useful to establish some form of debate around them.

Q Duhalde has said that he would not be President but he would possibly be a "piquetero", but at the same time he gives other speeches, systematically saying: "the country is over-run by anarchy", "we are heading towards a civil war", "there is a danger of a bloodbath", etc. Something like this was also stated by Alfonsin, "the Pope"[10]. Are these just words or does it represent something more serious?

A It seems to me in the short term they are just words. They're positions put with the goal of confusing and weakening the mobilizing process and the revolution in consciousness. But at any rate they are something of a warning that the ruling class is considering other alternatives ...As we said before, Duhalde's only strength resides in being able to persuade certain sectors of the population to support him by saying: "It's me or chaos". This was used many times before by Alfonsin and by Menem...but now we are in a different situation, because it seems to me that today the bourgeoisie has no organized structure for anything...If they are not able to weaken or discourage the mobilizations by other means, the idea that "anarchy is intolerable for any society", implies they will impose order at some point in time.

They are unable to address the people's demands, so they try to discourage the people, they try to wear them down, they try to cause divisions until the mobilizations can be defeated or suppressed. But today, repression is not the central policy...The instance that Duhalde carries out a repression, all the world will be against him. On the other hand, I believe that Argentina is a country "shut out" by the global capitalists, and in this sense, it seems to me, the threat must be taken seriously. In the short term, I don't see any "authoritarian" plan, but we must be alert for the medium term...But what's the "medium term" in Argentina?

We're in a very different situation from that in which we were living two years ago... In reality the situation of the whole continent is radically different and more fluid: look at the situation in Peru, Bolivia and Venezuela. The same is true for Brazil, which is an unknown quantity. And now with the war in Columbia, imperialism is not just carrying out a war against the FARC[11], it is setting in motion a programme for the whole continent. And in this context, Argentina could play an important role, because the political process here could show a way of confronting imperialism that would be effective and attractive for all the peoples of Latin America.

It is evident that with respect to Columbia, that if the situation advances there, it could be utilized as a significant example and could also produce a debate in Argentina. But in fact, the Argentine process has its differences with the rest of the Southern Cone in general and has a special interest for Latin America.

It's notable that these questions, which are really central, were pushed aside by the World Social Forum in Porto Alegre. The FARC and the Zapatistas were not allowed to participate and there was also a policy decision that the situation in Argentina would go unnoticed as much as possible.

I had a bad impression of the World Social Forum. The official events didn't depart very far from defending a so-called, "more humane capitalism", and there was a political bias, as I mentioned. However, the experience of the "unofficial" activities and the contact with thousands and thousands of groups and fighters of the anti-globalization movement, was worthwhile. You can't put a price on that. Of course, it was also enriching to hear Chomsky and Wallerstein and to participate in the debates with anti-capitalist fighters such as Chesnais. I also had the very valuable opportunity of meeting the activists of the shanty towns – members of the landless movement (MST) in Brazil... Just as the organizers of the Forum discriminated against the Zapatistas, I also felt an attempt to control opinions about Argentina. I, for example, was invited on to a panel and was then uninvited and replaced by a representative from ARI[12].

Q Finally, about "the question of power", in very general terms, one of the most complex and polemical issues: has there been any advance or elaboration on this?

A I don't know if there has been any progress...we have talked about this theme and underlined the value of a "counter-power" or an "anti-power", as some prefer to call it...In many popular assemblies, to take a concrete example, there were those who wanted to form employment bureaus and commissions to respond to the problems of the neighbourhoods. Thus the people are being given very rich experiences...and start to see in a more concrete way the formation of elements of a "counter-culture" that implies a solidarity practise of struggle against fragmentation and individualism, in opposition to capitalist culture, with the enormous strengths this gives to any collective action. We also see the beginning of the construction of a "counter-power", because in many ways the popular assemblies are discussing organizing society on the basis of a different model from the one that exists now and which is controlled by the ruling class...

We are not implying that the ruling class doesn't continue to hold power, something that we can't ignore because, definitely, it rules everywhere, and poses a very real tension, but the idea of exploring ways to end capitalism through a "counter-power", a power that would be so great, it would defeat the capitalist power, is reaffirmed by us...I'm not now posing the question of a cadre-party, which in a determined circumstance, in a determined wave of struggles, for example, successfully challenges bourgeois power, without the masses first constructing a counter-culture and a "counter-power" from below, made favourable by a process of struggle that may give us a "socialism from below", like Hal Draper says...

I'm not able to say how this tension will be resolved, and I don't rule out that because of this tension it may be possible to arrive at some point for the need of some kind of organization similar to what we have known in the past...but in any case, the centre of gravity of our activities will not be around building a party that leads, but in the autonomy that produces power and makes intolerable the existence of the ruling class, working, not for an exceptional conjuncture, but pointing to a situation unsustainable in time...

So, what I'm saying is very general and full of questions, and seems to me, takes something from the Zapatistas, but it's also different. It's a very different matter getting rid of the bourgeois state power, compared to limiting yourself to solving partial grievances, specific to affected groups...

We're posing a global questioning of society and the capitalist world, and we encourage autonomy to defeat world capitalism. I could add that, even leaving aside the evaluations that we could have about the strong and weak points of the Russian revolution – for example, the extreme minority character of the working class and the Bolshevik party, only circumstantially a majority in the Soviets – it seems evident to me that at that historical moment, there were conditions that today I don't believe could be repeated...

Today imperialism's political, economic, military and cultural power makes it impossible to think of defeating it, without first basing oneself on the rank and file, a people acting for itself, to advance and organise, disorganising the enemy: this is the basis of everything, and starting from there we must be open to all kinds of combinations from the organisational point of view...

We're saying that in Argentina the daily life of the people has changed and they are able to think of the possibility of a different world, but the people on the streets are feeling intense pressure to see how they can shorten the process of change, which will have repercussions on the political conjuncture in Latin America. There's a need to think through the problems of the transformation of society in a concrete way, and this implies thinking of the social transformation on a scale, not of one country, but of a region...the crisis in Argentina challenges us to think of a Latin American revolution, at least of the Southern Cone...It's quite unreal to think of a sustained Argentine revolutionary transformation if it doesn't achieve a synchronization with the popular masses of Brazil, who are a decisive factor in Latin America.

I have the impression that a large part of the left, in so far as it has been very electoralist in the current situation, has also gone back to being very nationalist... I include here the anti-imperialist demand such as "No payment of the external debt", which is handled like an election demand, and is not linked to a general framework... They pose voting for "No payment of the external debt" in a way that weakens the demand... Above all, this is so when they speak in the mass media.

I had a debate with the ARI in the Chamber Of Deputies but, really, I was up against several organizations on the left. Mario Cafiero[13], who questioned the payment of the debt and the foreign domination of the country, ended up saying "We're not against the IMF, nor with the IMF: our position is to do without the IMF... We have to live within our means." And I felt the need to polemicize against him, to point out to people that these speeches weaken the struggle... Because the reality is that in the European countries, the G7, everyone, says: "Go through the IMF". People ask us to confront this. One must know and say: yes indeed, we are going into a confrontation with the IMF, and we are going face to face with the imperialist countries: that is, we must stand up to the imperialist world, to world globalization and the barbarism of capitalism...

And in respect to "living within our means", Argentina has possibilities that other countries don't have, but only transitional, because the United States will not accept that "we could live within our means". They will not say "Ah, they don't want us? Good, then let them manage things themselves".

There will be a policy of isolating us, of harassment and of war. What is posed is a fight. For this one must provide a framework for the slogan "I'm not paying", a framework that is part of the struggle against imperialism and the barbarism of capitalism and globalization.

We need to think of ways of standing up to them, of uniting Latin Americans against them, but also primarily of winning the working people to take up this fight, with a serious policy, with an awareness of what is happening in the world, which includes knowing that in Latin America all the conditions exist for an integrated struggle which opens a path against a world designed by the United States. This is a fundamental debate among the left and is the great challenge that is posed before us in Argentina. It would be wonderful if other fighters, in different parts of the world, would continue and support this process. ☐

NOTES

1 *The Argentine president.*
2 *Confederation of Workers of Argentina.*
3 *National Front Against Poverty.*
4 *Fernando De La Rua, previous President, Social Democrat, representative of the Radical Party.*
5 *Combative Class-based Current.*
6 *Luis D'Elia, leader of the National Picketers' Block.*
7 *National Picketer's Block.*
8 *AFJP, organization of the pension system.*
9 *REPSOL-YPF, organization of the oil chemical and gas companies.*
10 *Ex-President, Raul Alfonsin, who resigned in 1989.*
11 *Revolutionary Armed Front of Columbia.*
12 *Alternative for a Republic of Equals.*
13 *Mario Cafiero, Peronist deputy in the Congress, from Buenos Aires.*

Interview translated by Jess MacKenzie and Ernest Tate

VENEZUELA

Chavez gets another (last?) chance

Emir Sader*

Latin America is living on the brink of a nervous breakdown. First in Paraguay, then in Ecuador, in Argentina and now in Venezuela, the presidents succeed each other at hourly intervals, illustrating the institutional instability of the continent's countries and the gelatinous character of the type of society which follows from the transformations which these same presidents promised would bring stability and security.

In the case of Venezuela, Hugo Chavez was elected with 70% of the popular vote (in 2000) after denouncing - correctly – the country's elites as characters in an 'oil farce'. They have indeed squandered the country's oil wealth by maintaining high prices without seeking to industrialize the country or to free Venezuela from the constraints linked to dependence on upheavals in oil prices. The Chavez government, through its minister, Ali Rodriguez, currently general coordinator of OPEC, contributed to an increase in oil prices by reintroducing a policy of quotas. Thanks to these resources, the Chavez government was able to implement redistributive social policies, reform the Constitution of the country and organize a number of elections and plebiscites that fully respected the rules of liberal democracy.

These transformations have not however changed the fundamentals of power in Venezuelan society. The media have maintained a solid front of opposition, around which résistance to the government is articulated, leaving this latter no space of expression outside the radio and TV interventions of Chavez himself. The supporters of Chavez have not succeeded in implanting themselves in the strategically central sector of the oil industry, whose technicians and trades

Continued on page 24

"Chavez is very much weakened, and it will incline him still more towards conciliation"

Interview with Douglas Bravo

Douglas Bravo, a Venezuelan guerilla fighter of the 1960s, is currently leader of the Third Way Movement (Movimiento Tercer Camino).
He was interviewed by Veronica Gago for the Argentine daily Pagina 12.

Will the conflicts continue?
Since February 27, 1989, and the Caracazo [an uprising against poverty and hunger in Caracas - ed], which mobilized 10 million people, two forces have faced each other: those fighting for social emancipation and those who are trying to impose neoliberalism.

This rebellion of the poor has maintained a high degree of institutional instability in the country. This is still the case now under a government which claims to institutionalize this popular reaction. I think that there will be a succession of coups, confrontations and insurrectional strikes.

I mean that there is a confrontation over the political regime, over oil, but the two currents that face each other are both neoliberal, even if they represent different tendencies. On the one hand there is the bloc that could be called the Fourth Republic, composed of the politicians of the traditional right, the bosses and their media, some putschist military elements and some 'moderate' trades unionists [social democratic or social Christian] in the CTV federation.

This bloc supports an old and classic neoliberalism in the distribution of wealth. On the other hand, there is a neoliberalism that is much more advanced in its philosophical conception of capitalism: this is the bloc that supports the government. What is lacking here is a third force, revolutionary and patriotic, capable of confronting the power of the bourgeoisie and imperialism. In this schema, how do we explain the fact that the people came onto the streets to defend Chavez and that the troops remained loyal to the president?

It is clear that there are two very distinct currents inside chavismo. One current, the minority one – including the higher officers in the Armed Forces, the Supreme Tribunal and the Executive – takes the economic decisions and the official ones from the ideological and political point of view. It is this current that makes chavismo continually lose cadres, which poses problems; for example if Chavez loses five more deputies, he will lose his majority in the National Assembly.

The other current, majority from the quantitative but not qualitative viewpoint, is that which came into the street to defend Chavez. It is composed partly of officers ready to fight to defend the government, even if they do not dominate the military apparatus, and also political sectors that believe in the Bolivarian revolutionary project.

What is the current situation of the government?
The Chavez government has emerged very much weakened from the coup. However, this fragility will continue if he implements the conciliatory discourse that he has adopted since his return to power.

Conciliation as Chavez conceives it is a new pact – like that of Punto Fijo [an agreement reached in 1958 between the Democratic Action (AD), COPEI (Social Christian) and Democratic Republican Union (URD) parties, after the fall of the military dictator, general Pedro Jimenez – ed.] – which does not take into account those who supported him and negotiates with the rightwing sectors which tried to overthrow him.

What position did your movement adopt during the coup?
Tercer Camino opposed the coup, we went onto the streets but we circulated a petition demanding the installation of a patriotic government.

What was your reference?
In the current situation a majority socio-political sector in the country – what one can consider as the patriotic and popular bloc, composed of civilians and soldiers, some currently in the government and others not – is in the process of elaborating a document that will be presented soon to President Chavez.

What is this proposal?
It amounts to a radical opposition to what we think will happen if Chavez pursues his policy of concessions, namely the privatization of oil, gas and basic services. Our initiative proposes, among other things, the expulsion of the right wing of the Armed Forces including some that Chavez is in the process of confirming in their posts, and the revision of measures seeking to create a consensus, like the acceptance of the resignation of the new leadership, appointed by him, of the oil company, the PDVSA. ☐

Continued from page 22

unionists continue to be affiliated to the union federations traditionally linked to the parties of the old regime like Democratic Action.

Chavez was in the process of undertaking a series of structural transformations: a package of measures, already voted through by Parliament, sought in the first place to begin a profound agrarian reform, but also extended to a series of other sectors, including the oil and fishing industries. However, the external and internal situation had already begun to change for Chavez. To the extent that the US economy passed from growth to recession, oil prices began to fall. Moreover, the internal employers' boycott deepened, with a flight of capital and the closure of productive enterprises.

On the other hand, through his 'Bonapartist' military style – to use the terms of the classic analyses - Chavez gradually isolated himself, leading to the simultaneous appearance of several fronts against him: he began to lose the support of groups which were initially in his camp in the beginning; he came up directly against the hierarchy of the Catholic church – which had been hostile to him since the beginning – and, to the extent that the deterioration of the economic situation aggravated the internal social situation, he began to lose popular support.

The opposition

The mobilizations against the Chavez government took on breadth with the adoption of the package of measures of December 2001 (the 49 laws that Carmona, the boss of bosses, wanted to suppress immediately during his 35 hours as president). These mobilizations were led essentially by a united front of the big companies, which functioned as a general command for the opposition, articulating the various private companies, the functionaries in the state owned enterprises, the Church hierarchy, the generalized discontent of the middle class, and counting on the external support of Washington.

To the extent that the coalition of Chavez supporters in parliament crumbled – he can only currently count on the support of barely half the deputies – the dissident groups are multiplying even inside the government. Beyond this, the popular layers and in particular the poorest sectors, which constitute the base of the régime and have benefited from the political measures adopted, remain unorganized, without any capacity of expression.

The oil companies' strike was the detonator of the decisive confrontation. Chavez could not tolerate a halting of production, which would have definitively financially strangled his government, while at the same time the functionaries in these enterprises could not accept the new leadership named by the President without risk of losing control of the main resources of the country, which would come under the direct control of Chavez.

While seeking to undermine the Chavez regime and its strategic economic axis, the opposition begin to score some points – even if it was only marginally at the beginning – inside the armed forces. Indeed the support of the latter was, with the oil and the personal charisma of Chavez, the essential basis of the regime's legitimacy. As Chavez weakened, the opposition began promoting 'saucepan concerts' and mobilized ever more people – from 150 to 500,000 people, it is estimated.

Coup and countercoup

The coup was launched by senior officers in the armed forces, following a number of deaths in the repression of the demonstration of Thursday April 11, 2002. Some of the victims were shot by government troops, others were clearly hit by sharpshooters and the indications are that these had been set up by the military sectors of the opposition [and the mayor of Caracas]. The government established by the coup pursued its goals without respecting any institutional procedure and was very open in its pro-employer orientation. Thus, it immediately named a big employer as president and presented a programme for the oil industry: the suspension of sales to Cuba; a distancing from the policies of OPEC and a rapprochement with the US. All this in a dynamic clearly leading to privatization of the oil sector.

The popular mobilizations were a little late, showing how poorly organised Chavez's popular base had been. However, when these mobilizations began they quickly generalized across the country, and the Palace of government was seized. Meanwhile soldiers loyal to Chavez rebelled, the Parliament met and unanimously demanded the right of the vice-president to take his place in the government, and the OAS (Organization of American States) condemned the coup and reaffirmed the institutional legitimacy of the Chavez government. The employer-turned-president resigned and was arrested, while Chavez returned. In his speech he said he was ready to readjust his government, while announcing that those responsible for the coup, in particular those in the press, would be punished.

Perspectives

What margin of manoeuvre does Chavez still enjoy? That depends firstly on his capacity to ensure that his project for the popular majority becomes a project for the whole of the country, striking at the axis of those forces which have already shown their determination to overthrow him. That would also depend on the capacity of the opposition to retake the initiative and renew its offensive.

Chavez's margin of manoeuvre has certainly diminished in relation to the armed forces, in Parliament and the oil industry. It is probable that the initial project has been exhausted, because it supposed a clear polarization between the popular masses and the elites, which leads to forms of confrontation which Chavez can no longer countenance if he wishes to recycle his image as that of a leader capable of negotiating his projects with broader sectors.

Moreover, both the traditional elites and Chavez himself have taken account of the solid popular and military reaction. We will see what lessons they draw from it. Chavez has already made a gesture of negotiation, accepting the resignation of the oil industry chiefs that he had himself appointed and whose nomination had led to the strike against his government. Nonetheless, to the extent that the blows against his base have multiplied, the team around Chavez has been reduced to its hard core, those least disposed to negotiation.

The coming weeks will show if the wounds suffered by the Chavez project continue to bleed and if its death has just been postponed or if he can give a new élan to the project that brought him to power. The continental context is favourable to him; the price of oil should rise. It will then be on the internal level that things will be played out, which will depend on his ability to organize his base, divide the opposition, punish those are most directly linked to the coup d'état and negotiate with the others. He must succeed in maintaining the essentials of his project, while packaging it and formatting it in such a way as to gradually enlarge the consensus rather than increase the number of his adversaries, as has happened in recent months. ☐

* Emir Sader is a Brazilian sociologist

SPAIN

The Communist Party of Spain (PCE) held its 16th congress in Madrid from March 1-3, 2002. We print below two assessments of the congress, together with an account of the crisis in the CC.OO trade union federation with the PCE has been closely linked historically.

ON THE PCE CONGRESS

Ángeles Maestro*

At the recently held 16th Congress of the Communist Party of Spain (PCE) there appeared, for the first time in the party's history, a nationwide platform that presented alternative political documents and put forward its own candidates to the Federal Committee and the General Secretariat.

This Platform, although conforming to the statutes of the party, had enormous difficulties in functioning that it is not possible to enumerate here, but in spite of this, the candidacy to the Federal Committee obtained 21% of the votes.

The PCE congress represented a further phase in the process opened at the 6th Assembly of the Izquierda Unida (IU) with the Alternative Document that was presented there. The development of events since October 2000 has confirmed the validity of the analysis put forward in the Alternative Document. In brief, the central elements are:

A: War, on a global and lasting basis, and the deepening of repression, are not accidental but rather strategic elements of capitalist globalization.

B: War and repression are constituent elements of the new order and the new so-called 'anti-terrorist' alliances. Social democracy, hegemonized by the Third Way, is a structural element of the new imperialism.

C: The response of global capitalism to the increasingly deep and extensive economic crisis is the intensification of the mechanisms of exploitation and the elimination of the vestiges of legitimation of the system: relatively 'progressive' taxation, systems of social protection, social, trade union and political rights.

D: The complicity of the great majority of the political and trade union forces of the left in these brutal aggressions expresses itself in the total refusal to lead a resistance and to struggle through effective general mobilizations.

E: The first consequence is a serious crisis of political representation, intensified by the generalized scandals of corruption linked to privatization. The increasing abstention on the left reflects the defeat of left reformist positions that scarcely conceal the adoption of neoliberal policies and complicity with war. The PSOE-IU pact in 2000, the defeat of the Olive Tree coalition in Italy or the foreseeable electoral collapse of the PCF, are good examples of it.

F: Secondly, there is the increasing loss of legitimacy of the leaderships of the majority unions, which are increasingly seen as an element of the state apparatuses.

G: The bankruptcy of political and trade union representation, most vividly seen in Argentina, but with a general character, is linked to the emergence of the 'movement of movements', which shows that the days of impotent defeat are over and that it is possible to go onto the offensive, providing the starting point is the recognition that another capitalism is impossible.

H: A radical critique of the system and a strategic commitment to deepening and extending social conflict are essential prerequisites for the construction of new and broad forms of unity. That means participation in government must be subordinated to the interests of the social struggle.

I: It is vital that the most advanced and more combative sectors of the labour movement form part of the anti-globalization movement to develop a dialectical relationship between social mobilization and intensification of the class struggle.

J: In the same way, the anti-globalization movement must link itself to the workers' struggle to advance in the recomposition of class unity, incorporating alternative values, the fight for peace, internationalism not only as attitude but as a method of work and the construction of forms of direct democracy.

The Platform questioned Stalinism in an explicit and radical form; in theory and practice, in internal political activity and in the very conception of power. Also it argued for a profound debate about the transition from Francoism and its consequences. In the words of one of its paragraphs: "Starting from the 13th Congress, the PCE initiated a timid criticism of the transition [from Francoism – ed.] and the political action of the leadership of the party during this period. In the 16th Congress it is necessary to go further and to consider if it makes any sense to maintain any loyalty towards a constitutional pact whose real consequences are the constant erosion of workers' rights and the reduction, until its disappearance, of democracy. We must consider if the construction of democracy does not rather necessitate the questioning of the present political system of our country and the updating of the central subjects that we defined in the project of democratic rupture, whose postponement decisively contributed to breaking the powerful popular movement constructed against the dictatorship".

The debate we raised in the PCE, far from being a short-term internal battle, relates both in theory and practice to the great question facing the fragmented and weak combative left in our country: the construction with many other people of a movement that can advance the viewpoint, as this year in Porto Alegre, that another world is possible only with socialism. □

* Ángeles Maestro was elected to the Central Committee of the PCE as a supporter of the alternative platform at the congress.

Fransisco Frutos, Gen Sec of the PCE

Neither half full nor half empty

Julio Setien*

In spite of the dramatic significance that this 16th Congress of the PCE had been accorded inside Izquierda Unida (some had presented it as almost a replay of the 6th assembly of IU) its development and results do not seem to have fulfilled such expectations. It could be seen as nothing more than an inventory of the diverse positions existing inside 'the party'. However, things are somewhat more complex; to clarify this, we will analyze some of its more relevant aspects.

If we rely on texts, resolutions and approved amendments it seems that, to take the concrete case of the Basque conflict, support for dialogue and therefore, the rejection of the banning of Herri Batasuna, prevailed. However, this is not apparent from the report of Paco Frutos, which, surprisingly, does not contain a single reference to the Basque problem or the question of the right to self-determination. More forcefully expressed is the orientation to work in the anti-globalization movement and to support combative positions in the CC.OO as fundamental axes of the PCE's work. A militant attitude remains towards work in the social movements; in the case of the unions this has led to a position (a dangerous one, considering the diversity of its membership) in favour of the critical current of the CC.OO.

Enormous confusion continued at the international level, with the PCE remaining imprisoned in the political loyalties of the old 'international Communist movement'; that led to the invitation to the so-called Communist Parties of China or Korea, to give two examples of which there are plenty more. This is reflected also in the placing on the same level of the Forum of Sao Paulo and that of Porto Alegre, or taking shelter in a single reference (and for some, that is already an advance) to 'possible political responsibilities of Milosevic'.

The political repercussions of the anti-globalization movement, on which an interesting reflection has begun, and the tremendous changes in the international panorama after September 11, do not seem to have opened a breach in the international politics of the PCE, which remains within the old parameters.

What impact will the outcome of the Congress have on the PCE's line within IU? It's difficult to say. Indubitably, the PCE as such is not extending its influence or political weight within IU. The reason is obvious: the PCE as an organizational bloc does not exist, but this is a question to which we will return.

It would also be possible to analyze whether, through its weight at the Congress, such-and-such a current of the PCE is going to acquire more or less influence in IU, but in the context of a zero sum game between such currents. Even in absolute terms, the global result of that sum has been decreasing since the creation of IU (if we take that as the moment of reference), considering the constant decline in affiliations the PCE has experienced since then. In the short term, it does not seem that the outcome of the PCE congress is relevant to the present correlation of IU forces.

At the organizational level, we can note the continuity of general secretary Francisco Frutos, based on a coalition with Llamazares. This time, the formation of a bloc around the platform 'Partido Vivo', led by Angeles Maestro, produced some surprising confluences. The final result gave an estimated 59% to the sector of Frutos, 21% to the Platform 'Partido Vivo' and 20% to the followers of Llamazares. Few changes, then.

PCE 2

The PCE maintains a high internal diversity. Practically all the plurality of IU has its reflection (often its origin) within the PCE. In fact, the three candidacies that confronted each other at the 6th Assembly of IU were headed by leaders of the PCE.

It is surprising, therefore, that we have the continued prohibition of currents in a party shot through with differences and divergences. Thus, given the nonexistence of authentic currents of opinion that could articulate the disparities in the political terrain, difference are expressed - with the exception of the 'Partido Vivo' platform – around nuclei of influence which cannot really be described from the ideological point of view.

Nevertheless, it would be unjust to finish the analysis at this point. These nuclei of influence are formed not only around the internal struggle for power but around very substantial divergences on how politics should be practiced in the PCE and above all in IU. And method in politics is no small thing.

The last part of this brief analysis starts from a note: the Congress served to bury, at least in this political cycle, the feeling generated since the electoral defeat of 1999 in broad sectors of the PCE, although not always specified publicly, summed up in the question: 'What use is the IU to us, if we score almost the same percentage of votes as we did the last time we appeared as the CP?' A question that reflects a reality on which there has been little reflection: the character of the PCE since the creation of the IU.

The PCE was the key to the construction of the IU, putting to the service of the project not only its ideas and the work of its militants, but a good part of its material resources. The initial political arc of the IU was composed of several tiny parties and a PCE that constituted 90% of IU affiliation. Since then, a double process has occurred: loss of the formal plurality of IU (although diversity from the political point of view remains) and gradual reduction of the presence of the PCE inside IU, where almost half of affiliates are no longer from the PCE

So, from an initial stage characterized by the generosity of the PCE towards the other much smaller component organizations of IU, we arrive at the current situation with an over representation of the PCE in the leadership bodies and public positions of IU in relation to its real weight in the coalition. What is the nature of the PCE today, then?

It is difficult to qualify it as a political current inside IU, because, as we said, the PCE is made up of several political currents that replicate the divergences of the PCE inside IU and vice versa.

It is a party, in the formal sense of the word, but is inserted in another formation under whose rubric it has contested elections for the last 16 years, as opposed to the nine when it presented itself as the PCE. Moreover, there is already a sense within the PCE that its strategic and not simply electoral project is the IU. With this there is the paradox that an organization that has existed for 81 years, that already was very plural, even in the last years of the dictatorship, acts like a single voice in another organization of which it forms part, IU. This distance between word and deed is a source of misunderstanding and frustration, a permanent hindrance to the development of IU and leads to a false question in the minds of many PCE militants: 'What use is the IU?' This renders difficult the complex analysis of the situation of the forces to the left of social democracy in Europe, the relation between mobilization and social articulation with politics, the influence of the contradictory construction of the Spanish state on a statewide political force and so on. In short, it remains difficult to evaluate if the PCE is going to be obstacle to the renovation and the opening up of IU or a factor in the resolution of the existing tension

It is possible that the greatest virtue of this Congress has been to leave things as they were, not to try to resolve things which in logically must be resolved within IU and in through the relationship of the latter with the most combative sectors of society. □

Julio Setienes is a member of Espacio Alternativo and was a leading PCE trades unionist in the years of the transition from Francoism.

THE CRISIS IN THE CC.OO

Pedro Montes*

Understanding the recent crisis in the Spanish trade union confederation, the CC.OO (Comisiones Obreras - Workers' Commissions) - or to be more precise, the crisis in its majority leadership - is not an easy task; the underlying differences are not clear or explicit and it is difficult to predict the consequences and the changes that may take place in the CC.OO.

In order to explain the crisis that has led to the dismissal of the second-in-command in the union hierarchy, organization secretary Rodolfo Benito, it is necessary to go back to the 7th Congress, held in April 2000, and also not to forget the outcome of the 6th Congress. In this latter, a 'Critical Sector' emerged which demanded a turn to the left and a revival of democracy and pluralism inside the union. Although the Critical Sector obtained a third of the vote and the posts on the Confederal Executive, they were effectively expelled from the leadership of the union during the four years prior to the 7th Congress.

At the latter, the Critical Sector again argued for a reorientation of union activity to confront and mobilize against a rightwing government that is implementing a severe and regressive neoliberal policy, without any trade union or political opposition worthy of mention. The Critical Sector, in spite of intense repression, practically replicated its result at the previous congress with 30% of the votes.

But the main objectives of the Congress were: the carve up of the majority's monopoly of power among its various factions; a very regressive reform of the statutes, severely limiting constitutional rights; and deciding on the succession to the outgoing general secretary, Antonio Gutiérrez.

Three candidates emerged, with possible minor political differences, but all defending the same documents on trade union strategy and the same anti-democratic attitudes. By common accord and with the blessing of Gutiérrez it was understood that the new general secretary would be whoever enjoyed the greatest support among the majority. The strongest turned out to be Ignacio Toxo, secretary of the metalworkers' federation, and Benito, secretary of the Madrid federation. In third place and far behind was José Maria Fidalgo, a member of the Confederal Executive, whose support was limited to that provided by the central 'apparatus' and the 'presidential' designation that Gutiérrez had conferred on him. The latter, on seeing the results of the 'primaries', contravened the previous commitments he had made and demanded the resignation of the other two contenders.

Fidalgo was the candidate who best guaranteed the continuity of the policy of Gutiérrez. He was the most rightwing candidate, albeit in a close-run competition with Toxos, the weakest and, therefore, the most easily manipulated. Benito yielded first, in exchange for a privileged position in the union and an excellent position (organization secretary) to prepare for a later assault on the post of general secretary. Toxo resisted, but in the end surrendered in the hope of launching a subsequent challenge from his powerbase in the metalworkers' federation. And thus the ideology-free Fidalgo (his point of honour is that he has never been a member of any political party), without firm support, with his power based to a great extent on the balance of forces, but in any case very rightist in conception, managed to become general secretary.

In his first two years Fidalgo has fulfilled scrupulously the expectations he had raised, accepting government policy without resistance, even applauding it, and negotiating and signing pacts with the Popular Party with an enthusiasm worthy of a better cause.

The union seemed in line with this strategy, but this was more apparent than real. In the first place, there is the anomaly represented by the situation of the Critical Sector, with almost a third of the union being excluded from the confederal leadership. Secondly, the 7th Congress had ended inconclusively. Toxo and Benito have not ceased to manoeuvre and prepare themselves for the assault on the general secretaryship at the next Congress. Still, nobody could have predicted the current crisis, its characteristics or the new alliances that have been forged. Suddenly, Fidalgo and Benito fell out, the first faulting the loyalty of the second. Toxo took his revenge, demanding the dismissal of Benito, which Fidalgo finally carried out, leading to the resignation of three Benito supporters from the Executive.

There have been no political explanations for what happened, apart from the stammerings of Benito. The crisis has not publicly had any component of ideological confrontation. Some glimpse the hand of Gutiérrez, accused of conniving with Benito out of spite because Fidalgo had displayed too much autonomy. The Critical Sector has maintained a correct position: opposition to the line of the union, rejection - which in no way implies support to Benito - of purges carried out over legitimate disagreements and demands to restore integration, plurality and democracy in the organization.

Independently of its origins or shadowy aspects, the crisis of the CC.OO majority will have important repercussions, internal and external, although the outcome is uncertain, because an unfinished process has opened and its causes are not too clear.

Internally, the old majority will end up either very divided (indeed it is already) or will simply break up; this depends ultimately on whether the followers of Benito choose the path of resignation or confrontation. If they decide to fight, they need to develop their own discourse and to demarcate themselves to some degree from Toxo's majority. We say Toxo's majority, because Fidalgo, although general secretary, has in the crisis lost his power which was sustained by the old balance of forces, and he has become a mere puppet of the metalworkers' secretary.

The new situation can be used to clarify positions and to open a debate in the union, on questions of concrete management as much as strategic areas, In short, it could help the Critical Sector emerge from isolation. But all these are possibilities, since the union has degenerated in its practices and ideological positions to such a dangerous degree that it is possible to ask if with the present framework, the present bureaucracy and the apparatus, it is possible to recover it.

At the external level, the most positive aspect of the crisis is Fidalgo's loss of authority and the weakening of the majority. Their willingness to agree to the PP's demands is so intense that the PP itself no longer sees the general secretary and the majority as representing the whole of the union, so that it will demand less of them and distrust more their ability to deliver the membership when signing regressive pacts or agreements.

It does not seem that the crisis can be resolved through an extraordinary Congress and it cannot be ruled out that the internal confrontations will get worse. A climate of increased political tension in the union would be positive after the miasma that the bureaucracy has imposed lately, but this can only happen for sure if the affiliates and the workers can pressurize leaders who are mired in routine administration, political resignation, manoeuvres and dirty games, obedience, docility and the cultivation of their own interests. Of course, the much more difficult task will be using this crisis to generate the change of policy and internal practices that this union federation needs in the adverse conditions imposed by global capitalism and the Europe of the Maastricht. □

* *Pedro Montes is a member of the leadership of the Critical Sector of the CC.OO, and is also a member of the Presidency of the Federal United Left, an activist in the State Assembly of Workers Against Capitalist Globalización, and a member of Quaderns Internacionales, an organization of supporters of the Fourth International in the*

RUSSIA: SIGNS OF CHANGE

The economic situation in Russia in 2000-2001

Aleksander Buzgalin

There is nothing surprising in the fact that the economic revival in Russia which began in late 1998 is now giving way to stagnation. Even when the recovery was only just beginning, independent experts were pretty accurate in their predictions of how long it would last: if Russia's economy was going to develop by inertia, then the factors which brought about the economic upswing would play themselves out in about two to two-and-a-half years. And that's exactly what happened.

Economic growth halted

The signs of an imminent downturn were already quite visible in the middle of 2000. Although the macroeconomic situation remained favourable (inflation was averaging no more than 1.5-2.0 percent per month, the money supply was slowly growing, the degree of monetization of the turnover of goods and services was growing, individual incomes were growing in real terms, and companies' long-term debts were decreasing), there were dangerous symptoms building up in the production sector. There was a downturn in company profitability in almost every branch of the economy. The short-term investment boom —which in any case had not affected all industries — began to drop off. In a number of branches of manufacturing industry, particularly in the consumer sector, investment growth did not simply slow down, but actually started to decline. The decline in profitability and fall in investments were directly linked, because over two-thirds of investment in Russian companies' capital assets comes from their own funds.

At the end of last year, these alarming symptoms were dramatically confirmed. In the last two months of the year, economic industrial growth gave way to a small decline in production. Does this mean that all the opportunities for economic growth have been exhausted, and the Russian economy is heading for another downward spiral in the protracted crisis?

There is no simple answer. Events may take various turns. To understand what realistic prospects for economic growth remain in Russia, we need to examine the reasons for the upswing that has now come to an end.

Where did the recovery come from?

In contrast to the stagnation now looming over us, the economic upswing of the last two years was truly unexpected. The catalyst was the abrupt change in Russia's economic policy in 1998, which external factors necessitated. The growing pyramid of domestic and foreign debt and the inability of the government to resolve this problem through a rational macroeconomic manoeuvre resulted in the financial collapse of August 1998. The fourfold devaluation of the rouble created highly favourable conditions for Russian exports (which were suffering at the time from an unfavourable world market) and adverse conditions for import. As a result, there was an increase in export incomes and economic growth in industries providing import substitution (mainly in consumer products) on the domestic market

Primakov's government exploited this growth in export income by making it compulsory for exporters to sell all their hard currency proceeds, which enabled the government to stabilize the currency market and secure an increase in tax revenue for the budget.

A second factor was the general rise in world prices for oil and some other primary products, which began in 1999. This did not simply increase the inflow of export income and tax revenue, but also had a strong knock-on effect on the economy. In the fuel and primary industries there was a growing demand for pipelines, drilling equipment, construction equipment and other engineering products. Investment in the oil sector grew at an annual equivalent rate of more than 90 percent.

A third factor — which does not get very much coverage, but which had a major effect on the economic situation in most secondary industries — was the fact that wages were halved in real terms as a result of the August 1998 financial crisis. This considerably reduced companies' production costs, increased profitability and allowed them to increase investment in their capital assets. In addition, this reduction in real incomes was an additional factor governing the shift in consumer demand away from imported products towards domestically produced ones.

The limits of market growth

This brief review of the factors influencing the economic recovery demonstrates that none of them was of a long-term nature. The world market is now gradually shifting towards a reduction in prices for fuel and primary products. Given the worsening economic conditions in the United States and the prospective depression in European economic activity, the trend towards a reduction in prices for these products will become even more marked. Import substitution in Russia's domestic market has already played itself out. It is not merely that the balance between imported and consumer goods on the domestic market has been restored: in 2000, as real incomes grew, there was a steady increase in the share of imported goods being bought by consumers.

A growth in incomes in real terms naturally creates a general increase in demand on the consumer market. However, this increase in demand mainly affects imported rather than domestically produced products. In addition, a growth in real incomes counteracts the advantages gained by a reduction in labour costs.

All these considerations were quite evident two years ago. In order to ensure long term and stable economic growth, the essential thing should have been to give the recovery an additional boost with some long-range strategies. The key one should have been to embark upon a modernization of the capital assets of the Russian economy.

The "2003 problem"

This is the name given in Russia to the problem of the serious aging of the capital assets. This was already a problem before the radical market reforms even began. The reforms themselves, which led to a fourfold cut in investment in capital assets, greatly exacerbated this problem. Between 2003 and 2005 a considerable proportion of the capital assets in such sectors as agriculture, energy, pipeline transportation, and the housing and utilities infrastructure will urgently need replacing. The winter of 2000-2001 has seen major failures in the heating supply system, gas leaks and explosions, and prolonged power cuts in a number of regions; these were only the first warning signs of the impending problem.

Russia must face the fact that it has no option but to implement a massive overhaul of the capital assets in almost every branch of the national economy. However, even the growth in investment which accompanied the economic recovery of 1999-2000 was not nearly enough to redeem the situation in any meaningful way. The government's current economic policy simply ignores this problem. Officials responsible for the economy continue to speak smugly of an economic upturn. And even when the problem is acknowledged — as with electricity — hopes for a solution are pinned on a market-based restructuring which is supposed to secure an influx of foreign investment on its own. For some reason the dismal results of the market-based restructuring of energy in California have not put our reformers off.

However, the secret to ensuring long-term economic growth lies precisely in resolving the problem of overhauling the capital assets. This is an extremely tough challenge, because the country is still suffering from a major lack of investment (both in terms of money and ideas). Mobilizing investment is of defining importance for the economy, because only a broad-scale modernization of the capital assets is capable of creating a rising domestic market for the manufacturing industry in the long term, and at the same time ensuring that Russian products become increasingly competitive.

A year wasted

The Putin administration which came to power in early 2000 has done nothing in the last year — not only in terms of developing a strategy capable of providing for an overhaul of the capital assets, but also in terms of eliminating those economic threats which are visible today. This is universally recognized, and the influential business magazine Expert writes about this quite openly. But does this mean that the worst case scenario has been realized? There are serious grounds for doubting that things would have changed for the better even had the Putin administration and the Kasyanov government adopted a more proactive approach. The government's and the president's existing draft solutions for a whole range of serious economic development problems (restructuring transport and energy, reforming the pension system and the housing and utilities infrastructure, and reforming education) are based on inertia and the single-minded liberal approaches which have already brought Russia seven years of harsh economic crisis. Applying them to the current situation would mean that instead of stagnation or weak, unstable growth, the country would be subjected to a new edition of the crisis.

All these reform projects have one feature in common. They all imply an increased burden on the end user, be it companies (as customers for electricity or rail services) or ordinary people (who will have to pay more for rail tickets, electricity and education, and make extra contributions to the pension system). Much we are told of the benefits of these reforms in the long run, however, their immediate effect will be a rapid and significant shrink in demand on the domestic market, which will have a depressing effect on the economy and will inevitably bring about a decline.

Engineering a decline is an easy trick — one our government is quite capable of. But the government failed to harvest the fruits of the recovery which caught it unawares, and failed to create the conditions necessary to allow it to allocate resources for an accelerated renewal of the capital assets. It did not even manage to balance the budget, when all tax collecting targets had been more than met. And again, all hopes are being pinned on the idea that the 'market will sort everything out' — all we need is a market-based restructuring of this or that industry, or this or that branch of the economy. The only good news is that neither the president nor the government seem to be in any hurry to implement these solutions.

It's not all that bad

Are there any favourable prospects for the Russian economy? It is hard to believe so — too many problems have accrued. However, we should not paint too gloomy a picture. There is no crisis looming in the short term. The Russian economy probably faces a slow down in the rate of development, and a period of slight decline. Even the mounting problems of upgrading equipment in various sectors of the economy will not in itself bring the economy to its knees. However, delaying their solution, in unstable market conditions, is fraught with risks. There is still some time in hand before these risks will pose a direct threat. This time could be used to find solutions.

Strong authority

Although generally speaking there remains an adherence to democratic values and market freedoms, most Russians lean towards the idea of a strong authority capable of reviving Russia as a great power (this goal secured most support among respondents — 42.4%), using state intervention in the economy to correct the results of market reforms with a view to achieving greater social justice, and limiting the profits of private capital.

It is this sociopolitical tendency that determined Vladimir Putin's victory in the presidential elections. Voters saw in him a man capable of strengthening law and order, gearing the economy towards the needs of the ordinary people, and defending Russia's national interests, while at the same time preserving democratic forms of government and the positive results of the market reforms.

There is no need to demonstrate that Putin's ability to meet these demands is in fact very doubtful, and on certain issues totally illusory. The initially effective war against the Chechen guerrillas, which began with Putin's ascendancy to power, eclipsed in voters' minds many other acts of Putin's which went against the mood of the electorate.

However, it is now clear that Putin has a very selective understanding of law and order, that he is even more inclined towards compromise with the West than Yeltsin was, and that his economic policy thus far is geared towards radical liberal ideas. This means that the voters will not see the expected rebirth of Russia from Putin, and he will not even manage to maintain the temporary period of economic growth.

The question is, how long will it be before Russia's voters admit to themselves that they have once again become the victims of unfounded hopes? These hopes may in fact linger on for a very long time, if — as with Yeltsin's re-election in 1996 — the electorate is not offered a convincing, attractive political alternative.

Where is the labour protest movement?

The Russian labour movement has of late been something of a mystery for political scientists and sociologists. The fact is that wages have more than halved in real terms during the years of market reforms, and even these wages are paid several months late; unemployment has risen to 12 percent in a country which just ten years ago provided almost full employment; enterprises are no longer in a position to provide their workers with most of the social benefits they offered in Soviet times; and the image and prestige of manual labour has fallen as low as it can.

Yet, despite all this, there is no visible activity in the labour and trade union movement. Even in the toughest years of 'shock therapy' (1992-93), the number of strikes actually fell. Moreover, after some increase in industrial action in 1995-97, the number of strikes again decreased. Notably, the vast majority of official strikes are held by teachers demanding that the state pay their salary arrears. In the eight years of reform a labour protest movement has not really taken hold. Yet not so long ago, in 1989-91, the country was rocked by miners' strikes, and the labour movement, which had suddenly made its presence felt after decades of silence, seemed poised to become one of the major factors in the social life of the new Russia. But those same workers, when faced with a dramatic decline in living conditions which has left one-third of Russia's population below the poverty line, have become astonishingly passive. Why has this happened?

The reasons for passivity

The low level of strike action in Russia is determined by a whole range of economic and social factors, all of which contribute to a decline in the level of labour protest. First, though workers' visible wages have fallen dramatically, there has not been such a catastrophic fall in consumption. The fall in consumption in real terms has been curbed by the fact that many workers have allotments on which they produce their own food, and by semi-legal and illegal moonlighting.

Second, strike action stands very little chance of success when the economy is in deep crisis and production is falling, and when many enterprises are working to less than a third of their original capacity. Industrial action is more successful in periods of economic growth than in times of crisis.

Third, the strike movement in 1989-91 met with unanimous public sympathy and support, and no resistance from the authorities. Since 1992 all the main media outlets have been unanimous in their condemnation of strikers. Management and the local and federal authorities have resorted to various means of putting pressure on the strikers — from prosecution and dismissal to acts of terrorism.

Fourth, workers have had no experience of organizing themselves in the struggle for their rights. The traditional trade union structures which have survived from Soviet times have gravitated, due to inertia, toward compromise with the authorities at all levels — from factory directors to the federal government; and the new alternative trade unions have turned out to be weak, small in number and prone to internal conflict. There is no tradition of mass demonstrations for solidarity by workers from different professions.

The labour movement is changing

During 1992-93, protests by hired workers initially took the form of ordinary strikes, which at best brought temporary and partial success, the fruits of which were consumed by the ongoing economic crisis within two or three months. If workers were given a pay rise, any additional money would soon be devalued by inflation. If workers were paid the wages owed them in arrears, the delays would soon begin again. Then protest began to take the form of acts of despair. Workers, medics and teachers began to resort to hunger strikes, and sometimes even protest suicides. But the effect of these actions was equally short lived. Soon the authorities and management stopped paying much attention to their employees' hunger strikes and suicides.

Eventually, in 1996-97, the workers resorted to blocking transport routes, and in 1998 the miners organized a long-term picket in Moscow outside the government building, with political demands. At first these actions had wide repercussions, because they affected the interests of a large number of people (the blockade of the Trans-Siberian railway by miners, for example, which lasted for several days). The authorities were forced to seek a compromise, and management quickly made concessions. But here again, even when they had gained concessions, the workers soon felt that what they had won was slipping through their fingers. And the stance of the authorities soon became much harsher: They resorted to the regular use of force to free up the roads, and began taking legal action against the organizers of the blockades.

So the methods tried by the workers did not bring them any real success. When the economic situation in the country was getting worse and worse, but the rich were getting richer and richer, these riches could only be growing at the expense of workers' income. If there is a fall in production, profits may be preserved either at the expense of workers' wages, or by selling off the enterprize's fixed assets (which, for the workers, also entails losing their job and their wages). No one was planning to part with their profits.

The first signs of change

It is only now, in the eighth year of radical market 'reforms', that the first signs of change in the Russian labour movement have begun to appear. As yet there have only been a few illustrations of the working people's new approach to struggle for their rights, and these illustrations do not represent the face of the labour movement. As yet they are merely signs of impending change. Nevertheless, some things are indeed changing.

Above all, the tactic of passive protest against intolerable economic conditions is starting to be transformed into an active struggle to change these conditions — albeit as yet only in individual enterprises. The forms of the struggle are also changing in line with this. To prevent the plundering of assets at their workplace, employees have taken recourse to workers' control, and when they have met resistance from the management and owners of the enterprise, they have resorted to sit-ins. The actions of employees at the Yasnogorsk Engineering Plant in Tula oblast provides an example of the establishment of workers' control. This battle began back in 1998. The workers tried to gain full control of the plant — they practically ousted the old management and held a conference to elect their own directors. However, the courts ruled that the workers' actions were illegal, and the 'worker-directors' were arrested. Nevertheless, the battle did not end there. The workers succeeded in securing the dismissal of the previous director and several members of the previous management. The factory strike committee set up an organ of workers' control — a shipping commission — which monitored the sale of the factory's products. Under pressure from the workers, the management was forced to recognize this workers' initiative, which allowed the workers to block any illicit deals struck to the detriment of the factory or concealed from the accounts.

As for sit-ins, there have been individual cases in Russia before now. Previously, occupying the enterprise was merely a way for the workers to bring production to a halt in the face of resistance from the management, the private security companies they had hired, or local authorities which supported the owners. But the last year or so has seen a growth in the number of cases where the workers assert control of the enterprise not to stop production — production is often brought to a halt anyway through the fault of the new owners — but conversely to ensure that work continues. This is also the aim of workers' control, which may be established without the workers' having to occupy the enterprise. The second factor which has emerged in relation to sit-ins is the growth of sympathy strikes by workers of different enterprises.

Workforce occupy factory

In Russia only about a dozen enterprises are effectively controlled by the workforce. It is nigh-on to impossible to find any information about them in the 'free' Russian press, but if such information should appear, it is usually reminiscent of the 'negative propaganda' designed to corrupt enemy troops during times of war. The more successful the workers' actions, the more resistance they encounter. The best example of this is the confrontation at the Vyborg Pulp-and-Paper Factory in Sovetskii in Leningrad Oblast. In 1993 the factory was privatized, with numerous violations of the law. Then the new shareholders and management bought the workers out, established almost full control of ownership and sold the factory on. This resale was also accompanied by numerous violations of the law. Suffice to say that the sale price was set at 4.5 times less than the book value of the factory, according to an audit by the Audit Office of the Russian Ministry of Finance. Ownership rights were transferred after a down payment of one-fifth of this sum. As a result, the new owners paid just 3.8 million dollars for the ownership rights to a factory which it had cost in the region of US$700 million to renovate in the 1980s, with help from Finland.

The other aspect of this deal was the absence of a genuine owner. The company which formally obtained the ownership rights was a typical 'dummy' company which provided false information. The company describes itself as British, but is not registered in Britain, nor are its owners British citizens. The effective owner was the 'vodka king' of Leningrad Oblast, a Mr. Sabadash. Naturally, they needed a pretext to sell the factory at a reduced price, so a pretext was concocted: In 1995-96, the factory was artificially bankrupted, and was put up for sale in 1997. The new owners announced their intention to retain just one lumber transshipment station from the factory. The Leningrad Oblast prosecutor challenged the result of the sale and ordered the suspension of the transfer of ownership rights to the new owners. But effectively the new owners continued to control the mill. At this point, the workforce occupied the factory, put its own guard in place, elected its own director and began to run the place independently.

Gunfire in Sovetsky

Why did shots ring out in Sovetsky? The answer is very simple — because the workforce quickly managed to get the factory working. The factory emerged from bankruptcy and became profitable, the workers were given a pay rise and were paid the back-pay owed them, the factory paid its taxes regularly and was in a position to fund social benefits for its workers. These actions were naturally considered unacceptable. On July 9 came the

RUSSIA

first attempt by a private security company (an unlicensed one at that) to take over the factory. This attempt was resisted by the workers. On the night of October 12-13 a second attempt was made, this time deploying a 'Typhoon' unit — used to put down prison riots — OMON special troops and a private security company. Units of interior ministry troops were on standby. In order to make life more difficult for the factory, the would-be owners managed to force the railways to stop providing wagons for the supply of raw materials and the shipment of finished goods. However, this time too the attack met with organized resistance from the workforce. The unarmed employees (60 percent of whom were women) blockaded the Typhoon unit in the factory management offices. The Typhoon troops, sensing that that battle was not going their way, beat several people up and took them hostage, shutting one woman in the fridge. The Typhoon unit caused untold destruction to the premises they were occupying. When the workforce attempted to enter into negotiations, the Typhoon troops responded by opening fire, wounding two workers. However, the "valiant defenders" of illegally-obtained ownership rights were forced to retreat down a corridor of OMON troops — such was their fear of the workers' wrath. They were perhaps right to be frightened. These workers had reacted so passively to the bankruptcy of the factory in the mid-1990s: They collapsed from hunger in the lines for humanitarian aid, but did not enter into confrontation. But now, having taken the factory into their own hands, they realized that they could make it work, and they had no intention of backing down. 'We will fight to the death', say these people, most of whom completed secondary or higher vocational training.

The lessons of the conflict

In the aftermath of the carnage at the Vyborg Pulp-and-Paper Factory, there were very different reactions to the conflict from different sections of Russian society. A stream of lies flowed from television screens and the pages of many wide-circulation newspapers: The workers were accused of seizing the property of others; it was they who had bankrupted the factory, they who avoided paying their taxes; they had resisted a legal ruling with weapons in their hands, and they had beaten up the 'rightful owner' of the factory, Mr. Sabadash, who was now in intensive care. None of these reports had any bearing on reality. Izvestia even demanded that tank units be turned on the workers, and that the factory be bombed instead of bombing Chechen terrorists. Such blood-thirstiness was not seen even in the 'democratic public's' calls for reprisals against the Supreme Soviet in October 1993. Journalists from the main television channels reiterated the slogans from the presidential elections of 1996 — 'there can be no review of privatization, otherwise there will be civil war.' Economic crime structures were using likable television presenters to make explicit threats of war against all those who challenged their right to steal and plunder with impunity. There was a different reaction from the workers of St. Petersburg and Leningrad oblast. A collection was set up for the factory's employees, and workers from the Leningrad Metal Factory formed workers' brigades to support the Vyborg workforce. The trade union committee at the Leningrad Metal Factory turned into a sort of headquarters for coordinating demonstrations of solidarity with the Vyborg Pulp-and-Paper Factory. The workers also found support in Moscow: The State Duma passed a resolution defending the actions of the factory's workforce, with only one vote against. An association called 'Academics for Democracy and Socialism' quickly dispatched a representative to the factory, and then with the assistance of a number of Duma deputies organized a press-conference for the representatives of the Vyborg factory.

So how will events unfold? We are facing a paradox. Workers are beginning to stand up and fight not just for their wages, but to maintain production, to ensure that companies operate profitably, and against asset stripping. In response, they are shown the full weight of state power, which defends the rights of 'New Russians' to obtain ownership by circumventing the law, to steal the workers' wages from them and to receive income by decapitalizing enterprises.

Who will win? Will other workforces follow the lead of the first people to organize workers' control? Will most of the population trust the political forces that support the workers' struggle? Or will those who dream of a Russian Pinochet win the day? It is too early to give a clear answer to these questions. But one thing is clear — the labour movement in Russia is beginning to change. Only events will show how quickly these changes will take place, whether this first surge will peter out, and whether individual attempts to establish workers' control will remain just that — individual cases. But by an irony of history, if Russia is to produce an effective entrepreneurial class then it is not the 'new Russians' who will be able to fill this role, but organized workers. ☐

EUROPEAN UNION

EU enlargement: from poverty to misery

G Buster

The enlargement of the European Union to include the Central and Eastern European countries (CEECs) has now reached the decisive moment. The European Council meeting in Gothenburg confirmed that it was an "irreversible" process and adopted a final schedule for the negotiations, which are to conclude by the end of 2002, thus enabling the applicant states to participate in the elections to the European Parliament in 2004. The European Council at Laeken in turn agreed that EU enlargement will include all applicant states with the exception of Rumania, Bulgaria and Turkey. For years now EU membership has characterised and conditioned the political horizon of the CEECs, justifying the neoliberal adjustment policies as the mechanism for systemic change. In the remaining twelve months æ and in the distinct transitional periods that have been arranged æ they will be required to pursue a definitive deep economic and administrative restructuring with, as its consequence, a sharpening of conflicts of interests. Because later, when full membership is a fact, the single market will act on the correlation of forces established in each of the states in question, determining who are the winners and who are the losers in this major social transformation.

After ten years of systemic change, public opinion in the CEECs views the membership process as the light at the end of the tunnel: they are distrustful of present sacrifices and hopeful that they will be of some use. The question is of some importance because when the negotiations are over each applicant state will have to hold referendums. And in recent years the situation has become somewhat clouded, with a majority of the electorate opposed to membership in such countries as Estonia and Latvia. But the latest survey by Eurobarometer shows a slight increase in support, with the potential yes vote hovering around 60%, although in some countries, such as Poland, 44% think the government is making too many concessions to the EU in the negotiations.*1

Where do the negotiations stand? Of the 372 chapters (12 countries, 31 chapters to negotiate), 334 have been opened for negotiation and 249 have now been provisionally closed. And of the 38 chapters yet to be opened, 24 have to do with chapters 30 ("Institutions") and 31 ("Other").*2 But the numbers are deceptive, for the 14 remaining chapters refer to the key issues and the hardest ones: agriculture, regional assistance policy, restructuring of heavy industry and state assistance, and post-enlargement financial provisions and budgets.

The negotiations are being held against an extremely complicated panorama of the differences between the CEEC standard of living and the EU average, the low agricultural productivity and the high percentage of the labour force in the rural sector, the continuing high number of workers in heavy industry, including the iron and steel industry with its barely disguised state subsidies, combined with unemployment rates as high as 16.5% in Poland. The CEECs æ above all Poland, which by its size is a special case æ are being told to drastically reduce their farming population and transfer them to other areas of production, while at the same time restructuring heavy industry and the traditional iron and steel complexes, with a social welfare system that is extremely weak and a fiscal crisis that puts paid to any increase in social spending. And all this in three years, haggling over the structural support and subsidies of the Common Agricultural Policy (CAP).

Not surprisingly, the actual process of negotiations and adaptation to the harsh dictates of the community has created a series of reactions within the CEECs, and above all in Poland. The recently elected coalition Social Democratic-Peasant Party government in that country faces a parliamentary opposition composed of more radical peasant parties and the anti-European Catholic far right. Now it is being forced to back down on the first point it had intended to negotiate with Brussels æ the transitional period for the purchase of land by Community citizens following enlargement æ amidst a major political scandal.*3

All of this æ the policy decision made at Laeken concerning the members of the initial enlargement group, the political situation in Poland and other CEECs, and the social consequences of the negotiating items æ makes much less likely the advances that had been anticipated under the chairmanship of Spain, a country, moreover, that is itself one of the more reluctant member states about enlargement since the process will lead to it losing out in terms of aid.

A little background

The neoliberal "shock therapies" that have jump-started the transition to capitalism since the fall of the Berlin Wall in 1989 have involved a sharp drop in GNP, impoverished a large sector of the population and produced structural unemployment ranging between 10 and 16% in all the CEECs.*4 There was no growth in most of these countries until 1999 and positive growth for the group as a whole only in 2000.*5

In 1993, on the basis of article 49 of the EU Treaty, the European Council, meeting in Copenhagen, established the political and economic criteria for CEEC membership. Following the presentation of their candidacy in 1994-95, the EU negotiated and signed with them the European Accords, a transitional mechanism to prepare for the membership negotiations, with a series of limited support measures, in particular the PHARE [Action plan for coordinated aid to Poland and Hungary], ISPA [Instrument for Structural Policies for Pre-Accession] and SAPARD [Special Accession Programme for Agriculture and Rural Development] programmes. The Committees and annual Association Councils have encouraged and supervised the CEECs' progress toward rapprochement with the harsh Community regime. By 1994, as a result of the policy of disconnecting the old regional division of labour in the CMEA (Council for Mutual Economic Assistance, a.k.a. COMECON), the EU had become the largest market for the CEECs, and accounted for 60% of their exports in 2000, although the EU has a trade surplus of 17,000 million Euros.*6

The Madrid European Council of 1995 asked the Commission for a study of the financial consequences of enlargement. The result, Agenda 2000, produced some extremely hard bargaining that ended only with the Extraordinary Council meeting in Berlin in 1999, which established some financial forecasts for up to December 31, 2006. During the transitional period, the criteria for distributing agricultural, regional and structural assistance will be the same for new and old members of the EU. In accordance with the calculations by the Commission in its day, these estimates should help to cover the transfers to the

EUROPEAN UNION

new members until 2007, when a new EU budget is to be approved. Concretely, 3,120 million Euros have been budgeted annually for the pre-accession programs and a total of 58,000 million Euros for the structural and agricultural assistance of the new members.*7

The basic problem

Enlargement will add 75 million people to the 375 million citizens of the EU, a 23% increase, but will increase the EU's GDP by only 4.5%. As The Economist warns, with more than a tinge of Malthusianism, "they are many and they are poor".*8 For a comparison, the EU's enlargement to include Spain, Portugal and Greece increased its population by 22% and its GDP by 10%.

The difference in income levels is enormous. The per capita GDP of the three Mediterranean applicants in 1980 was 66% of the Community average, but in the case of the CEECs the per capita GDP is only 38%, which will effectively reduce the per capita GDP of the expanded EU (with the CEECs) by 15%, which under the present rules entails some major transfers. While the population of Poland is equivalent to 10% of the total EU population, that country accounts for only 2% of the EU's total GDP. The respective figures for Spain in 1980 were 14% and 8%. The problem is that in the relatively sophisticated model developed up to now for Commission services, assuming that the present reforms continue "means that for the AC 8 [the Accession Candidates] and for the CEEC 10 as a whole [including Romania and Bulgaria], an average growth rate of 3 per cent per year over the period 2000-09 would still be achievable, compared to a prudent assumption of 2.5 per cent average annual growth for the EU 15 over the same period. Thus, catching up would continue, albeit at a very slow rate."*9 While we don't want to rain on anyone's parade, it is necessary to point out that the model is based on the 1994-99 growth data. But the most recent data and forecasts on GDP growth clearly demonstrate the effects of the international recession and the drop in domestic and external demand, with declines ranging between 1% for Hungary and 3% for Poland from the forecast growth in GDP for 2002.*10

The consequences of enlargement for the present member states are, under the same model, "extremely small, with as many negatives as positives".

The political consequence of this perspective for the enlargement negotiations is a hardening of the respective positions of the EU and the applicant states up to the final moment. With regard to the structural funds æ 213,000 million Euros between 2000 and 2006, or 35% of the EU budget æ the drop in regional per capita income through enlargement means that 11 of the 17 Spanish regions that now receive structural funding will lose it, and end up at around 75% of the Community average. Spanish Prime Minister Aznar attempted a kamikaze manoeuvre to reopen the discussion closed at the 1999 Berlin Summit and secure a minimal flow of structural funding after 2007 for Spain, threatening to block the German position of a seven-year transitional period for the movement of persons in the enlargement negotiations. We now know how the story ended, with the complete isolation of Aznar in the EU.

But in the new negotiations that will open after enlargement, in 2007, Spain's alliance with the CEECs by itself may manage to raise the bar to 90% of the Community average for the support programs or increase the proportion in the Community tech budget for structural assistance from 0.45% of the EU GDP to 0.66%, as a Commission study has suggested. In the first option, the CEECs gain nothing and, in the second, they will prefer an alliance with Germany, which in the end is the major contributor to the Community budget, in order to avoid the major EU powers definitively reforming the regional assistance system and drastically reducing such assistance as Schroeder has threatened. If Spain receives 1,000 Euros annually per capita in structural support, it is not hard to imagine what this can mean for countries like Poland or Slovakia.

Agriculture

The most difficult of the sectors left to negotiate is also the one that reflects the most dramatic differences. Seventeen percent of the labour force in the CEECs is in this sector, which accounts for an average 8% of the GDP æ comparable in importance to the figures for Spain, Portugal and Greece æ but a long shot from the EU averages of 4% and 1.5% respectively.

Again, Poland's situation (like Romania's) is exceptional, with 21% of its labour force in agriculture, producing 4% of the GDP. (The figures for Romania are 40% and 15% respectively.) In both countries more than 80% of the land is distributed in small family operations with very low productivity, and the two countries combined have the same number of farmers, 7.3 million, as the entire EU. In all the CEECs with the exception of Rumania, rural employment has declined by 4% since 1994. Poland alone has lost 600,000 rural jobs in this period.

The Commission model cited earlier forecasts annual reductions in rural employment in excess of 1% in the eight applicant countries of the first phase, and reductions of 2% in the public sector. For Poland, with its particular rural structure, which differs from the seven other first-phase applicants in which there have been major agrarian reforms since the Second World War, this means uprooting more than one million people from their farms over the next five years while at the same time reform of the public sector and industrial restructuring are throwing a further 250,000 persons into the street. It is hard to imagine the social consequences of all this, given that real levels of consumption in the countryside have declined by 50% in the last ten years, with poverty rates of 29.9% compared with the national average of 16.5%.*11

However, for the Commission the support programs linked to the CAP are incompatible with the necessary restructuring of the Polish countryside. It was the height of cynicism for Franz Fischler, European Commissioner for Agriculture, Rural Development and Fisheries,
to state, on January 10 in Berlin, that "Structural change in the applicant countries will take time, and we also have to take that into account in the much talked-about question of direct payments. For what would happen if the system of direct payments were to be embraced in full on the very first day of joining the EU? First, this would be yet another incentive to retain existing structures, and second, we would run the risk of social upheaval, because at a stroke farmers would be earning considerably more than other workers in the same region." *12

According to The Economist, "Under current plans, the CAP will not be fully extended to the Central Europeans because, Eurocrats claim, that would bankrupt the system, and there is no need for it anyway because prices for Poland's food will rise once it joins."*13

Unfortunately, the same Eurocrats state in their magazines that "Significant price increases with the accession should only be expected for beef, sugar, milk (and processed derivatives, butter and milk powder), and coarse grains (barley, maize, rye). ... Simulations indicate that, taking into account the combined effect of these factors, the impact of introducing the CAP in CEECs on agricultural prices in CEECs might be relatively small on average. It now appears that future developments of production in the CEECs, and the likelihood of a conflict with WTO constraints after accession, will largely be dominated by trends/changes in productivity, rather than by the introduction of the CAP."*14

Spain has now proposed a five-year transitional period for direct CAP assistance, in which the farmers would directly get only 30% of the assistance and the rest, without further details, would go to a fund for restructuring the agricultural sector. "The EU seems to be saying that we will have the same obligations as existing members, but not the same rights," says Pawel Samecki, one of the Polish negotiators.*15

Conclusion

Add to this scenario the reduction in state assistance and the restructuring of the steel industry, which has so far been postponed in most of the CEECs. Throw in as well the overwhelming Polish budget deficit and the fiscal crisis that it has produced and the failure of the social welfare system, which is barely comparable in the CEECs to those existing in the EU. Karol Modzelewski warned back in 1995 of the negative consequences of enlargement.*16 The only expected safety valve is the emigration of some 900,000 people from the CEECs to Western Europe in the first five years of membership.

But the cards are now distributed and, notwithstanding the severity of the negotiations during 2002, the CEEC governments, whatever their political complexion, will give in, one by one, at the last moment. They are convinced that non-membership in the initial group would have much more dangerous electoral consequences for their political future than a bad deal. In the end there is always the consolation that, once inside the EU, they will hold a substantial number of votes in the European Council – if the Treaty of Nice is ratified after Ireland's NO – and they can participate fully in the forthcoming negotiation of the community budget.

But the ground rules are about to change in the debate on the future of the European Union. The leadership of the major powers (France, Germany and the United Kingdom) is not prepared for interminable haggling and negotiations in the enlarged EU. And many brand new citizens of the EU in Central and Eastern Europe may end up, as Marx (Groucho) pointed out, "going from the most dreadful poverty to the most complete misery, thanks to their own efforts". □

NOTES

1. See "Initial results of Eurobarometer survey in candidate countries show broad support for accession"
(http://europa.eu.int/comm/public_opinion)
2. See Enlargement Weekly, January 7, 2002, with the full negotiating framework, country by country.
http://europa.eu.int/comm/enlargement/docs/newsletter
3. See EU Observer, "Poland tightens up position in talks", 19-12-2001
http://www.euobserver.com
4. For a summary of the social consequence of the transition and the social conflicts it has generated, see Agustín Maraver, "Trabajadores y Nomenclatura en la Transición", Cuadernos del Este nº 20, 1997.
5. EBRD (2001) Transition Report, European Bank for Reconstruction and Development.
6. For the evolution of the trading relationship after the European Agreements, see Joseph F. Francois and Machiel Rombout, "Trade Effects from the Integration of the Central and East European Countries into the EU", Sussex European Institute. The trend has been toward a balance in such industries as automobiles and automotive parts, electrical machinery, office equipment and telecommunications, as a result of the investments of European multinationals in those industries to take advantage of the differences in wages and other costs of production.
7. EU Enlargement DG, Enlargement of the European Union: An historic opportunity, may be consulted at
http://europa.eu.int/comm/enlargement.
8. For the following data, see DG for Economic and Financial Affairs, "The economic impact of enlargement", Enlargement Papers,
http://europa.eu.int/economy_finance. The Economist, "The door creaks open", November 17, 2001.
9. "The economic impact of enlargement", op. cit., pp. 30-31.
10. Consensus Economics, "Eastern Europe Consensus Forecasts", November 19, 2001
http://www.consensuseconomics.com
11. Gertruda Uscinka, "The social security system in Poland", special issue on social security in the CEECs, in the Belgian Review of Social Security, vol. 43, 2001, pp. 224-25:
12. Enlargement Weekly, January 14, 2002, "Fishler goes further on agriculture thinking"
http://europa.eu.int/comm/enlargement/docs/newsletter
13. The Economist, "Looking west, looking east", October 25, 2001.
14. "The economic impact of enlargement" op. cit., p. 57.
15. The Economist, "Looking west, looking east", October 25, 2001 and Michael Mann, "EU candidates may wait years for subsidies", Financial Times, January 8, 2002.
16. Quoted by Catherine Samary in her interesting article, "Ampliación de la UE al Este: ¿Qué alternativas de izquierdas?", Viento Sur nº 55, March 2001.

Article translated by Richard Fidler.

OBITUARY

Ross Dowson

Ross Dowson, who died on February 17, 2002 was the major personality in the Canadian Trotskyist movement from the early 1940s to 1974, when he left with a few collaborators to set up a group almost entirely devoted to working within the social-democratic New Democratic Party.

Dowson had played a key role in reassembling a Canadian Trotskyist organization, the Revolutionary Workers Party, near the close of the Second World War. The RWP's main activity was the publication of a bi-weekly 8-page newspaper *Labour Challenge*, with a readership that for some time numbered in the thousands. The group also contested elections, mainly at the municipal level.

The postwar period was a difficult one for the left in general and no less so for the Trotskyists, who were harassed and driven out of their positions in the trade union movement. The divisions that developed in the Fourth International (FI) forces, and the subsequent international split, have been well documented. The already weakened RWP effectively disintegrated.

Ross Dowson worked strenuously to reconstitute the Canadian section of the FI, first through the Socialist Education League, based largely in Toronto, then through the League for Socialist Action (LSA), which was formally constituted in 1961.

During the 1960s the LSA, like most far-left groups, attracted new members among young people radicalized by the Cuban revolution, the Vietnam war, and the developing women's liberation movement. Until the mid-1960s, the LSA was confined to English Canada. With the formation in 1964 of its Quebec counterpart, the Ligue Socialiste Ouvrière, the united organization (now the LSA/LSO) began attempting to analyze the Quebec national question and nationalist movement from a Marxist perspective. A consistent supporter of Quebec's right to self-determination, in 1970 it began actively supporting Quebec independence from the Canadian state.

Ross Dowson, as the organization's national secretary, was at the heart of all these developments. A skilled lithographer and printer by training, he spent almost his entire working life as a full-time paid staffer (at times the only one) for the organization. For the new generation of recruits in the Sixties and early Seventies, he was our major link to the older generation of class-struggle militants and Marxists who had built the labour and socialist movements in previous decades.

In the late Sixties Canadian Marxist academics, under the influence of the then-predominant dependency theory, tended to view Canada as a peripheral 'de-industrializing' subordinate satellite of the United States, de-emphasizing or even denying its status as a (lesser) imperialist power in its own right. Dowson became enamoured with this approach and, when it became a prominent theme in a broad left opposition current that developed within the NDP in 1969-72, he began to adapt to it politically, developing a theory of a new, progressive Canadian nationalism, in opposition to U.S. 'domination', that should be embraced (albeit critically) by socialists as a radicalizing force. In the early 1970s, a bitter debate on these positions broke out in the Canadian Trotskyist movement, and Dowson soon found himself in a minority.

After being decisively defeated at the League's 1973 convention, Dowson and about 20 supporters left the Canadian section of the FI to establish the Forward group, publishing a paper of that name for about ten years, and operated mainly in and around the NDP. The group functioned to some degree as a personal cult around Dowson. In 1988 Ross Dowson suffered a devastating stroke from which he never recovered. He spent his final years in an acute-care hospital.

Condensed from an article posted on Marxmail: http://www.marxmail.org/

Advertisement

Notebooks for Study and Research

The INTERNATIONAL INSTITUTE FOR RESEARCH AND EDUCATION shares the values of grassroots activists. Since 1986 the results of our work – on economic globalization, twentieth century history, ecology, feminism, ethnicity, racism, radical movement strategy and other topics -- have been made available through the **Notebooks for Study and Research**.

- **No 1** *The Place of Marxism in History* Ernest Mandel (40pp, ¤3.25, £2, $3.25)
- **No 2** *The Chinese Revolution - I: The Second Chinese Revolution and the Shaping of the Maoist Outlook* Pierre Rousset (32pp, ¤3.25, £2, $3.25)
- **No 3** *The Chinese Revolution - II: The Maoist Project Tested in the Struggle for Power* Pierre Rousset (48pp, ¤3.25, £2, $3.25)
- **No 4** *Revolutionary Strategy Today* Daniel Bensaïd (36pp, ¤3.25, £2, $3.25)
- **No 5** *Class Struggle and Technological Change in Japan since 1945* Muto Ichiyo (48pp, ¤4, £2.50, $4)
- **No 6** *Populism in Latin America* Adolfo Gilly, Helena Hirata, Carlos M Vilas, and the PRT (Argentina) introduced by Michael Löwy (40pp, ¤3.25, £2, $3.25)
- **No 7/8** *Market, Plan and Democracy: The Experience of the So-Called Socialist Countries* Catherine Samary (64pp, ¤5, £3.25, $5)
- **No 9** *The Formative Years of the Fourth International (1933-1938)* Daniel Bensaïd (48pp, ¤4, £2.50, $4)
- **No 10** *Marxism and Liberation Theology* Michael Löwy (40pp, ¤ 3.25, £2, $3.25)
- **No 11/12** *The Bourgeois Revolution*, Robert Lochhead (72pp, ¤6, £3.75, $6)
- **No 13** *The Spanish Civil War in Euzkadi and Catalonia 1936-39* Miguel Romero (48pp, ¤4, £2.50, $4)
- **No 14** *The Gulf War and the New World Order* André Gunder Frank and Salah Jaber (72pp, ¤2.75, £1.75, $2.75)
- **No 15** *From the PCI to the PDS* Livio Maitan (48pp. ¤4, £2.50, $4)
- **No 16** *Do the Workers have a Country?* José Iriarte "Bikila" (48pp, ¤2.75, £1.75, $2.75)
- **No 17/18** *April 1917: Coup d'état or Social Revolution?* Ernest Mandel (64pp, ¤2.75, £1.75, $2.75)
- **No 19/20** *The Fragmentation of Yugoslavia: An Overview* Catherine Samary (60pp, ¤3.25, £2, $3.25)
- **No 21** *Factory Committees and Workers' Control in Petrograd in 1917* David Mandel (48pp, ¤5, £3.25, $5)
- **No 22** *Women's Lives in the New Global Economy* Penny Duggan & Heather Dashner (editors) (68pp, ¤5, £3.25, $5)
- **No 23** *Lean Production: A Capitalist Utopia?* Tony Smith (68pp, ¤5, £3.25, $5)
- **No 24/25** *World Bank/IMF/WTO: The Free-Market Fiasco* Susan George, Michel Chossudovsky et al. (116pp, ¤8.75, £5.50, $8.75)
- **No 26** *The Trade-Union Left and the Birth of a New South Africa* Claude Jacquin (92pp, ¤5, £3.25, $5)

Subscription costs £18, US$30 or ¤30 for 5 issues; £30, US$50, ¤30 for 10 issues.

Notebooks published in **book format** by Pluto Press generally count as a double issue for subscription purposes. You can request back issues as part of your subscription. Back issues are also available for the prices indicated (outside Europe, add 20% for postage).

For Notebooks for Study and Research we prefer **payment** in euros, made by bank or giro transfer to Netherlands Postbank account no.1757144, CER/NSR, Amsterdam. Next best are cheques payable to P Rousset, either sterling payable in Britain or dollars payable in the US. Please avoid Eurocheques.

Please add 20% for postage outside Europe.

All **correspondence** to: IIRE, Willemsparkweg 202, 1071 HW Amsterdam, The Netherlands. Fax: 31-20-6732106. E-mail: iire@antenna.nl.

...is struggling to keep its head above water. Our new design aims to help readers to use the magazine and to get more people to read it. However we need both feedback and support to develop the new look of the magazine so that it meets the needs of our readers more fully.

With this issue International Viewpoint gains a simple cover statement: "news and analysis from socialists worldwide". This phrase sums up the uniqueness of the magazine in the English-speaking world. Part of the intellectual tradition in imperialist countries, especially in Britain and the USA, is to attempt to prescribe tactics for other countries. International Viewpoint takes a very different approach: it allows socialists in many countries to talk about their own struggles in their own words. Activists (and researchers) around the world recognise a powerful resource in IV and its sister journals Inprecor (French) and Inprekorr (German).

Of course, we also hope that the new design will help the magazine. Long-time readers will recognise it as our most fundamental redesign since International Viewpoint was launched twenty years ago

This issue of International Viewpoint not only signals a new design and a broader production team. It also reflects the greater momentum from the activists who use the magazine around the world. In the wake of September 11th, interest in the magazine has grown. Sales magazine have grown as a result, but unpredictably. This means that income from sales can be 50% above target one month, but 50% below the next.

A huge success for us is that donations from supportive individuals and organisations have paid one third of our expenses so far this year. Sales of the magazine still pay half of its expenses – the level that sales increased to last year. However, that still leaves a substantial shortfall which must be met in three ways:

First, monthly payments by our sellers would be a huge help. Our sellers do pay us regularly – but the frequency of payments matters. The gap between what we spend and what we get is more than covered by invoices that our supporters haven't paid yet. Sellers can pay us directly in any major currency, and we will send them more regular statements to keep them on top of payments.

Second, we need to combine your efforts and ours to increase our numbers of subscribers: both individual and institutions. We are producing a new subscription leaflet which reflects the new design of the magazine. If you would like copies of the leaflet, please email International_Viewpoint@compuserve.com

Finally, you can help us by taking a few copies of the magazine to sell to or share with potential subscribers.

Essential as these measure are, they won't work unless IV becomes more the magazine you need it to be. The suggestions and feedback we get from our readers are really valuable because you know what you need better than we do. This month, for example, readers from all over the world contacted us to let us know what sort of coverage of the French elections they wanted to see in the magazine. We want more ideas, criticism and comment – and, of course, more translators, proof readers, distributors and researchers. We look forward to hearing from you.

Give us your feedback, so we can

INCOME	£10,400
EXPENDITURE	£12,700
NEEDED	£2,300

INTERNATIONAL VIEWPOINT

10 issues delivered by airmail, for only:

Britain, Ireland	£30
Other European countries	50
Greece, Portugal, Turkey, East Europe	25
Australia, New Zealand	$85
Canada	$85
Rest of world	US $70
Non-OECD countries	US $35

First-time subscribers – 25% discount!

Britain, Ireland	£22.50
Other European countries	35
Greece, Portugal, Turkey, East Europe	20
Australia, New Zealand	$50
Canada	$50
Rest of world	US $50
Non-OECD countries	US $28

SUBSCRIBE!

NAME
ADDRESS
CITY
CODE
COUNTRY
PHONE
EMAIL

Send to/order from: INTERNATIONAL VIEWPOINT, PO Box 112, Manchester M12 5DW, Britain

INTERNATIONAL VIEWPOINT is available online at: http://www.3bh.org.uk/iv/index.htm

Document: C.E. Anderson & Associates
Mechanical Engineer: Schematic Design: Ove Arup
Design Development/Construction Document: McGuIre Engineers
Other Consultants: Oak structural Design Office, Scientific Air-Conditioning Institute, AALab, Mambo Atelier Niihori and others
Structure of the Building: Reinforced concrete structure, partly steel structure
Principal Exterior Material:
Wall panel: glassfiber reinforced concrete / Roof: metal louver, asphalt felt roofing / Openings: aluminum sash
Principal Interior Material: (classrooms)
Floor: linoleum floorings /
Wall: plaster board, paint finish /
Ceiling: perforated metal sheet
Period: 10. 2001 - 06. 2003
Publication: *PLOT02* Kazuhiro Kojima (A.D.A.Edita Tokyo, 2002)

House
Architects : Anne Lacaton & Jean Philippe Vassal,
with Emmanuelle Delage, Christophe Hutin, Sylvain Menaud
Location: Coutras, France
Use of the Building: Residential
Total Floor Area: 290 m^2
Number of Floors: 1
Height of the Building: 4.50 m
Client: Arlette & Pierre Guinchard
Constructor: FILCLAIR, greenhouse constructor
Structure of the Building: Steel
Principal Exterior Material: Transparent corrugated plastic
Principal Interior Material: Plywood
Period: 1999 - 2000
Cost : 64.800 Euros exclusive of tax
Awards: World award architecture 2001, Shortlist
Publications: *Archicréé*, France, n° 295/2000, p. 58
Baumeister, Germany, n° 9/2000, p. 80
World architecture, UK, n° 95/April 2001, p. 68
Lotus Navigator-Electa, Italy, n° 4/Nov 2001, p. 40
Verb, architecture boogazine, Spain, Actar Editor, p. 274

Neighborhood Center, Holmbladsgade
Architects: Dorte Mandrup Architects
Location: Holmbladsgadequarter, Amager, Copenhagen, Denmark
Project Type: Conversion and addition to an 1880 industrial building.
Use of the Building: Neighborhood Center (library, youth center, cafe, multipurpose hall, community related offices)
Site Area: 3.840 m^2
Building Area: 951 m^2
Total Floor Area: 3.600 m^2
Number of Floors: 4
Height of the Building: 12 m excl. roof, 18 m incl. roof
Client: Copenhagen Municipality
Structural Engineer: Dominia A/S
Other Consultants: Landscape: Dorte Mandrup Architects and Henrik Joergensen landscape architects
Constructor: 7 different crafts
Structure of the Building:
Existing building: Loadbearing columns and beams, loadbearing outer brickwalls.
Addition: Loadbearing concrete columns and in situ concrete deck. Loadbearing plywood construction.
Principal Exterior Material:
Existing building: Yellow brick.
Addition: thermo glass paneling in wooden frames, larch, and plywood.
Principal Interior Material:
Existing: Entrance hall: Maple veneer.
Addition: Plywood.
Period: 1999-2001
Awards: Copenhagen Cultural Foundation Award 2001
Publication: *Arkitektur* DK 8/2001

Seaplane Hangar H53, Cell Network DK Headquarters.
Architects: Dorte Mandrup Architects
Location: Margretheholm, Holmen, Copenhagen, Denmark
Project Type: Conversion of a former military Seaplane hangar from 1921. The Hangar is protected.
Use of the Building: Offices for Cell Network Denmark (internet solutions), 150 workplaces
Site Area: 5.180 m^2
Building Area: 1.782 m^2
Total Floor Area: 2.450 m^2
Number of Floors: Varies between 1 and 3
Height of the Building: 13 m
Client: Thylander & Co A/S
Structural Engineer: Torben Sejersen A/S
Other Consultants:
Landscape: Dorte Mandrup Architects in collaboration with Henrik Joergensen Landscape architects, Furnishing : Dorte Mandrup Architects ApS .
Photographer: Jens Markus Lindhe
Constructor: WR entreprise A/S
Structure of the Building: Existing building In-situ: Concrete beams, with light weight roof construction. New additional constructions: Steel
Principal Exterior Material: Wooden cladding, brick. New sliding wall steel construction and glass
In aluminum profiles.
Principal Interior Material: Birch plywood, white lacquered steel, parachute nylon
Designing Period: 06. 2000 - 09. 2001
Awards: Copenhagen City Foundation Award 2001
Publications: *Arkitektur* DK 8/2001, *MD* 2/2002, *Rum* 3/2001

Kindergarten in Yatsushiro
Architects: Mikan
Location: Yatsushiro, Kumamoto, Japan
Use of the building: Educational Facility
Site Area: 3.609 m^2
Building Area: 808 m^2
Total Floor Area: 663 m^2
Number of Floors: 1
Height of Building: 4.70 m
Client: City of Yatsushiro
Structural Engineer: Kanebako Structural Engineering
Mechanical: Tetens Engineering
Other Consultants: Gelchop Art Works (exterior furniture for children), Madoka Morikawa (frescos on exterior storage area)
Contractor: Wakuda Kensetsu
Structure of the Building: Wood
Principal Interior Material: glass and veneer plywood
Principal Exterior Material: glass and wood panels
Period: 11. 1999 - 03. 2001
Publications: Japan Architect, Shinkenchiku, Nikkei Architecture, L'Architecture d'Aujourd'hui

Elena Building
Architects: Laurent Ney
Location: Brussels, Belgium
Use of the Building: Apartment and office building
Site Area: 300 m^2
Building Area: 110 m^2
Total Floor Area: 450 m^2
Number of Floors: above ground 3, below ground 1
Height of the Building: 14 m
Client: Elena sa
Structural Engineer: Laurent Ney, Ney & partners
Constructor: GDC
Structure of the Building: Prefabricated concrete floor slabs concrete blocs
Principal Exterior Material: Western red cedar, glass
Principal Interior Material: Painted concrete, wood
Period: 11. 1998 - 03. 2001
Awards: Awards of Belgium Architecture, category "New construction," 2002 , Energy Awards Special mention of encouragement, 2002
Publications: *Carnet de route* Tome 3, Bois & Habitat édition 2001, "Immeuble de la semaine" *La libre Belgique*, édition 2-9 July 2001, "Guide de la nouvelle construction 2001"

The Furniture College Letterfrack
Architects: O'Donnell + Tuomey Architects
Location: Connemara, County Galway, Ireland
Use of the Building: Educational
Site Area: 3.75 ha
Building Area: Old Building 1.128 m^2
Total Floor Area: New Building 2.505 m^2
Number of Floors: above ground 2, below ground 1
Height of the Building: 12 m
Client: Connemara West
Structural Engineer: Christopher Southgate
Mechanical Engineer: McArdle McSweeney
Other Consultants: Peter Costello, Auantity Survayor
Constructor: Purcell Construction
Structure of the Building: Concrete and Timber Frame
Principal Exterior Material: Oak and plaster
Principal Interior Material: Concrete block work and oriented strandboard
Period: 1995 - 2001
Awards: RIAI Award 2001 / RIBA Award 2001 / AAI Downes Medal 2002
Publications: *Archi* n°4, August 2002, *RIBA Jourrnal* 108/3 March 2001, *Irish Architect* 169 July-August 2001, *OZ* Volume 22 2001

Information Technology and Electronics Institutes
Technical University, Graz
Architects: Riegler Riewe Architects Pty. Ltd.
Location: Graz, Styria, Austria
Use of the Building: University
Site Area: 17,209 m^2
Building Area: 4,187 m^2
Total Floor Area: 15,139 m^2
Number of Floors: 3
Height of the Building: 10 m
Client: Republic of Austria
Structural Engineer: DI Dr. techn. Stefan Rock, Graz
Mechanical Engineer: Ing. B. Hammer, Graz and Friebe Korp.OEG, Graz
Builder: Granit GesmbH, Graz and Strobl BaugesmbH, Weiz
Structure of the Building: Concrete columns + walls as load bearing elements
Principal Exterior Material: In situ concrete, in situ pigmented
Principal Interior Material: In situ concrete
Period: 1993-2000
Awards: Finalist of the 6th Mies van der Rohe Prize, 1999, Prize of the Austrian Cement Industry, 1999

Kanazawa 21st Century Muscum
Architects: Kazuyo Sejima + Ryue Nishizawa / SANAA
Location: Kanazawa, Ishikawa, Japan
Use of the Building: museum
Site Area: 26.965 m^2
Building Area: 9.559 m^2
Total Floor Area: 17.147 m^2 + 10.614 m^2 (underground parking)
Number of Floors: 1 basement and 2 storeys
Height of the Building: 15 m
Client: Kanazawa City, Japan
Structural Engineer: Sasaki Structural Consultants
Mechanical Engineer: P.T. Morimura & Associates, ES Associates
Structure of the Building: reinforced concrete and steel frame
Principal Exterior Material: glass
Principal Interior Material: pre-cast concrete, glass
Period: 04.1999 - 06.2004

House Tammimäki
Architects: Sanaksenaho Arkkitehdit Oy, Sanaksenaho Architects, with collaborators: Jari Mänttäri, Sari Lehtonen, Sakurako Funabiki (model), Agnès Baudot (exhibition)
Location: Lippajärvi, Finland
Client: Pirjo and Matti Sanaksenaho
Structure expert: Tero Aaltonen
Ventilation and sewer expert: Markku Kallio
Electricity expert: Juhani Mäntylä
Period: 1998 - 2002

Ilti Luce Office Building
Architect: UdA – Ufficio di Architettura
Location: Turin, Italy
Project Type: New building as elevation of an existing one
Use of the Building: Office
Site Area: 1.600 m^2
Building Area: 400 m^2
Total Floor Area: 400 m^2
Number of Floors: 1
Height of the Building: 4.5 m (10 m from the street)
Client: Ilti Luce srl
Structural Engineer: Ing. Antonio Cagna Vallino
Mechanical Engineer: Stefano Testa
Other Consultants: Arch. Giorgio Domenino (Project coordinator)
Constructor: Oria & Ferreri srl
Structure of the Building: Concrete and steel
Principal Exterior Material: Polymethyl methacrylate (PMMA)
Principal Interior Material: Aluminium, rubber, brick wall
Period: 06. 2001 - 06. 2002

Levis House
Architect: UdA – Ufficio di Architettura in collaboration with architect Davide Volpe
Location: Vandorno, Biella, Italy
Use of the Building: Residential
Site Area : 1,500 m^2
Building Area: 90 m^2
Total Floor Area: 85 m^2
Number of Floors: 2
Height of the Building: 6 m
Structural Engineer: Antonio Cagna Vallino
Structure of the Building: Concrete and steel
Principal Exterior Material: Concrete, wood
Principal Interior Material: Concrete, wood, glass
Period: 01. 1998 - 06. 1999

Villa Fujii
Architects: Motomu Uno + Phase Associates
Location: Kitasaku-gun, Nagano, Japan
Use of the Building: Villa
Site Area: 1,653.69 m^2
Building Area: 319.27 m^2
Total Floor Area: 318.27m^2
Number of Floors: 1
Height of the Building: 6.60 m
Client: Akio & Reiko Fujii
Structural Engineer: Masato Araya
Mechanical Engineer: Masami Tnno
Other Consultants: Toru Mitani (Landscape), Sachie Isaka (Lighting)
Constructor: Kitano Construction Corp.
Structure of the Building: Hybrid Structure (Reinforced Concrete + Steel)
Principal Exterior Material: Larch Board Paneling
Principal Interior Material: Marble/Oak
Period: 3. 1999 - 6. 2000
Awards: Architectural Design Commendation of Architectural Institute of Japan 2002, American Wood Design of the Year-Best of Residential 2002

"New Trends of Architecture in Europe and Japan" Committee

Honorary Members:
Juan B. Leña Casas, *Ambassador of Spain*
Poul Hoiness, *Ambassador of Denmark*
Ove Juul Jorgensen, *Ambassador of the Delegation of the European Commission*
Ignacio Berdugo Gomez de la Torre, *Rector of the University Salamanca*
Hakuo Yanagisawa, *Chairperson of "New Trends of Architecture in Europe and Japan" Japan Committee*
Tadahiro Sekimoto, *Chairperson of EU - Japan Fest Japan Committee*

Executive Members:
Ignacio Aguirre de Carcer, *Cultural Counsellor of the Embassy of Spain*
Eduardo Kol de Carvalho, *Director of Instituto Camões, Cultural Counsellor of the Embassy of Portugal)*
F. Javier Panera Cuevas, *Director of the Center of Photography, Service of Cultural Activities, University of Salamanca*
Manuel Vicente, *Vice President of Ordem dos Arquitectos*
Shuji Kogi, *Secretary General, EU-Japan Fest Japan Committee*

Advisors:
Alvaro Siza, Wiel Arets, Fumihiko Maki, Hiroshi Hara

Secretary General:
Fram Kitagawa, *Art Director, President of Art Front Gallery*

Coordinators:
Francine Fort, *Director arc en rêve centre d'architecture*
Rei Maeda, *Art Front Gallery*
Ikuo Kawase

Exhibition
Visual Concept:
Michel Jacques, *arc en rêve centre d'architecture*
Graphic Design:
Franck Tallon

Secretariat:
Art Front Gallery
Hillside Terrace A,
29-18 Sarugaku-cho, Shibuya-ku,
Tokyo 150-0088, Japan
Tel: +813 3476 4868
Fax: +813 3476 4874
e-mail: eu-japan@artfront.co.jp
http://artfront.co.jp/eu-japan/top.htm

arc en rêve centre d'architecture
Entrepôt, 7 rue Ferrère,
F-33000 Bordeaux, France
Tel: +33 5 56 52 78 36
Fax: +33 5 56 48 45 20
e-mail: info@arcenreve.com
http://www.arcenreve.com

Catalogue
New Trends of Architecture in Europe and Japan 2002
Supervised by:
"New Trends of Architecture in Europe and Japan" Committee
Publisher:
Fram Kitagawa
Published by:
Gendaikikakushitsu Publishers Co., Ltd.
Editing:
arc en rêve centre d'architecture
Design:
Franck Tallon
Translation:
Ikuo Kawase, Keith Vincent, Rei Maeda, Gila Walker

ISBN 4-7738-0203-0
Printed in Japan, 2002

「日本・ヨーロッパ建築の新潮流」委員会

名誉委員：
ホァン・B・レニャ・カサス（駐日スペイン大使）
ポール・ホイネス（駐日デンマーク大使）
オブ・ユールヨーゲンセン（駐日欧州委員会代表部大使）
イグナシオ・ベルドゥーゴ・デ・ラ・トーレ（サラマンカ大学学長）
柳澤伯夫（「日本・ヨーロッパ建築の新潮流」日本委員長）
関本忠弘（EU・ジャパンフェスト日本委員会委員長）

実行委員：
イグナシオ・アギーレ・デ・カルセル（駐日スペイン文化参事官）
エドアルド・コル・デ・カルヴァーリョ（駐日ポルトガル文化参事官）
F．ハビエル・パネラ・クエバス（サラマンカ大学文化活動機関写真センター部長）
マヌエル・ヴィセンテ（ポルトガル建築家協会副会長）
古木修治（EU・ジャパンフェスト日本委員会事務局長）

アドバイザー：
アルヴァロ・シザ、ヴィール・アレッツ、槇文彦、原広司

事務局長：
北川フラム（アートディレクター、アートフロントギャラリー代表）

コーディネーター：
フランシーヌ・フォール（アルカンレーヴ建築センター・ディレクター）
前田礼（アートフロントギャラリー）
河瀬行生

展覧会
展示計画：ミシェル・ジャック（アルカンレーヴ建築センター）
デザイン：フランク・タロン

事務局
アートフロントギャラリー
〒150-0033　東京都渋谷区猿楽町29-18　ヒルサイドテラスA
Tel: 03-3476-4868
Fax: 03-3476-4874
email: eu-japan@artfront.co.jp
http://artfront.co.jp/eu-japan/top.htm

アルカンレーヴ建築センター
arc en rêve centre d'architecture
Entrepôt, 7 rue Ferrère, F-33000 Bordeaux, France
Tel: 33 5 565 27 836
Fax: 33 5 564 84 520
e-mail: info@arcenreve.com
http://www.arcenreve.com

日本・ヨーロッパ建築の新潮流2002
2002年6月1日発行
監修：「日本・ヨーロッパ建築の新潮流」委員会
発行者：北川フラム
発行所：株式会社　現代企画室
編集：アルカンレーヴ建築センター
デザイン：フランク・タロン
翻訳：河瀬行生、キース・ヴィンセント、ジラ・ウォーカー、前田礼
印刷所：藤田印刷株式会社
定価：本体2,400円＋税